DECLARARI

Ron Pratt

© Copyright 2006 Ron Pratt.
All rights reserved. No part of this publication may be reproduced, stored in a retrieval system, or transmitted, in any form or by any means, electronic, mechanical, photocopying, recording, or otherwise, without the written prior permission of the author.

Note for Librarians: A cataloguing record for this book is available from Library and Archives Canada at www.collectionscanada.ca/amicus/index-e.html
ISBN 1-4120-8974-3

Printed in Victoria, BC, Canada. Printed on paper with minimum 30% recycled fibre.
Trafford's print shop runs on "green energy" from solar, wind and other environmentally-friendly power sources.

Offices in Canada, USA, Ireland and UK

Book sales for North America and international:
Trafford Publishing, 6E–2333 Government St.,
Victoria, BC V8T 4P4 CANADA
phone 250 383 6864 (toll-free 1 888 232 4444)
fax 250 383 6804; email to orders@trafford.com

Book sales in Europe:
Trafford Publishing (UK) Limited, 9 Park End Street, 2nd Floor
Oxford, UK OX1 1HH UNITED KINGDOM
phone 44 (0)1865 722 113 (local rate 0845 230 9601)
facsimile 44 (0)1865 722 868; info.uk@trafford.com

Order online at:
trafford.com/06-0730

10 9 8 7 6 5 4 3

DECLARARI INDEX

PART 1	1	PREAMBLE
PART 2	7	COUNSELLING & REHABILITATION (EKLEGETE)
PART 3	99	POLITICS; HISTORY; EDUCATION
PART 4	153	SIMPLE BASICS OF CHRISTIANITY

COUNSELLING & REHABILITATION

WHAT STANDARDS DO WE USE ?	9
PSYCHOLOGY / PSYCHIATRY DOES NOT HAVE THE ANSWERS	11
FREUD'S MEDICAL MODEL THEORY	20
THE CHURCH / CHRIST / FREUD	28
AUTOGENIC OR ALLOGENIC ?	42
NON - DIRECTIVE COUNSELLING	45
THREE ELEMENTS OF NOUTHETIC COUNSELLING	49
WHO SHOULD COUNSEL ?	53
MENTALLY ILL	54
CHILD TRAINING	64
THE REALM OF SKID ROAD	69
IN CONCLUSION	78
DISTRIBUTION OF EXLEGETE VIA REGISTERED MAIL	95
ALL TO NO AVAIL	97

POLITICS; HISTORY; EDUCATION

SYNTHESIS TO HON. PIERRE ELLIOT TRUDEAU	99
DISTRIBUTION OF SYNTHESIS	119
PETER CORCORAN LET'S TALK ABOUT SCHOOLS / EDUCATION	121

EDUCATIONAL PHILOSOPHY GONE AWRY	122
RE: TRAINING RECIPIENTS OF B. C. M .H. R.	141
SIMPLE BASICS OF CHRISTIANITY	153

THE RIGHT APPROACH

THE RIGHT APPROACH	156
GOD HAS SPOKEN	158
GOD HAS ACTED	161

MAN'S NECESSARY RESPONSE

WE MUST SEEK DILIGENTLY; HUMBLY; HONESTLY & OBEDIENTLY	162
THE CLAIMS OF JESUS CHRIST	167
CHRIST'S SELF - CENTERED TEACHINGS	169
CHRIST'S DIRECT CLAIMS	173
CHRIST'S INDIRECT CLAIMS	177
CHRIST IS TO BESTOW LIFE	178
CHRIST IS TO TEACH THE TRUTH	179
JUDGE THE WORLD	180
CHRIST'S DRAMATIZED CLAIMS	181
THE CHARACTER OF CHRIST	188
WHAT CHRIST HIMSELF THOUGHT	190
WHAT CHRIST'S FRIEND'S SAID	193
WHAT CHRIST'S ENEMIES CONCEDED	195
WHAT WE CAN SEE FOR OURSELVES	197
THE RESURRECTION OF CHRIST	200
THE BODY GONE	202
THE GRAVE CLOTHES WERE UNDISTURBED	208
THE LORD WAS RISEN	211
INVENTIONS	211
THE DISCIPLES WERE CHANGED	215

MAN'S NEED

THE FACT AND NATURE OF SIN	218
THE UNIVERSALITY OF SIN	220
BUT WHAT IS SIN ?	222
THE TEN COMMANDMENTS	223

THE CONSEQUENCES OF SIN

ALIENATION FROM GOD	232
BONDAGE TO SELF	236
CONFLICT WITH OTHERS	240
THE DEATH OF CHRIST	243
THE CENTRALITY OF THE CROSS	246
THE MEANING OF THE CROSS	250
CHRIST DIED FOR OUR EXAMPLE	252
CHRIST DIED AS OUR SAVIOUR	255
THE SALVATION OF CHRIST	264
THE SPIRIT OF CHRIST	265
THE CHURCH OF CHRIST	271

MAN'S RESPONSE

COUNTING THE COSTS	275
THE CALL TO FOLLOW CHRIST	278
THE CALL TO CONFESS CHRIST	288

THE INCENTIVES

FOR OUR OWN SAKE	290
FOR THE SAKE OF OTHERS	291
REACHING A DECISION	294
BEING A CHRISTIAN	305

CHRISTIAN PRIVILEGES

AN INTIMATE RELATIONSHIP	308
AN ASSURED RELATIONSHIP	309
A SECURE RELATIONSHIP	313

CHRISTIAN RESPONSIBILITIES

CHRISTIAN RESPONSIBILITIES	314
OUR DUTY TO GOD	316
OUR DUTY TO THE CHURCH OF CHRIST	318
OUR DUTY TO THE NATION	319
THE SEVEN STEPS DOWN AND UP	328
WE INHERIT CHRIST	335
CHRIST INHERITS US	335
THREE GREAT FUNDAMENTAL ERRORS	341
THE FOUR SOURCES OF ILLNESS AND DISEASE	341
WAS CHRIST NOT ABLE TO BRING PEACE TO WORLD?	343
NO ROOM IN THE INN FOR JOSEPH AND MARY	344

FOOD FOR THOUGHT

WHAT DOES IT MEAN TO "SAVED" OR "BORN AGAIN"	353
TO OUR BEST GOD ADDS THE REST	365

Pope John Paul II,
Vicar of Christ,
VATICAN CITY,
00120,
ITALY.

26 August 1998 AD

DECLARARI

PART 1

Blessed Vicar of Christ:

    Being convinced in my mind that the Roman Catholic Church will fall, not totally, but generally, also being well aware of the fact that the gates of hell shall <u>NOT</u> prevail against the Church of Christ. (Matt 16:18), there will <u>ALWAYS</u> be a remnant of the faithful few that will stand.

    However, it is axiomatic that the 'gates of hell' are in a fight to the death with Christ's Church, utilizing all the powers and deceptions that are at satan's command, through his angels, spirits, saints, servants and instruments. This assault may well accomplish a degree of success via deceiving and snaring even the 'elect', whom satan seeks to devour.

    Further, in keeping with Almighty God's usual modus operendi and Natural Law, He will do with the Roman Catholic Church as He did with Israel. (and for the same reasons), cut them off because they lost favour with God, due to their own unbelief, unfaithfulness, and arrogant stupidity.

We see, Your Blessed Holiness, evidences of scenarios that have historically prompted Almighty God's Wrath and INDIGNATION, rampant in the North American Church today. For example, the Edmonton Journal newspaper, (Edmonton, Alberta, Canada) published an editorial, with the headline "POPE SILENCES CATHOLIC THINKERS; REPRESSION WON'T STRENGTHEN THE CHURCH".

Since few Editors today actually go to Church, they can be easily duped by dissident theologians, in our Seminaries, endeavouring to get God in step with the people. Further evidence was seen on National television news broadcasts that showed some woman in Holland shaking her finger in Your Holiness' face, telling Your Holiness not to come to Holland to tell the people in Holland what to do.

Blessed be God in that He has in Yourself, Your Holiness, one who is guided by, and listens to, the urgings, councils and discernment's of The Holy Spirit, through the Scriptures, and NOT guided by the rebellious, liberal theologians of selfism. i.e. the United Church of Canada, and the Anglican Church of Canada.

Truly, "TO EDUCATE A MAN IN MIND, AND NOT IN MORALS, IS TO EDUCATE A MENACE TO SOCIETY". (Theodore Roosevelt).

We know that through it all, with Almighty God, Mercy triumphs over Judgment (Jas 2:13), and if our Church will turn back to God, as a Nation, He will heal our land. 2 Chron 7:14 1 John 1:9. In my opinion, if the Church will not do this, under the guidance and direction of your Holiness, the Church will fall parcae.

This Synthesis is dedicated to Your Holiness in support, in Christ.

The writer of this Synthesis has tried to address the falling Church Scenario for a long time, to no avail, being ridiculed and maligned by those that should have really known better. However, the ridicule and malice I experienced pales into nothingness, compared to the ridicule and malice Your Holiness is subjected to.(Father in Heaven, forgive them).

"When reasonable argument is lacking, mud slinging is a good substitute", & "Oppress via discrediting" are two oracles of satan's realm, and the most utilized weapons to attack God's Realm.

This synthesis is respectfully submitted to Your Blessed Holiness with ALL due respect and love, with the hope that if there is anything herein that will help to reverse the fall of the Roman Catholic Church parcae, PLEASE use that at Your Blessed Holiness' will, for THAT is the intended purpose for this Synthesis, to be of service to Your Blessed Holiness.

This Synthesis is in four parts: Part one is to respectfully pay homage to Your Holiness, support Your Holiness, and offering to help in any way that Your Holiness deems appropriate.

Part two concerns Poimenics. Priests and Ministers learn little about Counselling in the Seminary. Most begin their Priesthood with virtually no knowledge of what to do, and are soon in difficulty.

Some Priests, in an attempt to prepare THEMSELVES as counsellors, beg, borrow and devour as many books on the subject as they can...but these are of little help as they mostly contain and commend Rogerian methods or advocate Freudian principles, and when the Priest or Minister tries to put these into practice, they fail miserably as counsellors, because those methods and principles try to rationalize sin; pass it off as sickness, and if there is any religion at all, that religion requires God to get in step with the people.

Counselling deals with values and standards...matters Priests and Ministers ought to be quite competent with, yet they are not. Simply telling people what God requires of them and utilizing the Sacrament of Confession or Reconciliation, will produce much fruit.

It boggles my mind to see or hear of Priests and Ministers suggesting to parishioners with problems, to see a Psychologist or Psychiatrist, while at the same time, there is an unopened Holy Bible laying on the Priest or Minister's desk; they somehow have not come to recognize the Bible as <u>B</u>ASIC <u>I</u>NSTRUCTIONS <u>B</u>EFORE <u>L</u>EAVING <u>E</u>ARTH.

As our Heavenly Father has Angels, Spirits, Saints, Instruments and Servants to do His Will, satan also has angels, spirits, saints, instruments and servants to do his will. We CANNOT fight God's battles with satan's weapons.

Part three concerns Education, and simply makes the point that our Educational Philosophy has gone awry, due to replacing dialectic thinking with empirical thinking. People are no longer Educated, they simply receive job training.

Part four deals with basic Christianity, and it seems that much of that has been forgotten. It is absolutely necessary that WE get in step with God, and stop insisting God get in step with secular humanism.

It is clearly understood, there is nothing new or startling contained in this Synthesis. The contents are nothing more than the BASIC teachings of Holy Mother Church...The Holy See...the Roman Catholic Church. However, it seems that there are Cardinals, Bishops, Theologians, Priests and Lay People that have lost sight of these BASIC teachings, and need again, to learn the rudiments of the Faith. This Synthesis is addressed to them. Those that have lost their way due to slackness in Prayer, and Scripture Reading time (these must be balanced and in proportion), Devotions and Meditations. We must be DILIGENT in ALL of these areas of our life. Backsliding comes from slack abiding. And if the father of all lies snares enough of these people to take The Church out of Almighty God's favour, "the blood" will be required of their hands. To reiterate, this Synthesis is intended for them.

Blessed Vicar of Christ, this Synthesis is dedicated to Yourself, and presented to Your Blessed Holiness, with ALL due respect and gratitude, giving thanks and praise for Your Holiness' strength and courage in standing by The Holy See, faithful to Jesus Christ, and the teachings of the Blessed Holy Trinity.

Your obedient servant in Christ.

R.A. Pratt, Ph.D., F.B.F.S.

PART 2

DO YOU NOT KNOW ? HAVE YOU NOT HEARD ?
WAS IT NOT TOLD YOU FROM THE BEGINNING ?
HAVE YOU NOT UNDERSTOOD THE FOUNDATIONS OF THE EARTH ?
ISA 40:21

A SYNTHESIS ON THE BREADTH AND LENGTH AND HEIGHT AND DEPTHS OF THE UNFATHONABLE LOVE AND REALM OF GOD, AND THE BREADTH AND LENGTH AND HEIGHT AND DEPTHS OF THE UNFATHONABLE RESPONSE OF MAN TO THAT LOVE AND REALM, BY R. A. PRATT, Ph.D.,F.B.F.S.

TO QUOTE FROM A THESIS WRITTEN IN 1982...

13 AUG 1982

*EKLEGETE; RE COUNSELLING AND REHABILITATION.

1. WHAT STANDARDS DO WE USE ? When we attempt to ascertain whether or not something is right or wrong, good or bad within a clients response and (or) behaviour patterns, what standards can we use to measure against ? In my opinion we certainly cannot use the CLIENT'S standards because the client, to say the least, is confused, unstable, and would probably change standards many times, depending on the moods, feelings and circumstances of the various times. More often, the client is quite irrational, irresponsible, immature, insecure and suffering a slight (?) inferiority complex. Obviously, we cannot use the client's own standards to measure against.

Can we use the COUNSELLOR'S or the THERAPIST'S standards ? In my opinion, HARDLY, I know MANY counsellors and therapists that are worse off than any client they will ever see i.e. dry drunks; vindictive; spiteful; intolerant; can be conned or manipulated by ANYONE willing to "suck up to them" for those purposes; utterly incapable of the impersonal approach that is so vital; if the counsellor or therapist likes the client, the client is right and cannot do anything wrong, if the counsellor or therapist does NOT like the client, the client is wrong and cannot do anything right. And of course, the ever present, non-productive, most dangerous of all, those on ego or power trips; also the bleeding heart do-gooders or the 'milquetoast'.

* An asking; make a choice; choose.

In many instances, there is no fraternalism among counsellors or therapists. Ego, vanity and power trips, to varying degrees, in various combinations are quite common. Obviously, we cannot use the counsellor's or the therapist's standards to measure against.

The ONLY standards that I have found to be accurate, to the point of INFALLIBILITY, and totally reliable, are the BIBLICAL standards, and these standards are used within the Nouthetic Counselling and Rehabilitation technique.

Precautions must be suggested...first, I am aware that MY interpretations and applications of Biblical standards are NOT infallible; secondly, I do not disregard science, which is useful for the purposes of illustrating, filling in generalizations with specifics, and challenging wrong human interpretations of Biblical standards, thereby forcing the counsellor or therapist to restudy.

However, to quote Dr. Jay E. Adams, in the areas of Psychology/Psychiatry, "science has given way to human philosophy, gross theosophy and spurious speculation". I have found the various psychologies just as heavy with dogma as any religion. If dogma is statement pronounced true apart from evidence that any competent person can verify, theology and psychology/psychiatry are simple pot and kettle, neither have any ground to call the other black. Theologians are willing to acknowledge presuppositional faith, but psychology/psychiatry will not do so.

Masur is correct when he claims psychology/psychiatry and psychoanalysis became substitutes for religion, for the disillusioned middle class. Analysis is accompanied by ceremonies and rituals that resemble a religious rite; its concept, at best debatable, are repeated as articles of faith.

The Nouthetic technique utilizes Biblical standards not because of religious fanaticism, but simply because as a result of 7 years of research and experiment, the Biblical standards have proven to be infallible. THIS is the reason I have adopted Biblical standards, according to **GOD's** Laws.

2. PSYCHOLOGY/PSYCHIATRY DOES NOT HAVE THE ANSWERS. Psychology/psychiatry itself, is the first to admit they do not have all the answers. Yet, on the first day of a semester, the Professor said "the world is in a mess". He spent the next hour explaining how psychology was the world's only hope for sorting out that mess.

The newspaper headlines have not improved...crime is on the increase...our streets are becoming unsafe...there are demonstrations in our streets...the mental institutions and detox units, in spite of tranquilizers, still do a thriving business. As a matter of fact, psychiatry (the illegitimate child of psychology), which has made the most grandiose claims, is in serious trouble. The American Psychiatric Association made the statement (1955) that psychotherapy is today in a state of disarray almost exactly as it was 200 years ago.

The great revolution, psychology/psychiatry, has solved few problems...I wonder how long the gross errors of Freud will continue to plague psychology/psychiatry ?

Patients, failing to recover after YEARS of treatment and thousands of dollars later, have ALSO been wondering about the boasts of psychology/psychiatry. Some, getting worse, have begun to suspect that many of their problems are IATROGENIC (treatment induced). H. J. Eysonck, Director of the University of London Psychology Dept. wrote "the success of the Freudian revolution seems complete; only one thing went wrong, the patients don't get any better".

Psychotherapy has not yet been proved more effective than general medical counselling in treating neurosis or psychosis. In general, therapy works best with people that are young, wellborn, well educated, and not seriously sick.

Even Journalists have become aware of this disillusionment with psychology/psychiatry. Leslie Leber wrote an article in THIS WEEK MAGAZINE, 18 Sept 1966. He wrote "Once bright with promise, psychoanalysis today seems hardly worth the millions we are lavishing on it each year". In the U.S.A. there are approximately 18,000 psychiatrists, and about 9% are Psychoanalysts...many of these Doctors and their patients have begun to take stock...have the benefits of psychoanalysis justified the hours of torturous self-examination, the years of painful slow probing, the $25,000.00 or so spent for the "complete" treatment ? In short, are psychologist/psychiatrists and psychoanalysists worth the millions a year we lavish on them ?

The truth is that not only is the "dramatic breakthrough" and "cure" almost non-existent, but thousands upon thousand who have spent millions upon millions are not at all certain whether they are one whit less "neurotic" than before they began their five times a week, $50.00 a session trudge to the couch... but much more significant than the gradual disillusionment of patients, is the wholesale defection of analysts themselves from the Freudian fold. Many are now challenging the need for long drawn out excavations of the subconscious mind.

    Surveys show that of patients who spend upward of 350 hours in the psychologists/psychiatrists office for treatment, 1/3 shows SOME improvement over a period of three years. The fly in the ointment, however, is that the same percentage show <u>SOME</u> improvement <u>WITHOUT</u> psychoanalysis, or under the care of a regular Physician. As a matter of <u>FACT</u>, the same ratio showed <u>SOME</u> improvement in Mental Hospitals one hundred years ago, patients sometime improve <u>IN SPITE OF</u> what is done to them.

    Unfortunately, analysts often interpret the above mentioned improvements as a result of psychology/psychiatry...they fail to realize that other people who use other methods...i.e. hypnosis, electric shock, cold baths, the laying on of hands, the pulling of teeth to remove foci infection, suggestion, dummy pills (placebos), confession or prayer, produce <u>EXACTLY</u> THE SAME RATIO OF IMPROVEMENT.

    The adherents of this "EXAGGERATED" faith use it as a shield of illusion to conceal ugly reality. When we read in the newspaper that the alcoholic, rapist, the vandal, the emotionally disturbed etc. will be given "psychological /psychiatric care" we are assured that the problem is being effectively dealt with, and we dismiss it from our minds. I contend that we have no right to this 'EASY' absolution from responsibility. I contend MUCH <u>RE-THINKING</u> is called for.

Further, I contend one achievement Freud ought to be credited with, is the <u>LEADING</u> part his theories have played in the present collapse of the FAMILY, and RESPONSIBILITY, in modern society...ANOTHER is Freud's contribution to the fundamental presupposition of the "NEW" morality. In my opinion, as Christ proved to be God's man, Freud proved to be satan's man.

Freud adopted and popularized the "MEDICAL MODEL". This theory has been so widely popularized (largely by PROPAGANDA) by using the "MIRROR" words 'MENTAL ILLNESS' and 'MENTAL HEALTH'. The 'MEDICAL MODEL' has been so successfully implanted on our minds that most people <u>NAIVELY</u> believe that the root cause of the difficulties psychologists/psychiatrists deal with, are <u>DISEASES</u> and <u>SICKNESSES</u>.

Because the realm of present day Politics has been further compounded, complicated, and polluted by the church of Psychology/Psychiatry, let's take a look at THAT church: I refer to Psychology/Psychiatry as a 'church' for the same reasons utilized for the Educational church.

As soon as Psychology/Psychiatry is mentioned in connection with paganism and mysticism, the 'battle flag' goes up, and the 'battle' is on. (for your information, Psychiatry is the illegitimate child of Psychology).

Psychology, promoted by **EDWARD BERNAYS**, (a nephew of SIGMUND FREUD), was one of the most amazing and influential propagandist of the 20th century), popularized, via propaganda, Freudianism, and the Medical Model Theory. (For your information, propagandists are now known as Pr Flacks).

Bernays developed a 'scientific' method of managing behaviour, to which he gave the name N. B. 'Public Relations'. Bernays, believing that democracy needed wise and hidden manipulators, was <u>PROUD</u> to be a propagandist, and wrote in his book "Propaganda", Quote "If we understand the mechanisms and motives of the group mind, it is now possible to **CONTROL** and **REGIMENT** the masses, according to **OUR** will, without them knowing it". Bernays called this <u>"ENGINEERING OF CONSENT"</u> and proposed that, Quote: "those who manipulate this unseen mechanism of society, constitute an invisible government which is the <u>true</u> ruling power of a country."

It was via this same "ENGINEERING OF CONSENT" (Propaganda Programme) that Democracy was murdered, and the Destruction of the Labour Movement began, in Canada, in June 1945. The Multi-Nationals got their 'foot in the door", and the Programme of knocking Fraternalism out of the Labour Movement began. All via two Propaganda Programmes, i.e. <u>ENGINEERING OF CONSENT</u>, launched, in Canada, JUNE, 1945.

In almost every act of our daily lives, whether in the realm of politics or business; in our social conduct or our ethical thinking, we <u>are</u> dominated by the relatively small number of person (PR Flacks)... who pull the strings which control the public mind, **when the public mind is <u>not</u> governed by the Spiritual Standards of God, according to <u>God's</u> Precepts, Oracles and Commandments, which is the <u>only</u> defence a human being has against the propaganda of <u>Lucifer's</u> realm.** When <u>ANYONE</u> does <u>not</u> have that standard to measure against, they are easily duped, and to brainwash them is a very simple matter.

It appears not to have dawned on Bernays until the 1930's that his 'science' of propaganda could also be used to subvert democracy and promote fascism. That was when journalist Karl von Weigand told Bernays that Nazi Propagandist, Joseph Goebbels had read all Bernays books, and that Goebbels possessed an ever better library of propaganda than Bernays did.

"The most successful, longest running and deadliest propaganda campaign in history... Re TAILOR MADE CIGARETTES, was one of Bernays projects also." Quote from a book by John Stauber/Derrick Jenson, "War on Truth", March, 1999.

Psychology/Psychiatry enjoys the status of a 'science' thanks to PROPAGANDIST Bernays, and is well-integrated into our culture.

Consider for a moment all of the departments of a school district that are <u>based</u> on one tentacle of psychology/psychiatry or another – behavioural training for teachers; IQ testing:

Personality tests; counselling; and dozens more. And when we realize that Sociology is simply psychology applied to groups of people you can double that number.

Now think of the people in the police department, starting with the officers themselves, who are taught, and expected to use, psychological/ psychiatric training.

Think of the Justice System; Employment and Unemployment offices; Welfare Programmes; Children's Services; Public Relations Depts; - and those are only Government applications of psychological/psychiatric tentacles.

Psychology is fed to us daily via the media, TV and radio. There are even 'counsellors' with phone-in advice shows. Talk shows would be a wasteland without psychologist/ psychiatrists to air their latest pet theories.

First, however, we must look at the source of this so-called 'science'. The 2 great founders of psychology/psychiatry were Freud and Jung, a drug addict and an occultist, respectively. Freud's addiction to cocaine is well known; Less known is that Jung wrote many of his theories under the influence of a 'Spirit Guide', which he never recognized as a demon of Lucifer's realm. But Jung labelled it as a "Collective Archetype". (Jung was also much influenced by Edward Bernays).

The Leaders of the psych world that followed were hardly any better. Maslow, Rogers, Fromm, all of them "Made the trip east," And ended up in occultism. These three popularized, with the help of Pr Flacks (Propagandists), the now-dominant theory in both "New Age" and psychological/psychiatric thinking, that a high self-esteem is the solution to **ALL** psychological problems. They claim that people suffer from low self-esteem, and are driven to 'act out' bad behaviour to fulfill their unmet 'needs'.

"Sympathetic understanding, the kind you give to a person when he is sick with a physical illness is what the mentally ill person must have"..."the person with a mental problem is sick and can't help it", the psychologists/psychiatrists tell us...they blamed Dallas rather than Oswald for President Kennedy's death...when Charles Whitman picked off innocent passers-by with a rifle, they said society MUST be held guilty for the act...the murderer himself is no longer held responsible; "he can't help it" has become a popular phrase of psychologists/psychiatrists.

Psychologists/psychiatrists have been trying to dull, if not actually extract, the teeth of the law, and this is on the distinct Freudian principle that it is entirely natural for the criminal to act as he does, and quite unreasonable for society to make him stand trial for being his antisocial self.

One of the last questions I intend to research is "who has done our society the greater harm, the legal profession or the psychological/psychiatric profession."

The question "is psychology/psychiatry a pseudo science?" is being asked by more people. Even those that should know better, have been 'misguided' by this pseudo science...A Chaplain in a Mental Health institution gave the following address to a group of Ministers that were about to be posted as Chaplains to Mental Institutions..."first of all, there is little you can do as Ministers for people in a Mental Institution. Secondly, what you CAN do is support the patients' right to feel injured by others. Thirdly, it is important to understand that in a Mental Institution, people with guilt no longer are subjected to rebuke from others outside, the pressure is off, and in this way they quietly lose their guilt and get well. Fourthly, we must consider people in Mental Institutions (now get THIS (emphasis mine)) not as violators of conscience but a VICTIMS of their conscience. Finally, when we look at their erratic behaviour, it seems to be sin, but it isn't, the patient is not responsible for his actions. He can't help what he is doing; he's sick. Often he blames himself for what he can't help, for what isn't his fault, and this is the cause of his problems.

Consequently, bad behaviour as being blameworthy is taboo in a Mental Institution. The usual religious approach of responsibility, guilt, confession and forgiveness is no good here. The patients' consciences are already too severe. These people are morally neutral people, and all we can do is be ventilators for them". This Chaplain's speech sets forth the Psychological/psychiatric view of our time. Every point he made, I CHALLENGE in this Thesis. The sheer determination of this viewpoint, with its inevitable consequences, excusing the client for his behaviour is apparent. Lawrence Le Shan says that this philosophy has led to "the therapists attempt to excuse the clients' negative and undesirable behaviour on the grounds that it was determined by the past and so he had no reason to feel guilty about it".

Any man that deserts his wife and children, 'throwing them

to the wolves' because the 'going' got tough, SHOULD feel guilty about that desertion, because he IS guilty of that desertion behaviour... any man that abuses his wife and children, SHOULD feel guilty about the abuse, because he IS guilty of that abusive behaviour. Any wife that 'steps out' on a husband working hard and long hours to provide for his wife and children, SHOULD feel guilty about 'stepping out' on her husband, and IS guilty of that 'stepping out' behaviour. Guilt MUST be dealt with in the OBVIOUSLY correct manner; NOT ignored and forgotten about, for the sake of ALL concerned.

3. <u>FREUD'S MEDICAL MODEL THEORY.</u> Many problems; contradiction and error lay in the Freud theory and therapy that is the basis of our 'MODERN' Psychology/psychiatry. Freud saw the human being as 'torn within'.

Man, he said, have basic primitive wants, impulses and drives that seek expression. These Freud called the ID (sex, aggression etc.). But in man there is also the SUPEREGO (roughly equivalent to what more often has been called the SUBCONSCIOUS mind).

The SUPEREGO is socialized into the individual by parents, the church, teachers etc. Within the Freudian technique, the SUPEREGO is the CULPRIT. According to Freud, the problem with the mentally disturbed is an over-socialization of the SUPEREGO. An over-socialized conscience is overly severe and overly strict. Freud says the mentally disturbed are VICTIMS of the SUPEREGO. (bearing in mind that according to Freud each individual is their OWN standard of response and behaviour patterns...an error and contradiction). According to Freud, the EGO is the third part of man, and is the ARBITRATOR (or arbiter between the ID and the SUPEREGO) and is within the realm of the CONSCIOUS self or CONSCIOUS MIND; the ID and the EGO are within the realm of the CONSCIOUS self. The SUPEREGO functions on the level of responsibility, whereas the ID and the EGO function on the level of irresponsibility.

A conflict arises when the ID desires to be expressed but is frustrated by the SUPEREGO. The primitive 'wants' seek expression, but the overly severe SUPEREGO, standing at the threshold, hinders the ID from expressing itself in the conscious life of the individual. This battle, which takes place on the subconscious level, is the SOURCE of one's difficulties. The war of the flesh. ROM 7:13 – 25.

When the ID is repressed by the SUPEREGO, the person in conflict experiences what Freud called 'guilt felling'... these 'guilt feelings', however, are not feelings that stem from real guilt. Since the feeling of guilt is false guilt, one does not need to 'confess' as the Chaplain pointed out, but rather what he needs to do, is rid himself of false guilt. So, naturally enough, therapy consists of making one feel right by dispelling false guilt. The Psychologist/psychiatrist achieves this by taking a stand WITH the ID AGAINST the SUPEREGO. The Psychologist/psychiatrist seeks to weaken, dilute and defeat the SUPEREGO so that it stops making its victimizing demands. (each is his own standard remember). VENTILATION (an airing of one's pent-up feelings) is part of the process. Re-socialization according to 'reasonable and realistic' standards (individual standards) is the other CRUCIAL part. Freud loses sight of the power and NECESSITY of sex transmutation completely.

Here is an example of the present day application of Freud's principle...this record case history is at the A.P.P. tape library, volume #1, entitled "LORETTA". Albert Ellis makes a strong attack on Loretta's sub-conscious (SUPEREGO). He threatens that Loretta will never be released from hospital until she does away with her moral values...the following is excerpts from the tape...Ellis said "your problem actually is the fact that you have a lot of 'shoulds', 'oughts' and 'musts' (SUPEREGO). The main issue, as I said before, (in another interview) in my estimation, is that you set up a lot of 'shoulds', 'oughts' and 'musts' which, unfortunately, you were taught when you were very young. You were taught these by your father, your mother, your teacher and your church. If you did not have this concept of 'shoulds' 'oughts' and 'musts', which, unfortunately, is nicely defeating your own ends, then you would not believe it's wrong to have sexual relations with your best girlfriend's husband, and you would not be disturbed".

After an objection by Loretta to this attack, Ellis tells her "well, you're entitled to your views, but unfortunately, as long as you maintain them, you are going to stay in this hospital; when you change your views, you will get out. Loretta, still staunchly objecting, replies, "well, as long as we have air-conditioning, it might not be so bad." And the naive Chaplain blissfully adds "the Chaplain provides the Christian comfort and the Psychologists/psychiatrist provides the needed therapy and neither conflicts with the other."

The psychologist/psychiatrist in his therapy tries (and __MUST__ if he is to be successful) to get the patient to adopt HIS opinions as the patient's 'NEW' conscience; using his OWN moral standards as the client's 'NEW' standards. (ANOTHER contradiction).

The Priest/Minister is known to be limited in his training, abilities and tools, and therefore, MUST defer and refer people with problems to the Psychologist/psychiatrist. (according to Mental Health literature). In short, the Priest/Minister is not considered a counsellor or therapist. But <u>THIS</u> question never seems to get asked..."is Psychology/psychiatry capable or even a valid science ?"

Psychologists/psychiatrists do not operate as physicians. Their <u>GOAL</u> is personality and behaviour change, and their <u>METHOD</u> is VALUE ALTERATION.

Psychology/psychiatry is the URSURPTION of the work of the Priest/Minister. Freud anticipated this usurpation. He wrote to Pfister about the "enormous number of people who were not ill in the medical sense, but are nevertheless in extreme need of analysis". And predicted that "the cure of souls (the term used for Pastoral care) will one day be a recognized non-ecclesiastical and even non-religious calling". Thus, the introduction of the 'medical model' became the <u>MEANS</u> of usurpation. This usurpation has been <u>ACHIEVED</u> by declaring a host of people "sick" who are not, and taking them under the pale of Psychology/psychiatry.

If Freud's theory was correct, namely that trouble arises whenever the ID has been repressed by the SUPEREGO, then, REALLY, <u>OUR</u> day ought to be a day of widespread mental health rather than a day of unparalleled numbers with personal problems. For <u>OURS</u> is <u>NOT</u> a day of <u>REPRESSION</u> of the ID, but of <u>PERMISSIVENESS</u> in expressing the ID. If there ever was a time the 'LID WAS OFF', in which there is wide-open rebellion against family, authority, responsibility and maturity, <u>OURS</u> IS that day.

And yet, unprecedented numbers are in trouble. If Freud's theory was true, the most immoral people, or at least the most amoral people, should be the healthiest...in fact, the opposite is true.

People in Mental Institutions (generally speaking), and people who come to Counselling, INVARIABLY are people with moral difficulties or VICTIMS of people with moral difficulties. 'MORAL DIFFICULTIES' does not always mean 'sexual violations'... that is only ONE aspect of it. Immorality of every sort, irresponsibility towards God and man (i.e. the breaking of God's 'laws') is found most surely among people with personal problems.

A revolution is brewing...largely restricted to the field of Psychology. There are a growing number of vigorous individuals who have begun to challenge the accepted Freud and Rogers theory. Some of the names in this movement are Wm. Glasser; G.L. Harrington; Bill Mainord; Perry London; O. Hobart Mowrer; and Ron Pratt.

There are of course, many differences of opinion among them, some no better then the opinions they are revolting against. The essence of the attack by this movement on the institutionalized system can be summed up in a word...the new movement is opposed to the Freudian irresponsibility formulation.

The advocates of the revolution ask "shall we still speak of the repressed ID?" They reply "NO"! Instead, they say, it is time to speak of the repressed subconscious (SUPEREGO). again..."do we seek to remove guilt feelings?" "never"!

We must acknowledge guilt to be real and deal directly with it. Psychological guilt is the fear of 'being found out'. It is the recognition that one has violated HIS OWN standards; it is the pain of NOT doing as one knows he ought to do. These advocates of the revolution insist that ventilation of feelings must be replaced by confession of wrongdoing. They are speaking of 'behavioural' problem, not 'emotional' problems, and they are correct except for, in my opinion, their rehabilitation programmes.

People who are thought to be 'withdrawn from reality' (schizophrenia), are in fact, trying to avoid detection; they side with the 'wants' instead of the 'oughts'.

'Guilt feelings' are thought of as 'false guilt' by the Freudian theory; guilt over the ID/SUPEREGO conflict, rather than the violation of one's standards. A typical example on this point is 'how could Sue be guilty of wearing lipstick?' She would be guilty, if she wore the lipstick out of REBELLION alone.

G.L. Harrington worked in a Veteran's hospital in Los Angeles with 210 male patients, in bldg. 206 (the end of the line bldg.) and Bill Glasser in the Ventura State School for girls in California, showed an 80% success rate with HARDENED Sociopaths, in a structured, total responsibility programme.

There is another problem which stems from the 'medical model'...disease and sickness are often mysterious, especially to the layman. Disease comes from without, and serious illness must be cured from without, by another...the 'expert'.

The sick person feels helpless, and he turns to the Physician. The Physician, like the disease that invaded the patient, solves the problem from without. Thus, AGAIN, personal hopelessness and irresponsibility are the <u>NATURAL</u> results of the 'medical model'. If a person's problems in living are basically problems of disease and sickness, rather than problems of response and/or behaviour, he has no hope unless there is medicine or therapy that can be applied to his case. Since there is no medical cure for people in such trouble, they move from despair to deeper despair.

A study by Allport and Plos in 1960 showed that the language of Psychology/Psychiatry had five times as many terms implying passivity and being acted upon as it had terms implying action. The passive helplessness characteristic of Psychological/Psychiatric theory and practice, clearly consent with the 'medical model', and leads to helplessness as well.

The chaos and helplessness that has resulted, is seen even in the humour of our time. A modern folk song by Anna Russell for example...
"I went to my Psychiatrist to be psychoanalyzed,
To find out why I killed the cat and blacked my husband's eye.
He laid me on a downy couch to see what he could find,
And here is what he dredged up from my subconscious mind.

When I was one, my mommie hid my dolly in a trunk,
And so it follows naturally that I am always drunk.
When I was two I saw my father kiss the maid one day,
And that is why I suffer now from Kleptomania.
At three I had the feeling of ambivalence towards my brothers,
And so it follows naturally I poison all my lovers.
But I am happy now I've learned the lesson this has taught,
That everything I do that's wrong, is someone else's fault."

The 'VICTIM' theory is well illustrated by Sylling who teaches... unwed mothers are victims of their parent's problems. The sexual involvement on the part of the girl is incidental. This strange assumption leads him to conclude that her real problem is not wrong, but basic needs and desires her parents failed to meet.

Thomas S. Szasz teaches..."to argue that all men, even those labeled 'PARANOID' should be treated seriously, as responsible human beings, is like desecrating the Psychological/Psychiatric flag. It flies in the face of one of the major tenets of Psychology/Psychiatry as a social institution, namely that the actions of mentally ill persons need not be taken seriously in the sense of their being held responsible for what they do." This allogenic view leads to a general degrading of the human personality. Man is viewed as an irresponsible pawn. The Psychological/Psychiatric treatment offered clearly grows out of this presupposition. It's manipulative mechanistic orientation reveals the unscriptural anthropology which denies the image of God (distorted but inherent) in man. No wonder LOOK magazine in a 21 page spread 2 Feb 60 called Psychology/Psychiatry "the troubled science."

4. THE CHURCH/CHRIST/FREUD: Mowrer, (a noted research Psychologist who had been honoured with the Presidency of the American Psychological Association) challenged the entire field of Psychology/Psychiatry, declaring it a failure, and refutes the fundamental Freudian presupposition. Boldly he threw down the 'gauntlet' (to Humanistic Christians as well) he asked, "Has Religion sold it's birthright for a mess of Psychological pottage?"

Mowrer opposes the 'medical model', which removes the responsibility from the client. Since he is not considered 'blameworthy' his family MAY treat him with sympathetic understanding and make other allowance for him. This is because they think he can't help his 'sickness'. He is invaded from without, he must helplessly rely on 'experts'.

The 'Medical model' (from which the concept of mental illness is derived) takes away the sense of personal responsibility; as a result, Psychotherapy becomes a search into the past to find others (parents, grandparents, teachers, the Church, even society itself) on whom to place the blame. Therapy consists of siding against the too strict SUPEREGO (subconscious) which these (parents etc.) culprits have socialized into the 'VICTIM'.

With these 'patients' the problems are moral, NOT medical. They suffer from REAL (justified) guilt, not 'guilty feelings' (false guilt). The basic irregularity is not emotional, but BEHAVIOURAL. They are not VICTIMS of conscience, but VIOLATORS of conscience.   They must stop blaming others and accept responsibility for their own behaviour. Their problems can't be solved by ventilating their feelings, but rather by CONFESSION of them. Most of them are where they are not because they are sick, but because they are sinful. In counselling sessions I discovered with remarkable consistency that their main problems were of their own making. Others (parents etc.) were not their problem, they themselves were their own worst enemies...some of immorality and so on... many fled to institutions to escape the consequences of their wrong doing...some sought to avoid the responsibility of difficult decisions.

It's quite true, parental incompetence MAY be the CAUSE of a lot of problems, but the CURE is the CLIENT'S responsibility now. However, even in these cases, where incompetent parental handling HAS been the cause, the client can't be excused beyond the age of 14 years. The bad response and behaviour patterns developed or even instilled by the parents in these cases, at some point in time, became the CLIENT'S responsibility...the cure IS the client's responsibility from that point on. It is simply a waste of valuable rehabilitation time to dredge out where the parents went wrong...we must spend that time via directive counselling, telling the client what must be done to correct the problems, using the proper and ONLY infallible standards to measure against, Biblical standards. Since we CAN re-shape ourselves, WE are responsible for the shape we are in.

We might easily cut the source of supply to skid row, if we were able to intercept EVERY troubled employee while still with the family, home and job; through EFFECTIVE counselling and rehabilitation techniques. This would be, PREVENTATIVE therapy...and INTERVENTION.

There are a few good Employee Recovery Programs in existence, TRYING to do just that, intercept the troubled person while still with home, family and job. But they are fighting a loosing battle...trying to build a second floor onto a house that does not have a first floor... the first floor being EFFECTIVE counselling and rehabilitation techniques, capable of the NECESSARY restructuring of the client. I have had MANY clients referred as drug addicts or alcoholics, who in fact were NOT drug addicts or alcoholics...the addiction in fact was NOT the SYNDROME only a SYMPTOM. Treating the client as an addict would NEVER HAVE SOLVED his problem or rehabilitated the client,

Directive Counselling can achieve in weeks what (in many cases) Psychotherapy could not achieve in YEARS.

The 'Medical model' techniques begin and end with 'man'. Mowrer and Glasser fail to take into consideration man's BASIC relationship to God; neglect God's law; and know nothing of the power of the Holy Spirit in regeneration and sanctification. Their presuppositional stance must be totally rejected. The mentally ill CAN be helped, but we must turn to Scriptures, to discover how God, (not Mowrer) says to do it.

Mowrer and Glasser have shown that many of the old views ARE wrong, and I was right. They have exposed Freud's opposition to responsibility, but neither Mowrer nor Glasser has solved the problem of responsibility. The responsibility they advocate is a relative etc., changing human responsibility. They claim that each individual is their own standard, but in reality, there are no other infallible standards but the standards imposed by God. It is AMAZING to discover how much God has to say about counselling, and how utterly FRESH and timely His approach is, for this day and age.

It must be interjected here, that as with ANY theory behind ANY pseudo science, there is ALWAYS a certain amount of truth or 'half-truths' present, and it should be OBVIOUS where the 'truth' of 'half-truths' proceed from;..they proceed from one that is utterly incapable of any originality whatsoever, but is a 'master' at duplication, and a practiced deceiver. In my opinion, perhaps someone was trying to tell us something in the similarity between the word PSEUDO and FREUD.

To our chagrin, we must recognize that the Church is even in MORE disarray than the Counselling and Rehabilitation field. Just as we cannot agree, neither can the Church...i.e. God is BIG in Northern Ireland; God is BIG in Southern Ireland. In love for God they shoot and bomb one another, injuring or killing innocent people, old folks, women and children.

God is BIG in Lebanon too...they all believe in God...they kill by the hundreds for Him...if they can kill all the others (Christians, Muslims, Hindus etc.,) for God, they know they are doing Him a GREAT service, and will thank Him for being on their side, and helping them and supporting them so that they could kill all the aged, women and children of the other faiths.

God is BIG in Iran...I'm sure they thank God for helping them kill the other Muslims of their Muslim faith in Iraq.

God is BIG in Israel too...they thank God for looking more favourably on them than everyone else...they are number 1 with

God. Jews and Arabs each claim God is on their side, and thank Him for <u>THAT</u> and for supporting them. Once an Arab got even for God by shooting the Pope.

Why there were even times when the great religious leaders of the day helped God by forbidding, and even ejecting, the bad sinners from attending God's Church services...and the congregations helped God to keep the Church clean and nice by humiliating or ignoring the dirty, stinking, lice laden drunken bums so they wouldn't come back and disturb God's people. Even strangers are discouraged (angels unawares?) and shunned. The great Religious leaders of the day once sent great crusades to far off lands to utterly destroy the 'infidels' God had decided NOT to destroy, but rather leave them to be 'a thorn' in Israel's side, until the end of time, because of the disobedience of Israel, and to be a 'lesson' to the Israelites for all time. In spite of this, the Religious leaders decided to do God a favour and destroy the 'infidel's' for Him, or at least harass the 'infidels' via murder, rape, and looting.

God's biggest 'problem' is not the troubled employee, alcoholic, drug addict, sinner, skid row bum, reprobate, atheist, etc...God's biggest 'problem' is the failing instruments and servants; instruments and servants God had planned on using, at a certain point in time, but were not 'there' when God needed them, because they fell away and failed God via rebellion; lack of faith, confidence in God, and trust; disobedience; not willing to simply 'follow', they had to run on ahead of God, getting their own mucky hand in the situation, and fouling the whole job up royally. They felt God was not BIG enough to handle the situation, so they had better handle it <u>FOR</u> Him.

We in the Counselling and Rehabilitation field should know and realize that, just like the clergy, we are simply 'sparkers'... parishioners and our clients, IF reconciled, will go on to do far greater things than we will ever do, and that's the way it SHOULD be.

God gave '<u>THE CHURCH</u>' the mission and responsibility to care for the poor, the sick, the widow, the orphan and the family, NOT THE GOVERNMENT, and Churches that keep that money back from God by NOT looking after their mission, find that, that money somehow 'DISAPPEARS' and the Church folds up and shuts down, and the lesson is not appreciated or understood.

God did NOT give the GOVERNMENT or the Church the mission and responsibility to say how His creation or creatures should be dealt with or trained up, He kept that job for HIMSELF, to be carried out through HIS instrument and servants, in <u>HIS WAY</u>.

The buyer for a local Christian Book store estimated he had in stock, approximately 3,500 book that were trying to explain what the Bible says. In my opinion, no more is needed than a Bible and a copy of the Imitation, both, in my opinion, <u>INSPIRED</u> books. If a person cannot see what God is saying to them through these two books, they had better take stock of their relationship with God,.. something is radically wrong.

Pastors are told by Mental Health Associations that they could do serious harm to the client if they don't refer them to Psychologists/Psychiatrists. The only trouble with this 'convenient' solution, is that the people who were 'referred' usually came back worse off or no better. Counselling deals with values and standards, matters the Clergy ought to be quite competent and comfortable with, yet they are not.

Raymond Meiner has a point when he writes "the Psalmist in the 1st Psalm calls that man blessed who walks <u>not</u> after the counsel of the ungodly", yet the clergy in many cases are not capable of wise and good counsel. Parishioners are <u>forced</u> to go to the ungodly to find the solutions to their problems. It seems some clergy feel God is not able to meet man's needs and problems. The parishioners are sent to those whose 'insights' proved wrong, and whose advice, when put into practice, simply did not work.

As I learned more and more how to keep my muggy hands off 'things', more and more Biblical methodology begin to emerge, and the results became more and more. Scripture says it all about counselling people with personal problems. There is not a personal problem or a situation that a person might encounter in their lifetime that is not covered in Scripture. The symptoms are given, the syndrome named, and the treatment prescribed. This seems to be overlooked in Poimenics. Difficult problems i.e. from the relationship of madness; to demon possession; to the dynamics of psychosomatic illness, and the effects of guilt, are succinctly described in Scriptures.

Is much of what is called 'mental illness' <u>'ILLNESS'</u> at all? This question arose mainly from noticing that while Scripture describes drunkenness and homosexuality as sins, Mental Health literature describes them as 'sickness' or 'disease' or 'normal'. I have to say that the mental illness viewpoint is wrong in removing responsibility from the sinner, by locating the source of his problem in constitutional or social factors over which he has no control. Scriptures say that the source of these problems lay in the depravity of man's fallen human nature.

Could the 'books' be wrong in also mis-classifying other problems like depression, neurosis, or psychosis as 'sickness'? When the 'Psychiatric heresy' started to rattle around in my head, I thought of Mr. O. Hobart Mowrer and his works THE CRISIS IN PSYCHIATRY AND RELIGION and THE NEW GROUP THERAPY. He was flatly challenging the very existence of institutionalized psychology/psychiatry. He stated outright that he believed the current Psychological/ Psychiatric dogmas were false. He cited evidence that Psychology/Psychiatry had failed. Group therapy is unscriptural and therefore <u>HARMFUL</u>.

In Mental Institutions there are people labelled neurotic, psychoneurotic and psychotic; (people of all stripes) that can be helped by confessing deviant behaviour, and assuming personal responsibility for it.

A pamphlet entitled "some help for the anxious". by Merville O. Vincent notes that Freud sees anxiety stemming from internal conflicts, then he mentions a second school of Psychology/ Psychiatry that has taken a more interpersonal approach saying that the feeling of insecurity is the base of all anxiety. Sullivan teaches that anxiety comes from disturbances in one's relationship with others. The third school of Psychology/ Psychiatry is existentialist thinking. Vincent concludes "to summarize, anxiety may come from threats to ourselves, threats from within or without. Anxiety may come from our past, present or future... in the past we have memories, experiences and unresolved conflicts... in the present we have bills, deadlines, work, examinations and relationships with others that may cause anxiety... in the future anxiety is aroused by lack of purpose, and the awareness of death which makes life even more meaningless." Vincent interprets Christianity as meeting the needs that people have, according to the diagnosis of Freud... Vincent says that Christ's diagnosis of man's condition is similar to Freud's diagnosis. (using satan's weapons to fight God's war). CLEARLY, he does not understand either Christ OR Freud.

That is a gross over-simplification, and a total misunderstanding of either Freud or Christ. This 'BAPTISING' of secular theories has come to characterize Christian Counselling and must be totally rejected. Vincent's system demands autonomy for man.

Freud called himself a "completely Godless Jew", and a "pagan". For him Christianity was an 'ILLUSION' that had to be dispelled. He said ALL religion was a sign of neurosis. He said men need to get away from religion altogether. CLEARLY, URGINGS, COUNCIL AND DISCERNMENTS OUT OF satan's realm.

The 'big' words from mental health literature are REFER or DEFER, for the Clergy. Rather than refer or defer to those steeped in humanistic dogmas, those who have been CALLED to help other people out of their difficulties must answer (or resume) their responsibilities. PROPERLY trained in Scripture, Clergy are more competent than anyone else.

The Clergy began their concessions to psychoanalysis

early. A close friend of Freud, Askar Pfister (a 'liberal' minister) typifies the capitulation that has generally taken place during the last 100 years. The issue here is whether the non-medical complaints of clients are allogenic or autogenic.

Can humanistic dogma generate the 'fruits' necessary? Can dogma grounded on humanistic assumption of man's autonomy generate the 'fruits' necessary? This amounts to the denial of man's depravity and the affirmation of man's innate goodness. The need for grace and the atoning work is undercut or usurped, and the client is left with the husks of a legalistic work, and a 'righteousness' which will lead to despair since it divests itself of the life and power of the Holy Spirit. Did Eli fail to confront his sons in the past because he was too busy finding excuses for their bad behaviour? He would have done better to emphasize the word WHAT. Had Eli compared the behaviour of his sons to God's standards, he would have been able to help his boys.

Chapter 16, section 7, of the Westminster Confession of faith says "works done by unregenerate men, although for the matter of them they may be things which God commands; and of good use both to themselves and others; yet, because they proceed not from a heart purified by faith; nor are done in right manner, according to the Word of God; nor to a right end, THE GLORY OF GOD, they are therefore sinful and cannot please God, or make a man meet to receive grace from God; yet their neglect of them is more sinful and displeasing to God".

That is a well-balanced statement. It clearly says that the works done by unregenerate men, even though they be acts that

God commands, are of no value in making them fit to receive grace from God, nor are they of any merit before God.

Clergy must look at the client's problem in the light of God's explanation of why the problem exists, and thereby find the solutions. This is the Divine pattern for Counselling.

The Clergy is called to be a PARACLETE not a PARAKEET. when Paul speaks of the PARACLESIS (help or Counsel) which God gives via the Scriptures, it is obvious that he speaks of a Book conceived of as an authoritative directive aid to our perseverance and hope.

Rollo May clearly believes in man's autonomy. Moral neutrality stems from that belief. May tries to justify his views Scripturely: he writes "this brings us to the matter of moral judgments in Counselling. It is clear, first from a Christian point of view, that no one has a right to judge another human being; the command, judge not, is an incontrovertible, particularly since it was given a dynamic by Jesus' own life and psychotherapeutically in the second place, judging is un-permissible," "And above all" as Alder says, "let us never allow ourselves to make any moral judgments, judgments concerning the moral worth of a human being." Carroll Wise agrees with May, she says "We can say frankly that we see no place in pastoral care for the passing of judgment in terms of condemnation or name calling, or of moralistic preachments."

May's interpretation of MATT 7:1-5 is false. Not only are there situations of all sorts in which judging is essential, but the Scriptures specifically command believers to make judgments, although illegitimate judging IS forbidden. i.e. judging in a hasty manner, without evidence; judging others before straightening up one's <u>own</u> life is also forbidden; judging intended to denounce another in order to raise one's ego is forbidden. But judgments of moral values in Counselling are precisely what the Scriptures everywhere command. There can be no morally neutral stance in counselling. How can a Pastor 'accept' sinful behaviour, sitting back, non-committely, watching the parishioner struggle with a problem he can only bring his own hopeless, sinful response to ? Such neutrality is impossible to a Pastor.

Who is the source of all GENUINE personality change that involves sanctification? Who ALONE is the one who brings life to the dead sinner? It is time to ask, "who has bewitched you... having begun by the Spirit, are you now being perfected by the flesh?"

Why do the Clergy refer the products of parental incompetence who lack self control to one who has never been able to discover the SECRET of God's peace or self control? Outwardly, he may APPEAR calm, assured, patient; even suave... can this be his <u>actual</u> inward condition? Can he have the 'fruits' of the Spirit apart from the Spirit? An honest re-examination of our present 'SYSTEM' should be an honest consideration of the place of the Spirit in counselling. He is a PERSON not a 'force' or a 'law'. Counsellors and clients must respect the sovereignty of the Holy Spirit.

God has chosen to work through human agents, a fact He has CLEARLY demonstrated by giving gifts of ministry to His Church. He does NOT foolishly give gifts that He doesn't intend to be used. Human activity that neither acknowledges nor draws on the power of the Spirit, rebelliously seeks to circumvent the Spirit, and is, therefore, devoid of the power to effect what can only be brought about BY the Spirit. The Spirit CANNOT be usurped by human techniques. The prerequisite for sanctification is the Spirit's presence in the life of a regenerate person. The Spirit enables the client to put off the 'old' with his 'old' behavioural patterns, and to put on the 'new' with the 'new' behavioural patterns.

Response/Behaviour patterns may become DEEPLY etched over a period of time, i.e. almost as 'given' as the 'original'. Though habit patterns ARE hard to change, change is NOT impossible. What was 'learned' CAN be 'unlearned', an old dog CAN learn new tricks. So a client must <u>not</u> be allowed to plead that he is what he is and nothing can be done about it. Change for some clients is <u>DIFFICULT</u> to accept. Change is difficult because change means doing something 'new' something unusual, something not done before. Such change is a threat; clients are afraid of the unknown, and therefore unwilling to launch out into new adventures. This must be accomplished via directive counselling and advice. Role-playing, modeling, and rehearsal helps the 'change' process. The Counsellor/Therapist may respond negatively to see how the client will handle hostility or face anger. Have the client imitate consciously, and purposefully, that which is 'good'.

Since we CAN, via God's help, Grace, Power and Might RE SHAPE OUR SELVES, <u>WE</u> ARE RESPONSIBLE FOR THE SHAPE WE ARE IN.

In my opinion, the fact of the matter is this: Clients go through a definite downward cycle. (They go through this cycle continually.) (there are 35 chartable stages). At a certain point in the cycle, (the 'relented' stage) the client sort of 'comes to his senses', and would really and truly like to get off the 'merry-go-round', and genuinely wish to change their lives. They turn to some programs for help, and unfortunately, they do <u>not</u> get help but <u>are</u> in fact, reduced one more notch lower toward the level of the institutionalized iatrogenic, and away they go again for one more cycle period.

Outside of the 'relented' stage of the cycle,, the client CANNOT be helped... he doesn't <u>WANT</u> help...It is during this stage of the cycle the clients manipulative and con expertise is sharpest and at it's best, he can 'call the shots' and the counsellor/therapist will do (unwittingly) what the client wants. They will tell the counsellor, "you <u>really</u> are helping me"... "you sure solved my problems"..."You sure helped me a lot"..."you're the best counsellor/therapist I have ever had"... etc. then, (figuratively speaking) hand the counsellor/therapist a 'blank cheque' and the counsellor/therapist signs it. The client's 'cover-up' expertise is sharpest at this time, and the client can appear to be quite 'in tact'.

This cycle is repeated over and over again until the 3% of the 1% recovery rate is the only 'rehabilitated' figure that can be truthfully and accurately reported. The 3% mentioned are those that get <u>themselves</u> straightened around in <u>spite</u> of what they were subjected to; they would have recovered by themselves with no treatment whatsoever, other than what they might receive from their family physician, providing the family physician is <u>not</u> a 'pill roller'.

Euphoria is the next downward cycle already in progress.

Intellect (superego) over emotions (id) i.e. I over E ,is what is required, NOT E over I, (emotions (ID) over intellect (superego)), and this can only be accomplished via response and behaviour pattern adjustment, using directive counselling, and Biblical standards against which to measure. Role playing, modeling, rehearsing, and imitating are essential.

Group therapy is to be avoided entirely; it is harmful to total re-structuring, and impedes progress, seriously. Further, Scripture forbids Group Therapy.

5. <u>AUTOGENIC OR ALLOGENIC ?</u> People no longer consider <u>themselves</u> responsible for what they do wrong. They CLAIM their problems are allogenic, not autogenic. Instead of assuming personal responsibility for their Response /Behaviour patterns they blame society. Wayne Oats, for example, says that clients' actions are the result of the rejection and exploitation of the client by the community.

Once we blamed bad people for the environment, now we blame the environment for bad people. Society is easy to blame because what is <u>everyone's</u> responsibility is <u>NO ONE'S</u> responsibility...but even society is now being let off the hook..."ours is a sick Society" we are told, then blame grandparents, parents, (although justified in cases of parental incompetence), the Church, a school teacher or some other particular individual for the client's actions, making searches into the past to find someone on whom to pin the blame for the client's response/behaviour patterns. The fundamental idea is to find out how others may have wronged the client.

In seeking to excuse and shift blame, counselling is itself an extension of the problem it pretends to solve. The end result of such an emphasis is immaturity and irresponsibility, and it should be obvious that many of the problems we face today are DIRECTLY related to immaturity and irresponsibility. The entire basis of human maturity and responsibility is undermined. The natural outworking of this emphasis (to cite but two consequences) <u>PARENTAL INCOMPETENCE,</u> causing a lack of discipline, and <u>FAMILY STRUCTURE</u> has broken down.

The downward cyclical movement, (which is predictable, chartable and constant and common to <u>ALL</u> clients) is propelled via bad response/behaviour patterns to problems, which cause <u>additional</u> problems, further complicating and compounding, as the downward cycle continues, for as long as the downward cycle continues ad infinitum. If this cycle is not reversed via intervention, the client will fall or sink deeper into the cycle that is anxiously awaiting to devour the client. The cycle can only be reversed or broken by breaking out of faulty response and behaviour patterns, using directive counselling.

What is wrong with the "mentally ill"? Their problem is autogenic... it is in themselves. The FUNDAMENTAL bent of human nature is AWAY from God, (generally speaking), and will, therefore, naturally attempt various dodges in an attempt to avoid facing up to bad response and behaviour patterns, which will be of varying styles according to the short term success or failures of the particular responses made to life's problems. Apart from organically generated problems, (i.e. brain damage, toxic problems, insanity, gene transmission etc.) the 'mentally ill' are really people with unresolved personal problems. Much bizarre behaviour must be interpreted as camouflage, intended to divert attention from one's otherwise deviate behaviour. (geared toward the "Dick Tracey' type therapist in particular it seems.)

Bizarre behaviour sometime in the past was rewarded positively when it succeeded in deflecting attention from one's deviant behaviour. Therefore, on succeeding occasions, the client <u>again</u> attempted to hide behind bizarre actions; discovering that frequently this ruse 'worked'. When this occurs frequently enough, a pattern of such action is established. Bizarre behaviour then becomes the natural (habit) means to which he resorts whenever he is 'cornered' or 'in trouble'. It follows then, that bizarre behaviour is the product of a deceitful heart. If this pattern is not broken, his behaviour will become so deviant, that in the end, 'society' will institutionalize him. Behaviour can become totally unacceptable in a very short time. As his actions become more bizarre he finds that his behaviour tends to isolate him. His social contacts are broken off, and the 'society' that he NEEDS, so desperately drifts away from him as HE hides from it. He knows he is living a lie and his conscience triggers painful psychosomatic responses. So at last he becomes a very miserable person, externally isolated and alienated from others, and internally torn apart. To act as if he can be excused for his behaviour is an unkind thing to do. Such an approach only compounds and complicates the problem. It is <u>not</u> merciful to be non-judgmental.

A client diagnosed as a catatonic schizophrenic would shut up, withdraw, and build a wall, CHALLENGING me to break it down. Another, diagnosed as a manic depressive, whose ploy was to howl, cry and scream at the top of her lungs to get people to go away and leave her alone. (when I hollered back, telling her to sit down and shut up, she turned off her antics instantly and said "You can't talk to me like that, I'm sick", we then began the therapy sessions, and she was quiet. (Released from therapy 10 weeks later).

Hallucinations by those who use LSD etc., are REAL to them. Seemingly bizarre behaviour or gestures therefore, can make sense when they are rightly interpreted as a protective response. Reacting in a proper way mentally, to what is perceived wrongly.

6. <u>NON- DIRECTIVE COUNSELLING:</u> Stanley E. Anderson wrote "the counsellor/therapist should listen, show no authority, give no advice, not argue, talk ONLY to aid or relieve or praise or guide the client and to clarify his problem."

Some Theological Schools are reluctant to be directive regarding Pastoral Counselling, "The pastor is not to be judgmental, he is not directive, he is not moralistic."

<u>THIS</u> teaching is out of Lucifer's realm; NOT God's Realm.

Rollo May teaches (when a client asks "what steps shall I take?") "this is a crucial point. The client asks for advice. If the counsellor/therapist succumbs to the temptation with it's implicit flattery, and gives advice or even specific instructions, he short-circuits the process, and thwarts the real personality readjustment of the client. The counsellor must seize this as a means of making the client accept that responsibility himself."

May explains; "in the first place personality is not transformed by advice. True Counselling and the giving of advice are distinctly different functions. The Psychotherapists' do not mince words in their rejection of the position of advisor."

From Freud: "Moreover, I assure you that you are misinformed if you assume that advice and guidance in the affairs of life is a part of the analytical influence. On the contrary, we reject this role of the mentor as far as possible. Above all, we wish to attain independent decisions on the part of the patient."

Rollo May continues. "advice giving is not a counselling/therapy function because it violates the AUTONOMY OF PERSONALITY. (emphasis mine) Ethically one cannot do it, and practically one cannot."

On the face of it, this is absurd. But of more importance God says "listen to advice and accept instructions that you may gain wisdom for the future" PROV 19:20. The emphasis on the autonomy of man is widespread and destructive. Carroll Wise says "to the extent that a person has failed to develop autonomy or has lost it, he is sick".

The fundamental presupposition of the Freud / Rogerian system is perfectly consistent with liberal and humanistic thought, namely, that the solutions to man's problems lie in the man himself. Clients are thought to possess adequate resources that can be tapped by the use of non-directive techniques. Man is autonomous. Consistent with this presupposition in non-direct (or reflective) counselling, the Counsellor/Therapist becomes a wall on which the client bounces off his 'thinking'

(thinking out loud). As the client verbalizes in the presence of a counsellor/therapist, the counsellor replies reflectively, repeating the client's words in a more sharply focused form. Eventually, by this process, the client gains 'insight' into his problems and gradually devises a solution, thereby solving his own problems...According to Rodgers, men that do wrong must be 'accepted', not admonished. Responsibility is undermined by the idea of acceptance.

This should give us all some insight as to why clients are helped very little, and, in some cases, come from Counselling/Therapy worse off than they were before.

Rogerian Counsellors do not listen; listening is precisely what they do not do...Rogers instructs "the counsellor must be prepared to respond not to the intellectual content of what the client is saying, but to the feeling which underlines it. Objective facts are quite unimportant. The only facts that have significance for therapy are the feelings, which the client is able to bring into the situation".

Rejecting this theory in its entirety, the Nouthetic Counsellor/Therapist asks highly specific questions. The Nouthetic Counsellor/Therapist explains, discusses, gives information. The Nouthetic Counsellor/Therapist marshals evidence and persuades clients to undertake proposed action. The Nouthetic Counsellor/Therapist scrutinizes every area of the client's life for Syndromes, pointing our symptoms or conditions that need correction, ensuring he does not leave any undesirable or untreated syndromes or problems, in any area of the client's life. All syndromes or conditions, are dealt with, once and for all.

Nouthetic Counsellors/Therapists, look and listen in order to gather and see the symptoms, thereby ensuring the correct syndromes are identified. Listening means taking an interest in what another says and responding appropriately. The Rogerian stance, on the contrary, avoids applying declarations to personal problems. Nouthetic Counsellors/Therapists spend less time finding out how clients <u>feel</u>, they are more interested in discovering how client's <u>behave</u>. Voluntary changes in response/behaviour depend on intelligent decisions, and effect the emotions as a result, thus reaching the whole man.

Sometimes instead of speaking of 'mental illness', people talk about 'emotional problems'. This language is confusing. When a client feels depressed, high, anxious or hostile, there is really no problem with the emotions. The emotions are working only too well. It is true that his emotions are not pleasant, but the REAL problem is not emotional, it is behavioural. Solutions aimed at relieving the emotions directly i.e. chemical methods like pills or alcohol, therefore, must be considered to be relief of symptoms. People feel bad because of bad behaviour; feelings flow from actions. A good conscience depends on good behaviour. Bad behaviour causes a bad conscience, (guilt).

What must one do to set his conscience at rest? The same thing that he does to extinguish the red light on the dashboard of his car. He doesn't take a hammer and smash the red light, instead he gets out and lifts the hood to see what is wrong. His problem is not with the red light on the dashboard. He is thankful for the light, it has warned him early enough to do something about the REAL problem. Likewise, one's problems are not with his conscience. Conscience is his friend, warning him that there is something wrong with his behaviour. Conscience is an ALARM system, NOT a GUIDANCE system. One should not try to smash his conscience then. He should not put it to sleep with pills or any other means that would anesthetize it. If the red lights on the dash were inactivated, the driver might be likely to forget about the problem under the hood, which will grow steadily worse until there is a breakdown. The same is true of the man with an inactivated conscience. Such cauterizing of the conscience comes by ignoring its messages or by anaesthetizing it over a period of time.

7. THE THREE ELEMENTS OF NOUTHETIC COUNSELLING:

There are 3 elements in Nouthetic Counselling:

1, Admonish
2. Warn
3. Teach

That the mind must be influenced, presupposes the need for a change in the person confronted, who may or may not put up resistance. Nouthetic confrontation arises out of a condition in the client that must be changed; the purpose of Nouthetic confrontation is to effect personality, response and behavioural changes in a client.

Usual counselling techniques recommend frequent long excursions back into the intricacies of the whys and wherefores of behaviour. Nouthetic Counselling is largely committed to a discussion of the WHATS.

All the WHY that a client needs to know can be clearly demonstrated in the WHAT...WHAT was done? WHAT must be done to rectify it? WHAT should future responses be? WHY leads to speculation and blame shifting; WHAT leads to solutions to problems. In fact, the WHY is already known <u>before</u> the counselling is begun. This is why Nouthetic Counselling may be spoken of in terms of 'weeks' rather than 'months' or 'years'. We never understand the WHY more clearly than when the focus is on the WHAT. This is in keeping with the tree elements of the Nouthetic Technique, ADMONISH; WARN; TEACH. Nouthetic confrontation implies changing that in the client's life which is harmful to the client, to meet obstacles head on, and overcome them,

Nouthetic counselling/therapy embodies involvement of the deepest sort. This is again a contradiction of the Freud/Rogerian theory which says don't get involved; maintain a neutral non-judgmental posture; never express your own feelings, or view point. While the client is required to be completely open, the counsellor is to be completely closed...this is a double standard; any idea that, that kind of neutrality is possible must be dispelled.

Failures in Nouthetic Counselling are very rare. However, when a failure <u>is</u> experienced, it is difficult and complex to analyze. When the Counsellor fails to do his job adequately, (as for example, when he fails to uncover the client's pre-condition problem), other elements of failure are also present.

There are six dangers to be avoided within Nouthetic Counselling:

<u>DANGER #1:</u> Sometimes clients will interpret failures as success. i.e. the client wants to settle for something less than total reorientation or restructuring of their lives, or one area of their

life. They might settle for solutions to the immediate problem. They are willing to seek help in solving the incapacitating or performance problem rather than 'digging in' and rooting out the pre-condition problem, of which the performance problem was but one instance or symptom. Such premature terminations of counselling are to be considered failures, and the #1 danger.

DANGER #2: In it's fullest meaning, success is the attainment of the changes required, together with an understanding by the client of how the changes were effected, and how to avoid falling into similar bad responses and behaviour patterns in the future, and, what to do if, indeed he should do so. Attainment of only part of these goals must be considered a failure.

DANGER #3: The chief reason a Nouthetic Counsellor will fail is that he might become too sympathetic to the complaints and excuses of the client. Frequently, clients will tell a very pitiful tale. There is the temptation for the Nouthetic Counsellor to decide that 'this is indeed a special case'. If the Counsellor agrees, that under the circumstances, the client was not responsible for his actions, there is NOTHING that the Counsellor can do for that client. The Counsellor has placed himself in an impossible position. He has in effect denied the autogenic principal so crucial to Nouthetic Counselling. There are only two things for the Counsellor to do: 1. refer the client to the Chief Counsellor/Therapist, taking himself off the case. 2. (if he comes to his senses in time), admit his mistake to the Chief Counsellor/Therapist and the client, then continue properly from there. Counsellors fail when they become too sympathetic towards excuses and do not hold clients responsible for their behaviour, but they can **never** fail when they become truly empathetic (the capacity to participate in another's feelings or ordeal) towards the client. The first attitude is sympathy, the latter empathy.

When Nouthetic Counsellors become soft hearted, they are most unmerciful to their clients. The most kindly (empathetic) stance is to tell the truth, help the client to face up to his own bad response and behaviour patterns, and encourage him to make the changes necessary to rectify the situation.

DANGER # 4: Nouthetic Counsellors can also fail by coming to conclusions too quickly. It is possible to hear too little of the story or only one side of the story, and jump to conclusions. When Nouthetic Counsellors fail to dig down to the pre-condition problem, and only handle performance problems, the Nouthetic Counsellor has failed. Nouthetic Counsellors fail by becoming 'too involved' emotionally. They can never become 'too involved' in the 'people' sense, but they may get too involved in the sense that they allow their own emotions to cloud their judgement. When this happens, Nouthetic Counsellors have been caught by the same snare as their clients, who are so emotionally involved in their problems that they no longer think straight, but instead allow feelings to govern actions.

DANGER #5: Nouthetic Counsellors always face the temptation to become over-bearing in the use of authority, using authority for it's own sake, or failing to keep the Spirit's authority and the Nouthetic Counsellor's own opinions discrete. When this happens, the Nouthetic element of concern for the client's welfare disappears. The Nouthetic Counsellor might well misinterpret and misuse the Nouthetic system to his own detriment and that of the client.

DANGER # 6: To shorten what might become a long list of danger points, it is sufficient to say that Nouthetic Counsellors may fail in exactly the same way that their clients have failed. Consequently, it is important for the Nouthetic Counsellor to examine their own lives and their Nouthetic Counselling practices in the light of every failure they detect in others. Clients are strong reminders of human error, and in that sense, are among the Nouthetic Counsellor's most valuable teachers.

METHODOLOGY grows out of pre- suppositions. All Nouthetic techniques and methodology grow out of the presupposition, based on my experience and research, that the only standards to measure against, that I have found to be accurate to the point of infallibility and totally reliable and that will ensure the successful and complete rehabilitation of the client, are Biblical standards.

8. WHO SHOULD COUNSEL? Not all counsellors I know should be in the Counselling and Rehabilitation field. I have seen many examples of Clergy that should have been truck drivers (no disrespect to truck drivers intended), and truck drivers that should have been clergy. (This fact in itself is completely understandable. If we get out of God's way and stop interfering with Him, keeping our mucky hands off, He will provide all the help that is necessary, needed and required. i.e. when God's instruments and servants become disassociated from their souls, they invariably are not walking the path God intended them to walk for Him, HINDERED by satan).

The work of Counselling and Rehabilitation is not to be

something we CHOOSE to do... it is NOT within the realm of the 'do gooders' (who in fact do more harm than good). It is a work we are CHOSEN and TRAINED and <u>CALLED</u> to do, and we are <u>GIVEN</u> the necessary gifts and talents to do our work. In this way we are JUSTIFIED and in fact <u>REQUIRED</u> to peruse our work. It is <u>NOT</u> a work anyone is to <u>take</u> on themselves. Make no mistake, what we sow, we reap.

I am NOT a Theologian, and not discussing any doctrine. I am simply sharing my research, experiences and training, as a Teacher and Counsellor and Therapist, and this role I do not <u>take</u> on myself.

9.<u>MENTALLY ILL?</u> Time Magazine 3 November 1967 issue told the story of 'THE REVOLT OF LEO HELD". Held, a 40 year old, 5 ft., 200 lb. balding lab technician, at a Lockhaven, Penn. paper mill, had been a School Board member, Boy Scout leader, secretary of a Fire Brigade, Churchgoer and an affectionate father. He bickered occasionally with his neighbours, drove too aggressively and sometimes fretted about the job he held for 19 years, but to most of his neighbours and co-workers, he was a model, respectable and responsible citizen.

That image was shattered in a well-planned hour of bloodshed when Held decided to mount a one-man revolt against the world he feared and resented. After seeing his wife off to work and their children off to school, Held, a proficient marksman, pocketed 2 pistols, a .45 automatic and a .38, then drove his station wagon to the mill. Parking carefully, he gripped a gun in each hand and stalked into the plant, and started shooting with a calculated frenzy that filled his fellow workers with 2 and 3 bullets each. At least 30 shots were fired. A hastily formed posse found him at home, armed, and snarling defiance, "come and get me" and "I'm not taking any more of their bull."

    Puzzled officials discovered a tenuous chain of logic behind his actions. Mrs. Ram had quit a car pool, complaining of Held's reckless driving. Some of the victims were in authority over him, or had been promoted while he had not. Held had feuded over smoke from burning leaves, he had a spat over a fallen tree limb that enraged him, and he beat a 71 year old widow with a branch. Held's stolid surface had masked truculent resentment and rage. Mrs. Knisely suggested that "here was a man who was sick; and had he been sent to a Psychologist/Psychiatrist, this thing could have been prevented."

    The question is, was Held <u>really</u> sick? Was Mrs. Knisely right, wittingly or unwittingly? The Times Magazine answered the questions... the caption under a picture of a prostrate wounded killer said "RESPONSIBLE, RESPECTABLE AND RESENTFUL'. This caption put the finger on the REAL issue. Held was NOT sick, he was resentful. Yet, it is a significant sign of the nearly total acceptance of the 'mental illness' propaganda that Mrs. Knisely's first thought was "He's sick and needs a psychologist/psychiatrist."

    Held's true condition was recorded long ago, which describes people who harbour grudges, resentments and bitterness in their hearts. For a long while Held was able to cover the resentment with an outer gloss of tranquility and graciousness. But finally the resentment burst through. Outwardly Held seemed respectable, he appeared responsible; but inwardly his heart seethed with resentment. Held spoke with 'smooth lips'. At Church and as a member of the Fire Brigade he paraded in a glaze of respectability.

Anger, hatred, resentments and bitterness, bottled up within, give rise to seven other problems. When resentment at last grew to the boiling point, Held decided that he would kill everyone who, in his judgment, had wronged him. Although for a time hatred can be covered up, at length it will be expressed in the ASSEMBLEY (Public); all the feelings and attitudes harboured down underneath, WILL be revealed.

In exactly that way, Held eventually spouted forth his hatred in one dramatic public revelation of what he was really like. Not everyone of course, reveals his harboured inner resentments in exactly the same way. The 'NORM' however, will be "in public".

Mental illness is a misnomer. The case of Leo Held illustrates why I object to the concept of 'mental illness' and the vigorous propaganda campaign that has been conducted under that misleading misnomer. The fact is that the words 'mental illness' are used quite ambiguously. J.S.Brockover (Psychiatric Digest Mar. 1968 page 51) speaks of "the indefinability of mental illness".

Organic malfunctions affecting the brain that are caused by brain damage, tumors, gene inheritance, glandular or chemical disorders may validly be termed 'mental illness', but at the same time, a vast number of other human problems have been classified as 'mental illness' for which there is no evidence that they have been caused by disease or illness at all. As a description of many of these problems, the term 'mental illness' is nothing more than a figure of speech, and in most cases, a poor one at that.

Yet, the Clergy is called upon to become a chief proponent of the Mental illness view. He is urged to "help both the family and the community at large to accept 'mental illness' as a sickness, and not as a disgrace," (Ministering to families of the mentally ill. New York and the National Association for Mental Health handbook, page 4) and the clergy, in their ignorance, do so. I am aware of both organically based problems, and those problems that stem from wrong attitudes and response/behaviour patterns; but where is there so much of a trace of any third source of problems which might approximate the modern concept of 'mental illness'? The burden of proof lies with the Clergy who loudly affirm the existence of 'mental illness' as a disease. Biblically 'mental illness' does not exist. The only safe course to follow is to declare that the genesis of such human problems is two-fold, not three-fold.

A certain amount of confusion has been occasioned by the fact that physical illness may have non-organic causes, i.e. worry may cause ulcers, and fear may cause paralysis. These resultant disabilities are ordinarily called 'psychosomatic illnesses'. Psychosomatic illnesses are genuine somatic problems which are the direct result of inner physical difficulties. But illness CAUSED by psychological stress must be distinguished from illness AS THE CAUSE of psychological stress.

Responsibility is the ability to respond as man should respond, to every life situation, IN SPITE of difficulties. It is the ability to do good to those who despitefully use us; it is the ability to feed one's enemy when he is hungry or give him a drink when he is thirsty; it is the ability to overcome evil with good.

Responsibility is respond-ability; the ability to respond to any situation of life in accordance with Commandments, oracles and precepts. It is the ability to bear the weaknesses of those without strength, and not just to please ourselves.

Christian's accept one another only because they are 'brethren' in Christ. In all such acceptance, judgments about sin are made. Rogerian permissive 'acceptance' bears no resemblance to Christian acceptance in Christ. It is, therefore, irresponsible acceptance.

Most people KNOW why they are in trouble, even when at first they deny it. Nouthetic Counsellors operate on the assumption that this is so. They find that most people drop their defences, and 'tell it like it is'. Counsellors who pre-suppose that clients do not know the problem in their lives, tend to ignore or re-interpret genuine expressions of guilt and thereby discourage and confuse clients about the causes of their difficulties, and miss the vivid pictures of a haunting guilty conscience.

Clients with a guilty conscience are vulnerable people. They often become intensely self-conscious. Even innocent words frequently are interpreted as personal attacks. They interpret as personal affronts, acts that have no direct relationship to them, or, lacking the courage to do so, will object to some incidental feature. To call a person paranoid is to misinterpret the dynamics of his problem. A guilty conscience is a body-breaking load. Depressed clients whose symptoms fail to show any sign of a biochemical root, should be counselled on the assumption that they are depressed by guilt.

One word that is TABOO in Nouthetic Counselling is <u>CAN'T</u>. The client will be told "you can't say can't". No two cases are exactly the same, but the symptoms of a syndrome do not change.

A client's language not only indicates what he thinks, but also influences the way he acts and reacts. In Nouthetic Counselling the very use of certain words must be counteracted, because words are not only indicative of, but also influence thinking, attitude and response and behaviour. Some clients have excused themselves for years with the idea that their case is unique, and say something like 'but, you see, it's different with me'.

One of the IMPORTANT factors in Nouthetic Counselling is giving hope. When wrong response and behaviour patterns are pointed out to clients, it does not discourage him, but rather gives him hope; REAL hope, and one of the first things a client NEEDS is hope.

Nouthetic Counsellors do not let the client's adverse evaluation of himself go by unnoticed, and NEVER respond in ways that might minimize the client's bad opinion of himself. The client is probably RIGHT about the present worthlessness of his life. If a client says "I haven't been a good mother", the

Nouthetic Counsellor will reply "That's a serious matter...tell me about it... what have you been doing?" When Nouthetic Counsellors take the clients seriously, the client usually responds quickly, pouring out problems and failures. Taking clients seriously is an important way to give them hope.

Nouthetic Counsellors realize that sometimes personality is so distorted by mood- affecting drugs that it is difficult to know whether he is talking to the person or a pill. Whenever possible, the prescribing Physician must be contacted to determine whether or not the pills could be discontinued or at least modified during counselling, we <u>must SEE</u> the symptoms in order to determine the syndrome. I have had cases where I refused to work with a client until the use of drugs was eliminated or at least modified. No Nouthetic Counsellor can advise a client about medication unless he is a Physician. Whenever possible, he should become acquainted with a Physician whose judgment and advice can help the Nouthetic Counsellor to make his own judgment. Nouthetic Counselling does not take long when the Counsellor can lay his finger on the precondition problem, and there is proper motivation on the part of the client. Taking clients seriously is the first step. Minimizing inner turmoil is cruel.

Structure is the means of proper living. Lives restructured according to the Commandments, Oracles and Precepts are, by the very nature of the case, also restructured according to the principles on which the world and Society were constructed. Lives oriented to Biblical Standards do NOT clash with the structure of the world, but rather harmonize with it. Some ask "but is restructuring confining?" no; exactly opposite is true.

The train is free to run most rapidly and smoothly when it is 'confined' to the tracks. By its very nature most discipline is unpleasant. The chipping away of imperfections is a painful process, but the fruit of discipline is very pleasant.

Clients frequently comment about the important part that insistence on discipline played in the solution of their problems. Clients have often said "I appreciate that you did not let me get away with anything." For the first time the gimmicks, tricks and ruses that they developed to make others feel sorry for them, and coddle them, have been penetrated. Clients themselves recognize that this is why they have been helped, and they say "thanks" for it. (Actual quotations)

Bob and Barbara were not progressing very well in Counselling. They had made some minor gains, other problems had been solved, but it became evident that something was wrong; there was some underlying factor (or data) that had not yet come to the surface. I concluded they were 'dragging their feet', they were not working hard enough at their problem. (a re-evaluation takes place during the sixth week of counselling). They were told that there had not been adequate progress for the 5 weeks that they spent in Counselling. I said "something is wrong, and as far as I am concerned, if you don't tell me what the REAL issue is and get down to work, I'm through, I can do no more for you. I can only work with the data you give me." Probing in various areas produced nothing. Then I asked point blank "do you want to make a success of this marriage or not?" Bob replied sincerely, "Yes, I do"; Barbara said, "well, I'm not sure". There was the problem. Barbara was not working hard because she was not sure it was worth it. Then I said "if you don't make a SOLID commitment to save this marriage and family, I can't help you any further." Barbara confessed to Bob she was seeing another man, she apologized and asked Bob if he would forgive her and asked if he still wanted the marriage. Bob did on both counts. At the next counselling session (one week later), it was quite apparent that a great change had occurred. They were released from the program two sessions later, after making tremendous progress.

This case demonstrates the importance of motivation. Yet it is significant to observe that, as in this case, frequently, where motivation is absent, the client may be motivated by the consistent application of Nouthetic principles. Nouthetic methodology is adapted to motivation.

Counselling is not usually an enjoyable process for the client; hard decisions must be made and painful subjects must be discussed. Discipline is not pleasant either, but at length it produces the pleasant fruit of 'peace'. The Nouthetic Counsellor usually takes a person apart and put him back together again. Some clients that come for counselling have already had their lives ripped apart at the seams.

A 'nervous breakdown' is really a very advantageous thing. Nouthetic Counsellors look on a 'breakdown' as a 'break-up', not a 'breaking down'. During such times, old patterns, old ways, old habits that have failed are broken up. The client comes to recognize that he has not been meeting life's problems properly. And so in frustration the old patterns are abandoned, and the client for a time, is 'at sea'...He stands bewildered with many of his past patterns shattered at his feet. While he is standing in the rubble, properly, this affords him an unprecedented opportunity. He may now 'pick up the pieces' and restructure his life in a more thorough manner than he otherwise might have been able to do. God has relented FOR A TIME.

ANY life-shattering event that tears a person apart affords this opportunity. When one loses a job, when a divorce ruptures a home, when a child get into serious trouble, when someone loses face, when his life is falling apart, when a client is so deeply depressed that he doesn't know where to turn next, the Nouthetic Counsellor has an important opportunity and duty.

When viewed positively, disintegration of the past may be considered an advantage. If the situation is handled properly, when one's life is disintegrated, it can be altered much more readily, much more rapidly and much more radically, along Biblical standards, then at other times.

A study of completed cases will show that the more serious the problem, the more likely are the hopes of a FULL rather than partial success. Motivation as well as the complete disintegration of past patterns seems to be a strong factor. "How badly is the client hurting?" is an important question for the Nouthetic Counsellor to ask and answer. Clients who are 'set' for a radical change, are in a position to make great strides.

Group therapy is not used within Nouthetic Counselling because it is, to say the most, of dubious value, and to say the least, encourages "playing to the audience". I have seen many examples of participants in the group being more interested in showing their own 'knowledge' or 'insights' or using the group to manipulate and con 'staff', and would, therefore, do harm to others in the group being 'victimized'. 'The blind leading the blind' in most cases.

One question must be asked, does Nouthetic directive counselling, with its strong restructuring lead to client dependence? Doubtless the danger exists. But since the goal of Nouthetic Counselling is to lead the client into self-discipline, and self-reliance, methods for avoiding client dependence have been developed. Nouthetic counsellors,(who are teachers or coaches), find no more difficulty in making the transition than the clients do.

10. <u>CHILD TRAINING:</u> "What do Nouthetic Counsellor have to say about rearing children?" Is a question I have often been asked.

The cliche "if you want to see what's wrong with the children of today, take a look at the grandparents" holds quite true in a lot more situations than we are willing to believe or accept. Parents cannot give what they do not possess; Parents cannot come from a place where they have not been.

Parental Incompetence is <u>THE</u> problem in our Society, and is of such gigantic proportion, that it will take an all out CONCENTRATED AND COORDINATED effort on the part of the Church, Ministry of Education, Human Resources, Ministry of Health, Attorney Generals, Dept. and the Counselling and Rehabilitation field to correct this problem. There are far more parents with problems than children; however, at a point in time, the child becomes A problem WITH problems.

It was most refreshing and encouraging to hear Dr. Spock say at his birthday party, he now realizes he was wrong in his child training theory, and apologized for the harm he has caused Society.(a television news segment).

We were told "the child is by nature an exceeding delicate organism, and unless his society treats him with utmost consideration, his sense of security is jeopardized, and he will become neurotic. Events in childhood cause future psychological difficulties." (that will have to be dredged up in adulthood) and that " parents may injure the lives of their children by traumatic shock if they apply disciplinary measures, thus, the Scriptural instructions about corporal punishment must be abandoned," there by flatly challenging and opposing Biblical standards, and the Nouthetic technique.

We DID abandon them, and now, do not realize, or will not accept, the fact, that we are, today, reaping what we sowed.

It is interesting to note that Biblical standards reassure reluctant parents that Corporal punishment, <u>PROPERLY</u> administered, will <u>NOT</u> harm the child. As a matter of fact, spanking, <u>PROPERLY</u> administered, is a more humane punishment than many other more prolonged punishments which border on being more like torture than a punishment.

It is also interesting to note, that the first thing a baby <u>LEARNS</u> so do is to tell lies. Before the baby can talk or crawl, the baby can lead the parents to believe it is in dire straits and needs to be picked-up AT ONCE.

One lie has to be covered by a dozen more, ad infinitum. Bad habits are hard to break, but if they are NOT broken, they will bind the child tighter and tighter.

We must EXPECT the child to act sinfully. Biblical standards say that "foolishness is bound up in the heart of a child, but the rod of discipline will drive it far from him." They will manifest their sinful nature by sinful behaviour from their earliest opportunities. It is also interesting to note that sins by adults do not differ largely in kind, from those of their children. Consequently, with children, just as with adults, discipline takes the form of a battle against bad response and behaviour patterns.

However, there is one great advantage to child discipline; if the parents ARE aware of the kind of patterns that their child may develop in later life, (because these patterns/habits are formed from age 0-5 yrs., after 5 yrs., what was formed, begins to develop), then as parents, they will do all within their ability to instill and structure into the child, those patterns which are consistent with Biblical standards.

Whenever he sees the weeds of irresponsibility/ immaturity beginning to sprout in the child's lifestyle, he will root them out, and in their place, plant the seeds of responsibility and maturity. Parents should respond to the behaviour of children in an honest and appropriate manner. Only by such responses can they provide a standard by which the child may discover the social consequences of his behaviour. Such a response will NOT harm the child as some think, on the contrary, neutral (i.e. distorted) responses and erratic responses by parents, confuse and tend to encourage sociopathic attitudes in the child.

The child CANNOT avoid being wronged by people. While a parent should not purposely wrong the child, parents at times, do so naturally and inadvertently, in many ways. Such wronging will not be as injurious as some might think. Throughout life, people will treat the child wrongly. It is well that the first wrong doing the child experiences may come from those who love the child most, for IF IN LOVE they admit the wrong, apologize and make right what they have done wrong, parents teach the child much by their EXAMPLE.

Also, if parents teach children HOW TO RESPOND to wrongdoing, they teach the most important lesson of all. The key to parental discipline is to teach the children Biblical standard responses to wrongdoing. A child's problem is NOT 'insecurity', (as so often claimed), but failure to solve problems properly. And if the child does NOT learn these things at the parent's knees while he is young and surrounded by love, he WILL learn them later on in life, at the hands of cruel and indifferent people; and in addition, be required to pay the penalty and consequences of his wrong patterns, and for people he will hurt by these wrong patterns. He will be required to pay the penalty and consequences the proud, arrogant, irresponsible, deceitful, rebellious etc. MUST pay. Pray, that if this should happen, he be led to a Nouthetic Counsellor/ Therapist.

As children grow into their teens, the problems becomes less a matter of the parent structuring responsibility and discipline into the life of a child, and more a matter of helping the child to assume responsibility for structuring his own life. However the shift of responsibility MUST be a gradual process, that began many years before.

Now discipline becomes almost entirely the responsibility of the teenager himself, He must become a SELF-structuring, SELF-disciplined individual BEFORE he leaves his home. He can no longer claim that he is not responsible for his actions. Teen age is the time to grow up. It's a time when one should put away childish ways and put on mature love, It is a time when they should be taught to assume the obligation of SELF-DISCIPLINE, a word that appears frequently in Biblical standards.

Rebellion, so characteristic of teenagers, is NOT just a 'phase' that all children must pass through, IT IS SIN. Since this IS a period in which he is learning independence and self-responsibility, it is hard for the youth to resist the tendency, but resistance and help IS possible.

God has given parents FULL AUTHORITY, to be exercised UNDER BIBLICAL STANDARDS. The husband is to be the head of the home; the wife is to be his SUBMISSIVE help-mate, (providing, of course, the husband functions ENTIRELY within the confines of the Precepts, Oracles, and Commandments of God's Realm), and the children are to LOVE their parents, HONOURING and OBEYING parents. (These are the authorities under Biblical standards).

Within Nouthetic Counselling, we use a CODE OF CONDUCT SHEET (NCRC 7/1) which structures the PARENTS behaviour as well as that of the children. i.e. there is no place in the code for yelling. If mother screams as well as paddles, she has violated the code and must apologize and rectify the situation.

When parents and children begin adhering to a code, the whole household soon settles down. <u>AND KNOW THIS,</u> children APPRECIATE (and need to know) knowing where the 'lines are drawn'. If today a child can commit a serious crime with impunity, and tomorrow gets slapped across the room for some relatively minor infraction, he soon comes to the conclusion that there is no consistency in the home. Since the severity of each punishment RARELY fits the severity of the crime; and since punishments are unpredictable, he concludes that he might as well do whatever he wants. It is interesting to note that the communication breakdown cycle is EXACTLY the same today as it was in Adam's time. It is also interesting to note that every communication gap is preceded by a credibility gap.

No teenager can blame another for his bad response/ behaviour, even when he has been TAUGHT that behaviour from childhood. What he learned can be unlearned. Since we CAN re-shape ourselves, <u>WE</u> are responsible for the shape we are in.

I have seen many families fail because there were no children, but I have never seen a family fail because there were too many children. Truly, if God is not in the home, there will be no home.

11.<u>THE REALM OF SKID ROW:</u> While we are all very precious and important to God, some have greater or more important assignments or purposes than others. The more important the purpose, the more likely are we subject to being snared or sidetracked by Lucifer and/or his instruments and servants. In my experience and research, I have noticed, that those who end up on skid row are people that were EXTRA important Instruments/Servants of God, with special assignments that were snared or sidetracked by Lucifer and/or his instruments and servants.

If a skid row person IS reconciled, and gets back onto the path he was INTENDED to walk, he will go on to do far greater things than I will ever do. While Nouthetic Counsellors may be 'sparkers', skid row people will do far greater things. I have also noticed, that when this happens, skid row people are prospered ASTOUNDINGLY fast and thoroughly.

I once had a client from skid row, a 'drunken bum' sleeping on park benches, that had been a successful lawyer. Because of his alcohol addiction, he lost his practice, home, family, car, friends, and was disbarred. Once this person became reconciled and onto the path he was INTENDED to walk, within 5 years, he again possessed practice, home, family, car and friends. Things that have taken me 25 years to acquire. I have seen this many times.

There seems to be a possible 'second best' role in life available especially to people within the skid row realm. But at no time have I seen examples of a 'third best' possibility. It seems that 'second best' is as far as they are permitted to fall without having their mission scrubbed, and everyone loses; God, the Nation, the Community, and themselves.

The same thing therefore, can be said of people who are <u>HEADING</u> for skid row right now, from 'standing' but 'in trouble' homes. People that have their job, family and home, but are on 'thin ice' on all counts.

There is one common denominator that I have found with EVERY 'skid rower' I have EVER worked with, and that is...<u>A KEEN SENSE OF JUSTICE</u>. As perverted or warped as it may have become, underneath the layers of dust, debris and bad response behaviour it lays. It will be found to be quite intact and operational when the dust, debris and bad response behaviour is cleared away. Further, it is the thing that most often and surely trips them up, ROYALLY. These are those who might have helped stop the present trend of separation, deserted and broken homes, broken families. broken lives, divorce, crime, rebellion etc. and can still be.

Whether the addiction is to alcohol or drugs, the progression of the addiction is completely predictable and chartable from stage 1 (the beginning) to stage 35 (death). The period of time the client spends in each stage, however, is <u>NOT</u> predictable or charitable; I have never seen 2 cases that were the same; each case is uniquely different. Further, the progression by drug addicts is considerably faster than the progression of the alcoholic. Nevertheless, both go through the same 35 stages of the progression.

My research and experiments have shown myself that the word 'ALCOHOLIC' is the second most abused word in the vocabulary of the Counselling and Rehabilitation field. 'REHABILITATED' being the first most abused word.

Whether the addiction is to alcohol or drugs, I have found only one significant difference, the drug addict is more sinister than the 'alcoholic'. The stages (or phases) of the progression of the addiction is the same although the drug addict progression is faster.

For this Thesis, (Author's license), the word 'ALCOHOLIC' is meant to encompass ALCOHOLICS, DRUG ADDICTS, and EMOTIONALLY DISTURBED CLIENTS alike, because again, the progression and consequences of bad response and behaviour patterns is basically the same for all three groups of clients. Further, they are hitting skid road younger and harder every year.

People that display <u>EXACTLY</u> the same symptoms of a so-called 'alcoholic' that does not even drink, are called mentally ill. I have seen this many times.

There is no point in trying to counsel or rehabilitate a client while the ROD OF CORRECTION is being applied by God. (CONSEQUENCE time). At these times a client <u>CANNOT</u> be helped, and does not WANT help. The only client's that seek help during this time, are clients that are actually working a CON; working the system. To force help on the client at this time is only INTERFERENCE, and will not benefit or avail anything. However, incarceration might be necessary and advisable...a person is entitled to a freedom <u>ONLY</u> to the extent he is capable of the responsibility the freedom requires and demands, or carries with it. If not capable of the <u>RESPONSIBILITY</u>; not entitled to the <u>FREEDOM</u>.

Hypothetically, if we work with families, as they exist now, i.e. together, although on very thin ice in all aspects, through Employee Recovery Programs if the client is working, or through Human Resources, plugged into the Employee Recovery Program concepts, if unemployed, ENSURING the clients were referred to <u>EFFECTIVE</u> Counselling and Rehabilitation programs (or techniques), we could cut the source of supply to skid road and eliminate the skid road realm altogether.

However, <u>BEFORE</u> this is attempted we must STOP, realizing and admitting we have failed by doing 'things' <u>OUR</u> way, by putting OUR mucky hands to work, by simply interfering with, rather than helping, and this mainly by many people doing what they WANT to do, rather than what they SHOULD be doing, if they were walking the path they were created to walk for God.

The church, all levels of Government, Management, Labour, and the Counselling and Rehabilitation field will be required to work together, in harmony, if we intend to do something about the mess our society is in. Make no mistake, God is not mocked, what we sow we reap. (a warning; a law; and a promise, of God. GAL 6:7-8)

My research indicates that the so-called 'alcoholic' is not a true alcoholic at all, in the true sense of the word. I have found that they are simply RUNNERS; running not only from Biblical standards, but also from themselves, their families, their problems, and/or their situations. They suffer from the effects of the consequences of their bad response and behaviour patterns, problems, and nature.

They GLADLY admit to being an 'alcoholic', basking and indulging themselves, with pleasure, in the sympathy and molly-coddling extended to them because they are thought to be 'SICK' with a disease that they can no more be held responsible for catching than pneumonia, mumps, polio or any other disease or illness.

They con their way into treatment units rather than go to jail, by claiming to be 'alcoholic', rather than admitting to the REAL problems, which I have found to be spiteful; sensually sick; sneaks; cheats; liars; irresponsible; immature; impaired rationale, etc., in various forms; in various combinations; and to varying degrees. They can be quite rational, clever and ingenious; they are also expert manipulators and con artists, and can, at will, (and it IS at will), con others into taking them in on rehabilitation or alcohol programs to rest up; to clear up the physical; to get clothing; to avoid consequences; to get a little holiday etc. I had a client that had been considered a drug addict, and treated as a drug addict, for 14 years. The client was NOT a 'drug addict', the addiction was only a SYMPTOM of the REAL PROBLEMS.

At times, an 'alcoholic' will truly attempt to straighten out his life. It is of THIS group I now write. I will refer to this group as 'RELENTED' (author's license) for the sake of clarification.

The 'relented' is taken in on a program based on Freudian and/or Rogerian theories and is completely hamstrung.

The 'relented' takes the program, is somewhat relieved artificially, and released, usually in a state of euphoria, (euphoria is the next downward cycle already in motion), and from that point on, his problems have now become, in addition to the still untreated original problems, IATROGENIC. And to add insult to injury, he is counted as having been Rehabilitated.

The 'relented' has not been truly helped, and in fact, is reduced still one notch (stage) lower toward the level of the INSTITUTIONALIZED IATROGENIC FREE LOADER. (this come about when the 'relented' comes to be convinced, that the hogwash some counsellors/therapists feed him is true, and they finally learn how to con an existence out of a society, individual or government. (end of author's license).

Through research and experience, I have found the FACT of the matter to be this: the 'clients' go through a DEFINATE CYCLE. (they ALL go through this cycle CONTINUALLY) At a certain point in the cycle, (I call it the RELENTED STAGE), they sort of 'come to their senses' and would really and truly like to get off the 'merry-go-round' (bear in mind ALL go through this cycle continually, both the 'new comers' and the iatrogenic's), and genuinely wishes to change their lives. What in FACT is happening at this point, is that (as the Scriptures explain), GOD HAS RELENTED, AND IS GIVING THEM ROOM AND TIME TO REPENT; (God brings them down so that He can bring them up).

They turn to existing Freudian and/or Rogerian oriented programs for help, and unfortunately, they do NOT get help, but are in FACT, reduced one more notch (stage) lower toward the level of the institutionalized iatrogenic, (having passed through the RELENTED CYCLE WITHOUT INTERVENTION BEING ACCOMPLISHED), and away they go again, for one more cycle period. This cycle is repeated over and over again until the client either IS helped, or dies within the skid road realm. This cycle is repeated over and over again until the 3% of the 1%

recovery rate is the only REHABILITATED FIGURE THAT CAN BE TRUTHFULLY AND ACTUALLY REPORTED.

To illustrate the point: recently, I had a client whom for 14 years had been considered a drug addict, and was treated as such. This client was processed through drug program after drug program from the incarceration approach; through the methadone program; through the Maple Cottage and Maple Ridge approaches, to name but a few of the Rehab Units this client had been subjected to.

This client has never had a job and had been on Social Assistance for 11 years. The drug addiction was a SYMPTOM, not a SYNDROME. The Nouthetic Technique revealed this client's pre-condition problems were the syndromes of rebellion; irresponsibility and arrogance. Other syndromes (that developed via a natural progression, due to the pre-condition syndromes not being treated (intervention NOT accomplished)), that further compounded and complicated the case were: immaturity, profanity, stubbornness, harbouring, procrastinating, hostility, inferiority, insecurity, jealousy, hypocrisy, anxiety, depression, central nervous system disorder, obsessive compulsive reactions, depressive reactions (both neurotic and psychotic). WHAT person, in the state of this client would not drink or take drugs to get away from THEMSELVES ???

The addiction was in fact, NOT the SYNDROME, but only another SYMPTOM of many syndromes. Treating this client as only a drug addict simply further compounded and complicated the REAL syndromes (or problems). This client was a victim of parental incompetence originally, but became an institutionalized iatrogenic due to the incompetence, chaos and disarray of the Counselling and Rehabilitation field. This is NOT an isolated or uncommon incident.

As a general rule of thumb, if we want to know what's coming down the road for the youth of today, in approximately 5 years, listen to the words of the songs they are singing and listening to, TODAY.

Humour too gives some indication of where we are heading. In a joke book complied by Bob Phillips "MORE GOOD CLEAN JOKES" will be found the following letter to the American Secretary of Agriculture:

Dear Mr. Secretary:

My friend Mr. Bordereaux received a $1,000.00 cheque from the U.S. Government for NOT raising hogs and so I am going into the NOT RAISING HOGS business.

What is the best kind of land not to raise hogs on and what is the best kind of hogs not to raise? I would prefer not to raise razorbacks, but if this is not the best kind not to raise, I will gladly not raise dorcos or poland chinas.

The hardest part of this business is going to be keeping an individual record on each hog I do not raise.

My friend Bordereaux has been raising hogs for more than 20 years and the most he ever made was $400.00 in 1981, until this year when he received $1,000.00 for not raising hogs. Now, if I get $1,000.00 for not raising 50 hogs, I will get $2,000.00 for not raising 100 hogs etc.

I plan to start off on a small scale, holding myself down to not raising 4,000 hogs for which I will, of course receive $80,000.00.

Now these hogs I will not raise will not eat 100,000 bushels of corn. I understand you pay farmers for not raising corn. Will you pay me for not raising 100,000 bushels of corn, which I will not feed to the hogs which I am not raising?

I want to get started as soon as possible, as this looks like a good time of the year for not raising hogs.

Yours very truly,

Octover Brussard.

12. **IN CONCLUSION:** Put religious training back into our School System; give God equal time with Freud, Rogers, Darwin and the other champions of the pseudo sciences. It's true, God is not dead, nor does He sleep...neither is satan dead, not does he sleep. Once 'wheels' are set in motion, they grind to an inevitable end.

At whose hand the 'BLOOD' will be required is not within the realm of this Thesis, however, Scriptures say their blood will SURELY be required of someone. God is no respecter of persons (or denominations); if we are not WITH Him, we are AGAINST Him; we either gather with Him or scatter from Him.

The Nouthetic Technique is based on Biblical standards

NOT because of religious fanaticism, but simply because as a result of 7 years of research and experiments, it was found to be a FACT, that there is not a situation or a problem (syndrome) that we can possibly encounter in our lifetime, concerning response and behaviour patterns, that is not covered in Scriptures. The symptoms are shown, the syndrome is named, and the solution is given.

Using Biblical standards will impart subtlety, resourcefulness, wise conduct, knowledge and discretion, even to the retarded and simpletons. i.e. a retarded client, whom I met about 2 years after he had completed the Nouthetic program (he completed the Nouthetic program in 14 weeks) said to myself during our conversation "one of the first things I learned after the program was that if I have an open mind, be very careful someone doesn't come along and dump a lot of garbage into it". While the cliche was not original, the emphasis was on the right words, and he understood very well what it meant, and what he was saying. He displayed more wisdom than a lot of people that are supposed to be 'normal', on many topics.

The Nouthetic Technique was developed, perfected and adopted during a 7 year research project, at a cost of well over $80,000.00. Neither of my research projects were funded. They were at my own expense.

Both research projects were conducted through the Western Academy of Nouthesia Social Science, in cooperation with the Nouthetic Counselling and Rehabilitation Corporation, Vancouver, B.C., and Brantridge Forest School, Sussex, England.

The Corporation has been utilizing the OUT-CLIENT Program unit of the Nouthetic Technique since 1973, when the Nouthetic Counselling and Rehabilitation Corporation was established in Vancouver, B.C.

We prefer to intervene while the troubled employee still has home, job and family (even though 'on very thin ice' in all aspects), thereby eliminating the usual 'end result' of a person, if intervention is not accomplished soon enough i.e. skid road.

The Nouthetic Technique is based on the Nouthesia mode, coupled with an entirely autogenic approach. These are further coupled to response and behaviour pattern adjustment, using Directive Counselling, involving the whole family, excluding children 13 years old or younger.

We deal with SYNDROMES (problems); not SYMPTOMS of syndromes (problems), and will identify the PRE-CONDITION syndrome, which is the basis of all other syndromes. This is the last syndrome to be delt with.
We work back through the symptoms to identify the various syndromes (problems) involved, then deal with the syndromes (problems).

We scrutinize every area of the client's life for syndromes (problems), ensuring we do not leave any undesirable or untreated syndromes, in any area of the client's life. ALL syndromes are dealt with once and for all. It requires approximately 12 weeks for a client to complete the program.

We have been most active in the Employee Recovery Program field, this subject being part of our research projects.

In my opinion, the most serious problem facing the Employee Recovery Program field, is the incompetence and disarray within the Counselling and Rehabilitation field.

The employee that has a two or three child family, trying to support his wife at home, (to raise the family as only a wife and mother can), has not got a snowballs chance in hell. Yet, the FAMILY is supposed to be the BACKBONE of a Nation. When poverty comes in the door, love goes out the window. KNOWING this, we naively ask "how come the percentage of family separation; family break-up; divorce; mothers with jobs; single parent families; children born out of wedlock; crime; violence; rape; unrest and rebellion has more than DOUBLED in the last 20 years ? These percentages are ACTIVELY growing more and more each MONTH these days. At the present increase rate, the percentages will MORE than double again, within the next 10 years.

Workers' Compensation Board benefits are now being paid for mental or emotional disorders when the disorder is found to be CAUSED by the job. Within a few years, 'emotional disorders' will become a major drain on Workers' Compensation funds, nationwide. We had better get ready, NOW, with the necessary EFFECTIVE Counselling and Rehabilitation programs. This is, if nothing else, good ECONOMIC sense.

We within the Corporation have long been concerned with the mental health and 'mental illness' of employees, and those who have suffered incapacitating emotional disorders. However, we must remember, that there are two distinct concepts involved; one is Mental Health, the other is 'Mental Illness', then ask the question, "who pays the three billion dollar bill ?"

The Manhattan study claims the incidence of emotional problems, in the general population is one in four (25%), and estimate within the workforce, it is one in eight (13%), and the workforce percentage is increasing by leaps and bounds. This study also claims the incidence of emotional problems in any group, over a long enough time span, will approach 100%. This study was published in 1962.

At that rate, it is patently impossible for industry to contemplate conducting its affairs only with employees who are never subject to emotional problems. Therefore, it makes much more sense to rehabilitate and salvage an emotionally disturbed employee, rather than to terminate the employee, and run the risk of replacing the employee with one that is WORSE off emotionally, and that fact undetected because of the 'cover-up' expertise developed (in the interest of survival) by the job seeker.

We must not lose sight of this developing problem, that will prove to be a MAJOR expense for the Ministry of Human Resources, if we don't do something about it now.

There must be an AVOWED concern for the individual employee and his family; the day of the flash-in-the-pan reiteration for the employee and his family is dead...what is needed is GENUINE fraternal concern.

We within the Corporation have come to understand the on-the-job behaviour of employees with emotional problems, and how important it is to reduce the unhealthy stress inherent in some jobs, in order to PREVENT emotional reactions on the job. As

Time Magazine so correctly described it; "MENTAL HEALTH ON THE JOB; INDUSTRIES THREE BILLION DOLLAR PROBLEM".

Industries role in life (generally speaking) is NOT the fostering of Mental Health, but the creation of marketable products and services, in a competitive world, at a good profit. It is probably not really fair to hold Industry responsible for 'mental illness' of workers (again, generally speaking) because, by the time one enters the workforce, the personality is already well formed, or, at least largely determined, and, he/she is, ideally, realistically participating in the world. However, we must not lose sight of the fact that treating an employee like a child provokes childlike behaviour.

Within the Corporation, we try to develop definite trends toward SOME acceptance, by Unions and Employers, of reasonable RESPONSIBILITY for providing treatment for emotionally disturbed members or employees and their families. The 'trend' has not come very far because of the ineffectiveness of many programmes members and employees are referred or subjected to, TO NO AVAIL.

Early detection is essential. ('resist beginnings; all too late the cure, when ills have gathered strength by long delay'). Syndromes (problems) are far more amenable to treatment at their onset. When a person is NOT detected early, that person is on the road to becoming an institutionalized iatrogenic, if intervention is not accomplished.

As W. P. Gullander so rightly stated: "profound changes have taken place in the kinds of jobs available...some jobs are disappearing and some jobs are being created. Jobs calling for new skills, and the willingness to learn them, and adapt, requiring workers to change jobs. It will become the NORM for some workers to have three or four DIFFERENT careers in their lifetime, perhaps requiring them to move with their families to a number of different localities. There will be a RESULTING sense of ROOTLESSNESS and superficial relationships, to others in the community, when one doesn't expect to stay very long. The effects of rapid, frequent changes are discomforting to a person or family".(emphasis mine).

This quiet revolution is 'RATTLING OUR CAGE'; the three A's, accident, absenteeism and alcoholism are costing Industry billions of dollars a year. We must remember that friction can damage or destroy the sensitive human mechanism. People with problems show it in many ways; i.e. belligerent employees; the employee with the 'blues'; the exaggerated worrier; the suspicious; the selfish and greedy; the learners; and the person who has poor emotional control. They have no 'safety valve'; human beings persist in acting like human beings.

Between 1970 and 1975, I conducted a five-year research project, going onto every skid road between Vancouver and Halifax, to ascertain WHY ? In spite of all that was being done, nothing seemed to help, and in FACT, the clients were being helped very little, and in most cases, became worse.

It soon became quite clear to myself; the reason that not much was being accomplished, was that WE, in the Counselling and Rehabilitation field were doing the wrong 'things'. WE were not SOLVING 'the problem', WE were further

COMPOUNDING and COMPLICATING 'the problem', and turned our clients into iatrogenics in the process. And to add insult to injury, the less than 1% that we DID claim to help, in fact, recovered on their own (in spite of what they were subjected to), and were counted as having been rehabilitated.

Also, as a result of that research project, I developed an out-client program to deal with people that still had their job, family, and home, although on 'very thin ice' in all aspects, realizing the place to 'catch' the client was 'here'; BEFORE the client fell to skid road. I also developed a Residential Program (that WILL salvage people off skid road and Social Assistance, and recycle them back into society) to deal with clients that were missed, and fell through 'the net', and enjoyed no intervention while still on the job with family and home; people that progressed or deteriorated to the point where they fell to be within the realm of skid road. Skid road people, in my experience, will respond to an EFFECTIVE Residential Program beautifully, but not well to Out-client Programs.

One of the questions researched during the 1975 - 1981 research project was: "HOW CAPABLE OF THEIR RESPONSIBILITIES TO TROUBLED PEOPLE WITHIN THE WORKFORCE ARE LABOUR AND MANAGEMENT ?" My research has shown that neither Labour nor Management is capable of their RESPONSIBILITIES or OBLIGATIONS to troubled people within the workforce.

Also, during that research project we were phasing into practice, the theories and techniques developed during the 1970 - 75 research project, working out the 'bugs', and developing a Modus Operendi and Methodology that has PROVED to be completely effective and successful.

During the 1975 - 81 project I addressed a large seminar re establishing Member Assistance Programs, to be established by Labour Unions for their members, at S. F. U. in October 1977, at the request of Ann Harley, Program Coordinator, S. F. U. Continuing Studies, and Mr. Art Kube, Regional Education Director, Canadian Labour Congress.

During this research project, the Corporation became involved with 'troubled' members of Unions and Management, and discovered the answer to the question: "WHY DO MEMBER ASSISTANCE PROGRAMS AND EMPLOYEE ASSISTANCE PROGRAMS EXIST ONLY ON PAPER, AND WERE INEFFECTIVE, BY THE FOURTH YEAR OF THE LIFE OF THE PROGRAM ?" I determined the answer to be, that Labour AND Management were trying to build a second floor onto a 'house' that did not have a first floor. (the second floor being the modus operendi and methodology of the Member/Employee Recovery Program concepts; the first floor being the competence and effectiveness of the Counselling and Rehabilitation field). This scenario was further compounded and complicated by the FACT that those within middle and upper management of both Labour and Management threw stumbling blocks at the 'program', even attempted to scuttle the 'program', IN ORDER TO KEEP THEIR OWN 'SKELETON'S IN THE CLOSET. i.e. they themselves were being 'flagged' as troubled employees.

During both of my research projects, at every opportunity, I shared my findings with Government, Labour and Management; the most recent, a theorem written 12 December 1981, based on actual case histories, 69 pages, and a brief to the Standing Committee on Labour, Manpower and Immigration dated 13 January 1982, 44 pages.

The last two questions I intend to research are:

1. WHO HAS DONE OUR SOCIETY THE GREATEST HARM, THE DISCIPLINE OF LAW, OR THE DISCIPLINE OF PSYCHOLOGY/PSYCHIATRY ???

2. HOW DID THE B. C. FEDERATION OF LABOUR AND THE LABOUR RELATIONS BOARD BECOME SO STYMIED BY, AND BOGGED DOWN WITHIN, LEGALISM, ABANDONING FRATERNALISM ???

Labour's methodology must be based on FRATERNALISM or MORAL principles, (principles that are easily sidetracked via legalism), NOT legal concepts.

Identification of 'troubled ' people is not always difficult. An employee was seen at the request of his Supervisor. The man regularly used a disconnected telephone on the wall near his lathe, (before making any major decisions), to talk with, and obtain advice from three sources; Bing Crosby, Harry Truman and God, in that order. Without impugning the consultative qualifications of these sources it can be said, with a fair degree of confidence, that this was not normal behaviour.

On the other hand, paranoid ideas (delusions of persecution etc.) may be described with seeming clarity and logic by a person who appears to be quite intact.

There are numerous clues to the identification of an emotional problem: alcohol/drug abuse, manner, demeanor, interpersonal relationships, deterioration of work performance etc. But in MANY instances, there are no obvious clues...The person may be harbouring within himself, and masking from the rest of the world, a pitiful and painful anxiety or depression. It must also be accepted that some of these problems are transient or self-limited, or are resolved (more or less) successfully by the person without intervention by others.

There are psychoneurotic and obsessive compulsive personalities within a company that Supervisors or Managers would classify among their very best workers, because these individuals set such high standards of performance for themselves. They work well in Industry, for a long time, but at CONSIDERABLE cost and discomfort to themselves and others around them. However, eventually, they SPIN OUT.

The relationship between a person's work and mental health is basic, both to human satisfaction and to Industrial productivity. Employee Recovery Programs are often established only AFTER something went wrong...AFTER the crisis. We must have an eye to PREVENTION as well as TREATMENT. When complaints are discussed and resolved, IMMEDIATELY, absenteeism, accident and employee turnover rate go down.

Industry CAN document the fact that two-thirds of it's job loss is CAUSED by personal factors; that 80 - 90% of it's accidents are based on the 'human factor'; that employee turnover, absenteeism, accidents, scrap, and alcohol/drug abuse are MAJOR problems; in a sense, to be dealt with PRAGMATICALLY.

Industry ENCOURAGES people to seek Counselling help on the one hand, then penalizes them for doing so by rejecting their applications for employment, if it is stated that they have received such treatment. Such attitudes are neither humane, logical nor common sense, in terms of the realities of the modern world.

There are companies whose attitude towards 'troubled employees' is 'terminate rather than rehabilitate'. Management feels that there are enough people 'out there' looking for work, that it is best to get rid of the 'troubled employee' and replace him, with someone else, thereby getting rid of problems within the workforce, saving money for the company.

This attitude came to light after it was noticed that every employee that availed themselves of the Employee Assistance Program (through the Industrial Nurse) was terminated or resigned (because of pressure) within three months maximum. The Industrial Nurse resigned over this issue.

This unscrupulous Management feels it saves money with this attitude, they consider that attitude as a source of revenue (or a reduction in overhead costs) in that they are spared the expense of bearing with 'troubled employees'. Hardly fair to a competitive company with scruples and integrity, that IS willing to bear the expense.

The unscrupulous management was assured their attitude

was wrong, and that eventually, they would be swamped with 'troubled employees' due to the fact that the percentage of 'troubled' people within the workforce was increasing by leaps and bounds, and that with every passing day, the company stood more of a chance of replacing a troubled employee with someone WORSE off. The management spurned this opinion, and continues in their 'terminate rather than rehabilitate' attitude.

We are OBLIGATED to the troubled employee and his family and friends, in terms of personal anguish and the loss of an opportunity to live and work productively. We must be OBLIGATED to the goal of PREVENTION.

Our motives may stem from COMPASSION, or from a need for human PRODUCTIVITY, but our success will profit everyone concerned. However, I am afraid that only when finding a satisfactory replacement for the 'troubled' person is bothersome, troublesome and difficult will REHABILITATE RATHER THAN TERMINATE be seriously accepted, without reluctance. Industry tends to 'improve', 'alter' or 'discontinue' Employee Recovery sentiments according to its need for manpower, not according to the needs of manpower.

The problems of Metropolitan areas are problems of stress, sharing, selfishness, greed, overlap, and increased leisure time; automating Industry is creating surplus manpower that is relatively unskilled and uneducated. I need not tell you that our complex, uneven, crowded and frenetic society has achieved some horrors that we MUST do something about.

We are in the midst of a 'knowledge explosion' within the Counselling and Rehabilitation field. As our understanding and insights increase, we will face a growing awareness of the need for a 'loom' on which to 'weave' all this 'knowledge' into a useful 'fabric'. Without conscious planning, the separate parts often have CONFLICTING METHODOLOGY AND INTERESTS, together with great duplication of effort. Great and diverse interests must be brought together in a common working relationship.

In my opinion, and according to the established cycle that seems to have engulfed the general public for the past 100 years or so, within the next year or so, a great hue and cry will arise to chastise and condemn the Counselling and Rehabilitation field, for not being of much help in this day...we may even be accused of being ineffective.

We must remind the general public , we in the Counselling and Rehabilitation field should not be expected to bear TOTAL responsibility, because of the FACTS of urbanization; industrialization; parental incompetence; bad government; apathy; lack of realistic cooperation between Management and Labour; selfishness; greed; irresponsibility; immaturity; pretension; rebellion; arrogance; lack of fraternalism, tough love, education, guidance and direction, within Labour; legalism; lack of taking a responsible stand on moral issues; non-participation in general; forgetting that Democracy only works when <u>EVERYBODY</u> PARTICIPATES etc. , has produced at least SOME of the problems.

We in the Counselling and Rehabilitation field MUST,

however, bear the responsibility for the institutionalized iatrogenic trend we have created or developed within society. We must learn to intervene at the PLACES of stress, and at the TIME of crisis, with individuals, groups and communities, and to reverse the institutionalized iatrogenic trend we so inadvertently caused. However, we must have HELP, and this must be in cooperation with Business and Industrial community, as well as with Labour, Governmental and the Church communities. We MUST have sufficient competence to cope with the problems, because we have now reached the point of no return; where 'RADICAL SURGERY' is required. Therefore, the support of the above-mentioned communities is <u>CRUCIAL</u>.

We must remember well the wisdom and judicious counsel of Dr. Alexander H. Leighton regarding the "FATAL TRILOGY; underestimation of client load; inadequate staffing; and insufficient funds".

In my opinion, Dr. LEIGHTON'S book CARING FOR MENTALLY ILL PEOPLE (Cambridge University Press, 1982) should be the basis for the necessary and much needed re-organization and 'RADICAL SURGERY' required within the Counselling and Rehabilitation field.

Further, in my opinion, Dr. Alexander H. Leighton, Professor of Psychiatry and Preventative Medicine, Dalhousie University, Halifax, N.S. should be commissioned, together with Mr. John W. Seager, Executive Director, Greater Vancouver Mental Health Services, Vancouver, B.C., and Dr. Jay E. Adams, to form and establish a Royal Commission that MUST be established, to bring stability, good order, direction, coordination, cooperation, and the much needed QUALITY and EFFECTIVENESS, within the Counselling and Rehabilitation field in Canada. (let Canada take the lead in this project; we CAN do it, we HAVE the necessary resources).

Thereby eliminating the chaos, disarray, wasteful and harmful duplication of efforts, and the ineffectiveness that has entangled, and is binding tighter and tighter, the Counselling and Rehabilitation field.

Dr. Leighton would bring to the Royal Commission wisdom, knowledge, and the crucial ingredient, and stabilizing force, of SERENITY. Anyone that has read Dr. Leighton's article in the CANADA'S MENTAL HEALTH magazine, JUNE 1982 will understand why I make that recommendation.

Mr. John W. Seager would bring to the Royal Commission wisdom, knowledge and the other crucial ingredient , honest, open, frank and above-board STRAIGHT - FORWARDNESS.

Dr. Jay E. Adams would bring to the Royal Commission the necessary ingredient of an honest new approach to Counselling and Rehabilitation, together with the necessary clinical evidence that CHANGE is of the utmost importance if we are to be effective in the Counselling and Rehabilitation field.

We MUST support training of more competent persons to work within the Counselling and Rehabilitation field, AND become a potent ally of Labour, Government, Business, Industry, and the Church, in our common goal to control via education, the bad response and behaviour patterns of our population.

Our treatment of the 'troubled' person has been, at its worst, inhumane, and at its best, less than adequate in the light of our knowledge. Labour, Government, Business, Industry, and the Church must demand QUALITY and EFFECTIVENESS in the services we provide; and WE must guard against resenting the pressure to assume OUR responsibility.

WE must remember we have precious little knowledge (practical knowledge) of private enterprise; and that we tend to belittle the lack of practical knowledge in the field of human relations, as used by Industry, in their daily dealings with their employees; and belittle Industries attitude toward persons that have been treated for emotional problems or 'mental illness'. We must ALL learn the SUPPORTIVE value; we MUST cooperate to effect the necessary changes, ideally with Dr. Jay E. Adams, Dr. Leighton and Mr. Seager at the helm.

This Thesis, *EKLEGETE written and released under the auspices of Brantridge Forest School, Western Academy of Nouthesia Social Science, and the Nouthetic Counselling and Rehabilitation Corporation.

The case histories and Research Project Methodology, and results, have been given to the Alcohol and Drug Commission of B.C., in a spirit of cooperation and sharing. Receipt of the above mentioned material was acknowledged via a letter from the Commission signed by Mr. J. H. Symons, his file reference T2-1 PLANNING, DATED 13 JULY 1978.

R A Pratt, Ph.D., F.B.F.S.

---

* an asking; make a choice; choose.

DISTRIBUTION via registered mail.

Most Rev. Angelo Palmas,
Apostolic Pro-Nuncio.

His Highness Bishop Sotirios,
Eastern Orthodox Church.

Most Rev. E.W. Scott,
Primate, Anglican Church.

Commissioner Pitcher,
Salvation Army.

The Rev. D. Anderson,
Canadian Council of Churches.

Rt.Hon. Pierre Trudeau,
Prime Minister of Canada.

Rt.Hon. Edward Schreyer,
Governor General of Canada.

The Hon. Joe Clark,
Leader of the Opposition.

Dr. M. Hislop,
Riverview Hospital, B.C.

Dr. J. Smith,Chairman,
Alcohol Drug Commission.

Mr. Ed Broadbent,
Leader, N.D.P. Party.

Rt. Hon. Peter Lougheed,
Premier,Province of Alberta.

Rt. Hon. Bill Bennet,
Premier, Province of B.C..

Rt. Hon. Howard Pawley,
Premier, Province Manitoba.

Rt.Hon. Richard Hatfield,
Premier, Province of N.B.

Rt.Hon. Brian Peckford,
Premier, Newfoundland.

Commissioner J. H. Parker,
Northwest Territories.

Rt.Hon. J. Buchanan,
Premier, Nova Scotia.

Rt.Hon. William Davis,
Premier, Ontario.

Mr. John Russell, C.E.O.,
Alcohol/Drug Programs,

Rt.Hon. James Lee,
Premier, Province P.E.I.

Rt.Hon. Rene Levesque,
Premier, Prov. Quebec.

Rt.Hon. Grant Devine,
Premier of Saskatchewan.

Commissioner D. Bell,
Yukon Territory.

Marc Lapointe, Q.C.,
Labour Relations Board B.C.

Hon. Lloyd Axworthy,
Employment & Imm. Canada.

Hon. Monique Begin, Minister,
Health & Welfare Canada.

Hon. Herb Grey, Minister,
Industry, Trade & Commerce, CAN.

Hon.J. Chretien, Minister,
Justice, Canada.

Hon. C.L. Caccia, Minister,
Labour Canada.

Dr. L. Kerwin, President,
Research Council Canada.

Hon. Grace McCarthy,
Minister, Human Resources.

Hon. R. McClelland,
Minister of Labour.

Hon. James Chabot,
Minister, Govt. Services.

Dr. K, Friedman,
Ombudsman of B.C.

Hon. A. Mc Eachern,
Chief Justice, B.C.

His Honour L.Goulet,
Chief Judge, B.C.

Judge L. Bewley,
Retired.

Mr. G. Dalton,
B.C.Police Comm.

Mr. B. Robinson,
Corrections, B.C.

D. McDermot,
Cdn. Labour Cong.

Jim Kinnard, Pres.,
B.C. Fed. of Labour.

Hon. Robert Caplan, Solicitor General of Canada.

Bill Smallie, Director Cdn. Labour Cong.

Hon. W.B. Campbell, Minister Veteran's Affairs Canada.

Art Kube, Director Cdn. Labour Cong.

Mr. Andre Fortier, President, Social Sciences & Humanities Research Council of Canada.

Dr. A.L. Leighton, Dalhousie Univ.

Hon. Dave Barret, Leader of opposition, B.C.

John W. Seager, Greater Vancouver Mental Health Ser.

Hon. Allan Williams, Q.C. Attorney General of B.C.

Mary Ford, Sociology Div. Van. Ref. Library

Hon. James Nielson, Minister of Health, B.C.

Terry Moore, C.K.N.W. Radio, Van.

ALL TO NO AVAIL...the resulting attacks upon myself by the Psychological/psychiatric interests, and the Alcohol Drug Commission were vicious, scathing, reviling, persecutory, and insulting, indefatigably. However, I was not required to resist unto blood. And when I get home, I will be able to say, to my Heavenly Father..."I tried"..There <u>are</u> those who unwittingly assist Lucifer without realizing that fact. However, we should never be alarmed when satan hinders us, because that in itself, proves we are on the Lord's side, and are doing The Lord's work. It is an oracle, within Lucifer's realm; "WHERE REALISTIC

REBUTAL IS NOT POSSIBLE, MUD SLINGING IS A GOOD SUBSTITUTE"..."OPPRESS VIA DISCREDITING".

To this day, the Freudian/Rogerian theories continue to usurp the role of the Priest/Minister, and are destroying North American society, taking liberal, humanistic, unthinking Cardinal's, Theologians, Bishops, Priests/Ministers and lay people down with them, via their apostasy, heresy, gross theosophy and spurious speculation.

Truly, Lucifer had his hour, but God will have His day; not one of the above people, who were in a position to DO something about the matter, will be able to stand before the Great White Throne on Judgement day, and be able to say "BUT LORD, I DID NOT KNOW THAT", to their chagrin. What fools we mortals be.

However, I was elected to the rank of FELLOW, as a result of that Thesis, and those research projects. AMEN. "IN RECOGNITION AND APPRECIATION OF CONTRIBUTIONS TO THE ADVANCEMENT OF KNOWLEDGE".

R. A. PRATT, Ph.D., F.B.F.S.

PART 3

5 Nov 1982

The RIGHT Honourable
 Pierre Elliott Trudeau,
 Prime Minister of Canada,
 Parliament Bldgs.,
 Ottawa, Ont. KIA 0A2
 Honourable Prime Minister:

Re your three 15 minute Telecasts.

As a Counsellor in the Counselling and Rehabilitation field for the past 29 years; working down in the muck and the mire, at the grass roots level, with all sorts of degenerates and jerks, I have experienced some very disappointing and frustrating moments. Your telecast topped anything I have ever experienced to date. Not because of you Sir, I suspect; but because of Governmental Bureaucracy.

Please understand Sir, this Theorem is NOT intended to be derogatory, slighting or insulting; I respect your Office too much for any of THAT nonsense.

Although I am certainly disappointed and frustrated, this Theorem is an attempt to rub minds with you. To 'rub minds' with you is, in my opinion, a right of mine; I've watched you grow from a kid riding a motorcycle, in a leather jacket, with a swastika on the back, in the early 1940s, to the Office of Prime Minister of Canada.

Obviously, you are seriously out of touch with reality. As a Social Science Researcher, this situation brings to my mind only one question: HOW THE HELL DID THAT HAPPEN ?

A recent letter to me from your office d/14 Sept. 82, signed by C.A.Ozoux, gave me a clue; that letter sent me back to my files, and I noticed the reply for my letter d/8 June 82, was signed by Edward Gorecki. These two pieces of correspondence were very important to you, in my opinion; they outlined the results of two research projects I had completed.

On closer examination of my files, I noticed that every acknowledgement I have ever received (when an acknowledgement was sent), for all information and findings I ever forwarded to you, were signed by various and sundry people over the last 9 3/4 years, but never by yourself.

At every opportunity, I shared the findings of my research projects from 1973 to Sept. 1982,(which was the Thesis EKLEGETE, which summarized the data gathered from two research projects, and the receipt or acknowledgement for the Thesis was signed by C.A.Ozoux).

Obviously, governmental bureaucracy has taken it's

toll. You probably never even saw ONE of those pieces of correspondence; it seems to me, that you were trapped by your own bureaucracy, and I wasted a lot of valuable time. Only one thing went wrong; everything I warned against since 1973, CAME TO PASS.

PLEASE; Mr. or Mrs. or Miss Bureaucrat, reading this Theorem, PASS IT ON to the Prime Minister, as a favour to himself and Canada. DO NOT send me a letter telling me how much "Mr. Trudeau appreciates having your comments", then throw it into file 13. At this point in time, Mr. Trudeau and Mr. L.B.Pearson are running neck and neck for the dubious title of the one that has done Canada the greater harm, damage and injury...give Mr.Trudeau a break, pass this on to him; PLEASE.

At this time Mr. Prime Minister, in my opinion, there can only be one of three possible explanations or answers to the question "HOW THE HECK DID <u>THAT</u> HAPPEN?"
1. you have surrounded yourself with a bunch of 'ya men'; (people that only tell you what THEY think you should or want to hear, keeping reality from you);
2. you are suffering from the Autism Syndrome;
3. you are hurting Canada via a subtle, diabolical plot; (conceived and prompted because of hostile sentiments and ingratitude expressed by what you consider to be, an ungrateful Canadian population, I would suspect)

The question can, and will be answered, by what I see coming out of Ottawa, after you have read this Theorem. Please read it; not to believe nor to contradict, but to weigh and consider.

Had the correspondence sent to you in March 1973 reached you, we would not be in the mess we are today. In that correspondence I warned you of what the multinational Corporations were up to, and suggested you re-enact the Wartime Prices and Trade Board Act, to stop them from hurting Canada, and also that immaturity, irresponsibility, parental incompetence, selfishness and greed were becoming major problems that must be dealt with. Your bureaucrat on that occasion (the twit), said you thanked me for sharing my comments with you, then told me that "these things were NOT happening".

You ask Canadians to "pull together"; "believe in each other; "trust each other" etc. Sir, if that were possible, we would not be in the mess we are in today. The problem that the multinational Corps. dictate Canadian labour economics more than the Government can, (close the mines in Quebec because Brazil offers G R E A T E R profits than can be stolen from Canada, but selling their products at Canadian prices, NOT the cheaper Brazilian price) coupled to the fact that, with the percentage rate of troubled people within the population increasing by leaps and bounds, as it is, (and it looks like it will more than double within the next ten years) (surely the Social Sciences & Humanities Research Council of Canada are keeping posted on these trends ?), further coupled to the fact of the incompetence, ineffectiveness and disarray that has entangled, and is binding tighter and tighter the Counselling and Rehabilitation field, the far greater percentage of the population are simply NOT capable of what you ask of them. And when it finally comes to light that I am right, don't blame the population; blame the bureaucrats that should have kept their fingers on the "pulse" of the population, but did NOT do so, or at least didn't tell you about it.

TRUST??? How can I trust even my own Government? Trust the global corps that can, and do, more to HARM a Country than the Government can do good to HELP the Country ? Trust politicians that come out of meetings on topics that are of VITAL importance to me, and tell me via the media "no comment" or "the meeting was fruitful' and (or) treat me as though the things that are discussed in those meetings are none of my damn business ? Canadian against Canadian ? how about the global corporations against the Canadian problem ???

Believe me Prime Minister, I am NOT paranoid...it is NOT unusual or beyond possibility for politicians to shaft ROYALLY the population they pretend to serve; it is NOT unusual for global corps. to rape and ravage a population, then laugh at the people for allowing them to do it...don't you realize these things ? want proof ? read on...

Because multinational corps are new, bold and POWERFUL, they cross the frontiers of academic disciplines as easily as they cross national frontiers. Any serious attempts to understand what they are doing, or the meaning of what they are doing, involves a journey into politics, social science and economies.

The men who run the global corps. are the FIRST in history with the organization, technology, money, and ideology to make an attempt at managing the world as an integrated unit.

Geo. Ball, former Under Secretary of State for the U.S.A.,

and Chairman of Lehman Bros. International said "we are able for the first time, to utilize world resources with an efficiency dictated by the objective logic of profit".

Jacques Maisonrouge, of I.B.M. fame, said "simply by doing it's 'thing'; by doing what comes naturally in the pursuit of it's business objectives, global corps. are ushering in a global shopping center, in such a way as to maximize global profit". He also adds "the boundaries that separate one nation from another are no more real than the equator".

Success or failure of global corps. are measured on global profit; on fundamental efficiency in creating profits; NOT on social impact in any country...the growth of global profits.

The rise of the global corporations has produced organizational revolution as profound in its impact and implications for man, as the Industrial Revolution, and the rise of the Nation-State.

In 1973 (remember?), the annual sales of global corps., compared with the gross national product of Nations, show that G.M. is bigger than Switzerland, Pakistan, and South Africa; that Royal Dutch Shell is bigger than Iran, Venezuela, and Turkey; that Goodyear Tire is bigger than Saudi Arabia.

By their extraordinary power, global corps. transform the world political economy, thereby transforming the historic role of the Nation-State. This power does not come from the barrel of a gun, it comes from the means of creating wealth on a worldwide scale.

In the process of developing a New World, Managers of

global corps. like G.M., I.B.M., Pepsico, G.E., Shell; Volkswagen, Exxon, and a few hundred others, are making daily business decisions that have more social impact than those of most Sovereign Governments, on where people will live; what work (if any), they will do; what they will eat, drink and wear; what sort of knowledge schools and Universities will encourage; as well as dictating what the society will be like.

The whole thought of such diabolical unconcern for a Nation or it's people, especially when the Nation is the home and Country of themselves and their families, might be thought of as a pill that is simply 'too big to swallow'. May I point out..this total unconcern, greed, selfishness, not giving a damn for the people, duping the people by what ever means is necessary, even to the point of outright lies and con-shots, is nothing new... we experience this every day of the week in these times; the metric conversion program is a prime example.

These distorted, disgusting, loathsome, .deceitful, cheating, devious, pregnant with destruction and subversive tactics; in an out-rightly bold, callous, openly blatant fashion, first dared to be OPENLY displayed in Canada, in 1945. The occasion was the Federal Election 11 June 1945 and the Ontario provincial Election 4 June 1945; the incidents were the utter destruction of the C.C.F. Party; and the beginning of the end for Labour.

To quote from a book by Morden Lazarus (Boag Foundation) entitled THE LONG WINDING ROAD will be essential as evidence.

The forerunners of the present day global corps. were businessmen in the 1940's.

During the B.C. provincial election of 1941, the CCF election slogan was 'victory abroad, security at home", and the election platform included public ownership of the war industries. This, naturally, very much upset the industrialists. The industrialists were well aware of the fact, that, a war enables them to make multi- million dollar profits.

The C.C.F. was saying what the Labour movement said during World War 1 i.e. "conscription of wealth if manpower is conscripted, and an end to wartime profiteering". To this the industrialists replied that "industry and wealth are already conscripted, and the C.C.F. was merely hitting a straw man".

Just-how misleading the industrialist's statements were, was not made known until 8- Feb 1945. On that date, the Bank of Canada reported the working capital of the 625 war industry businesses increased by over $316 million from the fall of 1939 to the spring of 1942, and that the largest 129 companies made the largest gains, i.e. half the total of all 625 companies. (to date, no one has determined which war made the most Canadian Millionaires).

The industrialists were also aware of the fact that Canadian Labour was getting too strong; although they knew how to handle the problem at the moment, the industrialists didn't want the problem to get any bigger. The industrialists were thinking of the Oshawa, Ont. G.M. strike in. 1937, when 4,000 men went on strike for a first Union Agreement. The Liberal Premier of Ontario, Mitchel Hepburn was VIOLENTLY opposed to the strike because 'if unions were allowed to get into G.M., they would spread into the mining industry of Northern Ontario". Hepburn started up a 'special' police force (made up from the

Ontario Provincial Police), known as "HEPBURN'S HUSSARS", and was prepared to use them to break the Oshawa strike.

But the Mayor of Oshawa, Ont. threatened to counter with the city Police Force if those "sons of Mitches" so much as crossed the city limits. The strike lasted 6 days and was orderly and peaceful.

Up to 1937, the C.C.F. Party grew and became very strong. Something had to be done about them. Premier Hepburn, businessmen and the mining Companies, with the aid of the press, scared the wits out of the public about unions and communism. The Liberals swept to a landslide victory in the Ontario Provincial election of 1937, crushing the C.C.F. Party.

The first important lesson had been learned; "OPPRESS VIA DISCREDITING" ...WHEN REASONABLE REBUTAL IS LACKING, MUD SLINGING IS A GOOD SUBSTITUTE"..."the general population CAN be conned via propaganda; they're not overly bright".

However, Labour's fight against Hepburn's crude attempt at dictatorship, and the realization by the general population that they had been duped, caused an aftermath that helped Labour plant their banners throughout the auto industry, the steel mills, electric, rubber, mining and other industries, where they'd never been before.

Starting in 1940, pro.-C.C.F. sentiments in Unions was rising rapidly, and the C.C.F. Party membership was growing fast. In the Ontario Provincial election of 4 Aug 1943, when we went to bed on election night, the C.C.F. was tied with the Conservatives in seats won. When we woke 5 Aug 1943, the Torries had 38 seats, the C.C.F. 34, and the Liberals had 12. The C.C.F. was the Official opposition for the first time in history. C.C.F. membership in Ontario rose to record levels; a total membership of 800,000.

In the Saskatchewan Provincial election of 1944, the C.C.F. Party won 50 of the 55 seats.
The C.C.F. in Nova Scotia had peaked.

This was enough for the industrialists and big business... if they were going to continue to "call the shots"," the C.C.F. had to be e1iminated"..."there would be no 'profiteering' under a C.C.F. Government".

The C.C.F. Party in Ontario and across Canada, came under increasingly VIRULENT hammering from PR FLAKS like Gladstone Murray, who headed a Company called Responsible Enterprise, and Montague Sanderson,(the "bug man"), Reliable Exterminators'. Very LARGE contributions were made by big business interests,(a veritable 'who's who' of Canadian big business), towards the anti-C.C.F. campaign, and the press cooperated like trained seals, but with much less intelligence.

The anti-C.C.F. campaign strategy was engineered and handled by paid hirelings like the man from Missouri,U.S.A., Burdick Trestrail, an Industrial Psychologist. And PR FLAK. (PROPAGANDIST).

The closer the elections came, (4th & 11th June 1945),

the more money was poured into the barrage of anti-C.C.F / LABOUR. propaganda; propaganda of the most contemptible kind...charges that C.C.F. Government would mean "muscle men and gangsters"; that "the C.C.F. was Nazi"; "anti-British; revolutionary" etc. and so on. NOT just from the paid hirelings who published and distributed Nationwide the poisonous pamphlet "STAND UP AND BE COUNTED" (patently anti-Semetic into the bargain, because the C.C.F. leader Mr. Lewis was Jewish), but also from prominent politicians like Premier Drew of Ontario, and also from well-known businessmen coast to coast.

To show just how widespread and insidious the anti-C.C.F / LABOUR campaign was, I'll quote from Weekend Magazine, 26 Feb 1977, from an article about Lloyd Shaw. "Lloyd ran for Parliament in Halifax in the 1945 Federal election.(a C.C.F. candidate). He might even win. But when the Prime Minister King Government and the business interests brought out the TRESTRAIL Pamphlet,(it went into every home in Canada), (the pamphlet was anti-Semitic;(David Lewis, the C.C.F. Federal leader was Jewish)); the "C.C.F./ LABOUR was communist" etc., "just the dirtiest literature imaginable".(speaking of the day after the pamphlet had been distributed into every home in Canada via Canada Post), "going down the street the next day - and it wasn't just imagination - the whole atmosphere changed, just that quick". "it was a shattering of the C.C.F." And the beginning of the end for Labour.

With meager election funds, both provincially and Federally, and small staff, against the slanderous onslaught, the C.C.F. was helpless; trade unions were virtually speechless.

The Communists were secretly lined up with the Conservatives to beat the C.C.F. Provincially, and with the Liberals Federally.

Ted Jolliffe, Ontario Provincial C.C.F. Leader, on 24 May 1945, on a provincial radio network, charged Premier Geo. Drew with maintaining a 'secret police' force, out of public funds.

The Ontario Government's secret police force was in charge of Capt. Osborne-Dempeter (of the Ontario Provincial Police), whose job it was to link up all non-conservatives with the communist party. He held...illegal Union Cards so he could attend Union Meetings.

Union Offices were rifled; documents taken; spies were sent to Union Meetings; blacklists of people of whom Premier-Drew's Gestapo disapproved were prepared, and businessmen were given the blacklists to check against their Employee name lists. The blacklist of names was made available to the paid propagandists.

(all this information, and more was made available to Ted Jolliffe by O.P.P. Constable John Rowe, who was Capt. Osborne, Dempster's assistant since 1944, when the secret police force was set up).

Premier Drew, of course, denied the charge completely, and appointed a Royal Commission to investigate the charges. The Royal Commission would, or course, meet AFTER the election. In the meantime, the lesson learned in the 1937 Provincial election i.e. "OPPRESS VIA DISCREDITING" ..."WHEN

REASONABLE REBUTAL IS LACKING, MUD SLINGING IS A GOOD SUBSTITUE"...and "THE GENERAL POPULATION CAN BE CONNED VIA PRPAGANDA" would be utilized to the fullest extent.

On 28 April 1949, a front-page headline read "JOLLIFFE VINDICATED". There WAS a 'Gestapo'. Jolliffe's charges that there was a secret police force in Ontario were proven by findings of the Lebel Royal Commission (4 Years later). The Chief of this special branch of the Ontario Provincial Police was dismissed. The Deputy Commissioner was relieved of his duties, and the spying was ordered to cease. On 29 July 1945, the Trades and Labour Congress demanded that Premier Drew stop spying on Ontario Labour.

EVERY Canadian, truly interested in what happens to Canada, owes a debt of gratitude and thanks to Morden Lazarus for his honest, and completely thorough investigation and reporting on Canadian Labour via his book THE LONG WINDING ROAD, and ALL Canadians must read the book, AND LEARN. See what's possible when big business and politicians team up Honourable Prime Minister, especially when they know how to 'work the system' ?

What global Corps. are demanding, in essence, is the right to transcend the Nation-State, and, in the process, transform it. Carl A. Gerstacker, of the Dow Chemical Co. says "I have long dreamed of buying an Island, owned by no Nation, and of establishing the world headquarters of the Dow Company on that truly neutral ground of such an Island, beholden to no Nation or Society".

A company spokesman for a principal competitor of. Dow, Union Carbide, agrees: "it is not proper for an international corp. to put the welfare of ANY Country in which it does business above that of any other". Christopher Tugendhat points out "The global interests of the world company are separate and distinct from the interests of every Government, including it's own Government of origin".

In terms of Management and Ownership, all global corp. are either American, British, Canadian, Dutch, French, German, Italian, Japanese, Swedish, or Swiss, (most are American), in outlook and loyalty, they are becoming (or became) companies without a Country.

Extraordinarily high profits on low over-seas investment is the norm. For example, in 1972 United Brands REPORTED 72.1% return; Parker Pen 51.2%; Exxon 52.5%; by 1973 America's seven largest banks were obtaining 40% of their profits from abroad, up from 23% in 1971. Was the money being loaned at higher or lower interest rates than we (Canadian consumers) could get at home ? How about the Royal Bank of Canada ?

Now, in 1982, that the Nations' Banks that tried to sucker or milk (or are milking) (are) (getting smart ?) are not able to repay the loans, public tax dollars are being used to pay, so that the banks will not be forced into bankruptcy.(i.e. American Government secretly paying the loans of Poland). These same banks, however, have no qualms about forcing small businesses at home into bankruptcy...public tax. dollars are not available to small businesses.

Business International warns it's Corporate Clients..."The Nation-State is becoming obsolete; tomorrow, it will, in any meaningful sense, be dead - and so will the Corporation that remains essentially- National" A new breed of globalists have launched an attack on the Nation-State more radical. than anything proposed by World Federalists.

The men who run global corps,(aware that ideologies, like soda crackers, travel well, only if skillfully packaged), are putting great energy into marketing a new gospel that has more potential to change the face of the earth, than even the marketing miracles that have brought Holiday Inns and Pepsi-Cola bottling plants to Moscow and Coca-Cola to China.

Roy Ash former head of Litton Industries and President Nixon's budget director and Chief Consultant in Managerial Matters, feels "nothing can stop an idea whose time has come". Men like Ash know that their vision of a world without borders, is the most important product they have to market (or sell). The extraordinary role they are proposing to play in human affairs challenges what Arnold Toynbee calls "mankind's major religion, the CULT of Sovereignty". In my opinion, what Roy Ash was able to deliver to the global corps will prove to be 'chicken feed' when compared to what George Shults will have delivered, when the truth becomes known, a few years from now.

Manhattan Bank, calls for a massive public relation campaign to dispel the dangerous "suspicions" about the corporate giants that lurk in the minds not yet able to grasp an idea whose time has come. Remember the slogan of the global corps. yesteryear, INVESTMENT ABROAD IS INVESTMENT IN CANADA ? (this, of course, coupled with the lesson learned in Canada in l937; can there be any doubt as to the success of that 'public relations' campaign via PROPAGANDA) ?

David Rockefeller calls for a "crusade of understanding" to explain why the global corps should have freer rein to move goods, capital, and technology, around the world, without the INTERFERENCE of Nation-States, realizing that such a crusade calls for the public relations campaign of the century. In my opinion, the campaign will be much like the "Burdick Trestrail Syndrome" (the campaign used by Trestrail in Canada, when the industrialists and big business teamed up with the Liberals, Conservatives, and the Communists to 'do a number' on the C.C.F. Party / LABOUR 1944/45). The campaign probably would be quite successful because what happened then, has been forgotten 3 generations ago.

The new globalists are well aware of the problem Rockefeller is trying to address. Geo. Ball says "Corporations do have the power to affect the lives of people and Nations in a manner that necessarily challenges the prerogatives and responsibilities of political authority. How can a National Government make an economic plan, with any confidence, if a Board of Directors, meeting 5,000 miles away can by altering it's pattern of purchasing and production, affect in a major way, the Countries economic life ?". The global corps' answer to the charge of being a political usurper, is not to DENY the extraordinary powers they seek to exercise in human affairs; but to RATIONALIZE it.

The continuing struggle for National identity is the unifying political theme of our day. The Chairman of Unilever, one of the earliest and largest global corps, warns his colleagues..."the Nation-State will not wither away, a positive role will have to be found for it".

In Canada and the United States, the most seriously damaged members of Society is organized labour; Singer Sewing Machine reduced it's main U.S.A. plant from 10,000 employees to 2,000 employees; General Instruments cut it's labour force by 3,000 in-the U.S.A. and increased it's labour force in Taiwan by almost 5,000. Remember what Massey Ferguson did with its labour force ? (the same thing).This process shows no sign of stopping. The globalist's claim the net effect is a net increase in jobs, because the stimulation of new industry is greater than the job displacement in older industry. This is how the laying off of 3,000 in the U.S.A. and hiring 5,000 in Taiwan is being rationalized.

Thousands of Canadians are losing jobs because of plant relocation; that other workers, in other places may be getting jobs in the process, is small comfort to the unemployed breadwinner. The latest statistics that I am using indicates global corps employ cheap labour, under what can only be called or described as 'sweat-shop conditions'; 60% of the male workers of Hong Kong work 7 days a week, for about one dollar a day. (1974 stats). Is this what you are asking Canadian workers to do? Control the PRICES and WAGES, as per the Wartime Prices and Trade Board Act, and THEN Canadian labour could work for less. The global corps lay off the Canadian worker, have their products produced at a dollar a day, but sell the product at the price using Canadian wage scales, not the one dollar per day wage scale; and the Government assists the global corps to do so. And to add insult to injury, because of the fact that when Poverty comes in the door, love goes out the window, and family separation is the NORM in this situation, the very backbone of the Nation,(THE FAMILY), goes down the tube, taking Canadian Society with it. Who was it you wanted me to trust ? the Government ? Canadian big business ? the global corporations ?

The disclosure of ITT's efforts to bring down the Allende Government in Chile (Chile became a major concern after the nationalization of Anaconda's and Kennecott's copper mines), have confirmed widespread fears that the global corps not only have too much power, but that they also abuse that power.

According to a former U.S. Ambassador to Chile, the C.I.A. spent $20 million dollars to defeat Allende; the line of bank credit shrank from $220 million to $35 million in the first year of Allende's Government. I wonder who paid the cold hard cash dollars to generate unrest and subversive activities in Chile, and hollered C 0 M M U N I S T S for all the world to hear, and condemn Chile ?

The global corps are in a position to dominate large Governments (like Canada and the U.S.), dislocate National economies, and upset world currency flows. Corporate Managers have the power to shift capital, develop or suppress technology, and mould public moods and appetites; to the extent that even the most powerful Governments (increasingly in the more industrialized Nations), worry about their ability to control global corps. whether the global corps should be welcomed, barred, or fitted with a legal straightjacket is shaping up as a prime political issue in most Countries. Where does Canada stand on this issue ?

The attitude of young people around the world, toward

global corps is a cause for particular concern; it will be fuel for revolutionary fires.

The developing confrontation between the global corps and it's enemies, promises to influence the shape of human society in the last part of this century, more than any other political drama of our time. The global corps are winning in that fight as of this date; they have a 33 year head start right now; may I remind you Sir, that when I first brought this matter to your attention, they only had a 22 year head start.
Can you please advise what the MONTHLY interest dollar value is on all of the loans Canada has, and must pay ? (Not the loan amount, just the INTEREST amount).
You would stabilize the Canadian economy over-night, if you had the courage to get the married women and mothers out of the workforce, and back into their homes, to look after their families, as only a Mother can, and also had the courage to re-enact the Wartime Prices and Trades Board Act, so that the bread-winner COULD afford to feed his family, and still be able to buy a home for them, and have an annual vacation with them, on ONE pay cheque. You would have to control everything...medical, dental, and legal fees; room rents, suite rents, house rents, house prices, interest rates etc.(as was done during the second world war; remember ?

This would sure cause one heck of a commotion within the population (ESPECIALLY from the selfish and greedy) and the global corps, but it would save Canada, the Canadian Society, and Nation.

However, from my experiences at the grass roots level,

within the Counselling and Rehabilitation business, I suspect the Canadian people, on the whole, are NOT worthy or capable of Democracy.. if this IS so, we will know soon enough...we will lose Democracy. A law of nature dictates, that a person is entitled to a freedom, only to the precise extent that person is capable of the responsibility that freedom demands, or carries with it.

Please Mr. Prime Minister, ask C.A. Ozoux to give you the copy of the Thesis EKLEGETE I sent you, and read it for yourself. I would appreciate your thoughts on the topics discussed. Perhaps the next time you are in Vancouver we could meet and rub minds for an hour or two, privately and informally.

My Prayer is that you will 'take the bull by the horns' and get things straightened out; if not, I guess I will have to get into politics and do it myself. Surely, you would not wish THAT on the Canadian people ?

May I also suggest, Mr. Prime Minister, that you read the book GLOBAL REACH by Richard J. Barnet and Ronald E. Muller, in order to gain insight that will be of vital importance to you, as Prime Minister of Canada, regarding Global Corporations... PLEASE ?

You are in a position to do a lot of good for Canada, or let Canada go down the tube. In this day and age of terrorist activity, if the 'radical surgery' required is not performed, there will be one hell of a blood-bath if Canada is thrown into a major depression and many more bread winners lose their jobs, their homes and their families.

If what we are experiencing IS a diabolical plot, you are doing a SUPERB job; if it is inadvertent, you are in a position to do something about it. However, it will require some L 0 N G and REALISTIC hard looking and DOING. Rest well assured Prime Minister, I will do all I can to help you from this end and level .Respectfully yours.

Your obedient Servant.

R A Pratt,Ph.D.,F.B.F.S.
President.

Cb/RAP
Photo copies:
The Honourable Ed Broadbent
The Honourable Joe Clark
The Honourable Dave Barrett
The Honourable WM. Bennett
The Right Honourable Edward Richard Schieyer,
Governor General and Commander in Chief of Canada

Mr. Peter Corcoran, 4 March 1985
Project Director,
"Let's Talk About Schools",
School District # 81,
Box 87,
Fort Nelson, B.C. VOC IRO.

Dear Mr. Corcoran:

May I express my gratitude and appreciation to The Project Committee of Fort Nelson, and The Hon. Jack Heinrich, Minister of Education, for the privilege at presenting the following presentation.

This presentation is intended to make constructive and objective observations, from a Social Science point of view.

Since having earned a Baccalaureate in Psychology over thirty years ago, I have seen the Discipline go awry, to the point where I now consider Psychology, Psychiatry, Political Science, and Social Science pseudo sciences. PLEASE, don't let that happen to our Educational System.

This opinion is based on the fact that within any true science, where fact disproves the hypothesis, the hypothesis is amended accordingly. Within the above mentioned Disciplines, if the FACT cannot be adjusted to accommodate the hypothesis, the FACT is quietly set aside.

Over the last fifteen years in particular, my attempts at 'sounding the alarm' have been totally ignored by colleagues, and Government, even though my election to the rank of

FELLOW ("In recognition and appreciation of contributions to the advancement of knowledge") was a result of those papers and lectures.

This difficulty, in my opinion, has come about, due to fact that Educational Philosophy is also, (if not already gone) going awry.

Fouille wrote "Uniform education, similar training, common beliefs, more than make up for differences in racial stock'. Obviously, education, more than any other ingredient, will develop or destroy a National Character, and has great influence on the destinies of Nations. National Character seems to run parallel to the development of Educational Philosophy, rising or falling with Educational Philosophy.

It seems the degree to which the process of Educating is successful, depends on the skills employed in making use of the various tools of communication available for this purpose.

From a Social Science point of view, an Educational Program must have a number of essential components if it is to be successful i.e. it must be carefully planned; it must be directed to a clearly defined need; those to whom it is addressed must be motivated to take an active part; the programme must be skilfully administered; there must be a continuing assessment of the results.

Dissemination of a curriculum alone, I consider useless, and cannot be considered an Educational Programme.

Each component has its particular merits, but each has very decided limitations in carrying the full brunt of an Educational programme on its own. Objectives must be formulated, and a plan must be developed.

For an example, an Educational Programme is much more likely to bring about a change in attitude, or a course of action in terms of stated objectives, if it is focused on a particular group. i.e. the narrower and more precise the age group, the easier it is to plan a programme that will focus sharply on the needs of that particular group.

The broader and more diverse the interests of the group, the blunter, you can be sure, will be the impact of any Educational effort. The homogeneous group is easier to motivate than the heterogeneous group. The more highly motivated a group is, the easier it is to plan an Educational Programme that will have the potential for success.

It never seems to occur to us that there might be a REASON why so many people make a failure of their lives.

In my research, I found most people cited such things as "lack of superior ability" (this predestines and confines the vast majority to failure from birth, without a chance...I proved this to be false), and "lack of adequate capitol" (this makes dollars, and not the person, responsible for success or failure...I also proved this to be false).

The REAL factor, I found, was fitting the proverbial 'square peg in a round hole'. I found most failures were MISFITS. Most 'failures' would have been a success in the field where they best fit and belong.

Failures are not foredoomed; success does not just happen.

Each and every individual on the face of the earth has a purpose, and is quite unique.

Students must fix the RIGHT goal, not just ANY goal. They must be able to define SUCCESS.

Most students I have worked with were going through school without a real goal at all...they never thought of having any purpose in life...they were not going anywhere in particular. If we don't know where we are planning to go, how can we ever expect to arrive there?

Most had no AIM...they were merely victims of CIRCUMSTANCES (they thought). They never planned purposefully. They allowed themselves to drift, making no effort to master or control circumstances.

Students must fix the RIGHT goal. They often fix goals for which they have little or no aptitude, then drift into inaction. The RIGHT goal will arouse ambition, incentive, determination, will power, and excite vigorous and determined effort...it will fire them with incentive.

There must be preparation to achieve the RIGHT goal... education and preparation. How can one expect to accomplish a purpose without acquiring the 'know-how' ?

Students are not taught the fact that humans do not come equipped with instincts complete and intact.

Dumb animals never need weary their brains with 'book learning'. A new-born calf does not have to be taught how to walk...it starts immediately to get up on it's infirm and uncertain legs. It may fall down on the first or second attempt, but in a matter of a few moments, it stands. The calf doesn't have to reason out any GOALS. It requires no textbooks nor teaching. It INSTINCTIVELY knows its goal... DINNER, And it knows, also INSTINCTIVELY, the way...it proceeds immediately to the first meal. Birds build nests by INSTINCT; no one teaches them how.

Of course, dogs, horses, elephants, dolphins, etc. can be taught and trained to do tricks. But they CANNOT reason, imagine, think, plan, design and construct different things. They do not acquire knowledge, perceive truth from error, make decisions, and employ will to exercise self-discipline according to their own reasoned wisdom and decisions. They cannot develop moral or spiritual character.

Humans must be taught and learn. We can learn to think and reason, to conceive a new idea, to plan, design, and construct. We can investigate, experiment, and invent.

But we have to LEARN; to STUDY; to be EDUCATED, to be prepared for what we PROPOSE to DO. One of the first things we need to learn, is THAT WE NEED TO LEARN.

Once we have learned enough to choose a goal, we must then learn the way...to acquire the additional Education, training, experience, to give us the know-how to achieve our goal.

If we fail to set definite goals, we have no specific aim, and we neglect the specialized Education to make possible the attainment of our purpose.

We must be broad enough to realize that 'Education' includes not only 'book learning', but also personality development; leadership; experience; knowledge; contacts; and observation.

There is then, a RIGHT and a FALSE Education. In my opinion, the entire system and Education philosophy in this country neglects to recapture the TRUE values. The basic and most essential knowledge, the TRUE VALUES; the MEANING AND PURP0SE OF LIFE; the WAY TO PEACE; and HAPPINESS; and ABUNDANT WELL-BEING; these BASICS are never taught. This decadence in 'modern' education; this tragic 'knowledge gap', must be corrected within the Education Philosophy that seems to have gone awry.

Right Education must teach that all things are a matter of CAUSE AND EFFECT; that for every 'result', whether good or evil, there is a CAUSE. True Education would teach the cause of this countries evils; of personal and collective troubles, so that they may be avoided. Also, it must teach the cause of the GOOD results, so that we may know how to win them, instead of the troubles. Right education must not stop at teaching to live, it must also know, and teach, the PURPOSE of human life, and how to fulfill it.

Decadent Education Philosophy has spawned many student revolts, and produced violence and chaos! ANOTHER significant tragedy of our times.

Education Philosophy in this country, seems to be disseminating false education that has come down to us from unthinking, philosophizing, misguided pagans who lack a knowledge of the TRUE values and PURPOSES of life, according to GOD'S Commandments, Oracles, and Precepts.

Good health is a subject of Education. MUCH sickness and disease (estimated at 90% to 95%) comes from faulty diet.

We may laugh at people who dip small mice into a sauce, and, holding them by their tails, drop them as a delicious delicacy into their mouths. (NOT suggesting we eat mice). If we do laugh at them, they will laugh back at us, and tell us that mice eat clean grain and clean food only, while we dip slimy, slithering scavenger seafoods into a cocktail sauce, and consider THEM a delicacy. We can find canned eel and rattlesnake on fancy store shelves. Why? Because humans know very little at birth. We have to LEARN, but most of us don't know that! And what we don't know, We don't KNOW that we don't know!

Most of us have grown up eating just whatever seemed to taste good, and whatever we saw others eating. There has been little Education or even study about what we ought, or NOT to eat. God's dietary laws are completely ignored. i.e. eating meat and drinking milk at the same meal. If we know a person that does, habitually eat meat and drinks milk at the same meal, then we know a very nervous person, with bad nerves. Eating meat and drinking milk at the same meal produces a toxic poison that damages the nervous system. THAT'S why God tells as not to do that.

Mental attitude has considerable influence on physical condition. Negative thinking, fear, worry, discouragement, etc. I've heard it said that any dead fish can float downstream, but it takes a live one to swim up-stream. An inactive person will not accomplish; accomplishment requires DOING. A half-hearted effort may carry one a little way toward his goal, but it will never get him far enough along to REACH his goal. Put a constant 'prod' on yourself, drive yourself, or you will lag, let down, and stagnate. Without energy, drive, constant propulsion, a person cannot expect to become truly successful. (All precepts of God).

Students need to LEARN determination and resourcefulness. When sudden emergencies arise, then, of all times, one needs a clear mind, calm nerves, rapid thinking, and sound reasoning. One needs a cool head, to quickly get all the facts and make a wise decision, then act on that decision. (More precepts of God).

Students need to LEARN perseverance...stick-to-itiveness. There ARE times when one appears to be totally defeated; all is lost; apparently, that is. One is then tempted to give up and quit, when just a little more faith, just a little more determined hanging on and perseverance would have turned apparent certain failure into glorious success. (More precepts of God).

Another important component of Education we seem to have lost sight of is simple SINGING. Singing is important for two reasons: I. It activates a certain portion of the left brain. 2. If we want to know where the students will be in about five years, listen to the words or the songs they are singing or humming today. Songs have a TREMENDOUS influence on our character development. i.e. listen to the words of the songs the children are listening to today via N L Radio. (Another precept of God). Have you ever seen two people involved in a serious fist-fight, singing while they were fighting ?

Is it possible that the Living God might be a factor in determining the success or failure or one's life ? Few have thought so.

Would it not seem axiomatic that, IF there is a compassionate, beneficent Creator standing by, ready and willing to give us emergency help as a last resort, it would have been more sensible to have sought His guidance and help all along?

Few, it seems, will ever rely on their Maker and life-sustainer until they feel helpless and in desperate need. Even then, the motive too often is SELFISHNESS. Freedom from fears, and worries, peace of mind, security, protection, happiness, abundant well-being, the very source of their supply is the Great God. Since it all comes from Him anyway, why not tap the SOURCE from the very beginning?

But in our day of pseudo sciences, sophistication, vanity, gross theosophy, and spurious speculation, it is not fashionable to believe in a Creator. In this deceived Country, knowledge of God now finds little or no place in 'modern' Education Philosophy.

Many so-called 'successful' people had 'goals'. They sought happiness in vanity, pride of status, money, material acquisitions, and similar pursuits. They seek the approbation of others, and engage in backslapping to invite it. But, like an actor's applause, (the word make me think of applesauce), it doesn't last, and leaves them flat, with an inner hunger for something that will satisfy. So they become restless and discontented. Their bank accounts may be full, but their lives are empty. They started out with wrong goals. They had not discerned the true values, but pursued the false values. They inherited a handful of wind.

A particular family comes to mind; a multimillionaire family. Due to parental incompetence, the end result was that both their son and daughter ended up committing suicide, after a life, (as short as it was), of alcohol and drugs. The family 'success' was not long lasting, and not long remembered. Their 'success' will not live on after them.

It would be possible for me to give many examples of rich and famous people in Vancouver that phoned myself around 2 or 3 A .M., and I found them weeping, and lamenting the utter emptiness of their lives; literally not able to stand themselves, when they were alone with themselves, however, professional ethics forbid this.

They had money, and lots of it, but their lives were empty. Their life-long struggle; the contestant striving "after Wind" and false values; the sneaking; cheating; lying; stealing; being sensually sick; in various combinations and to varying degrees, left in its wake a trail of fears, worries, apprehensions; disappointments; heartaches; troubled consciences; discontent; empty lives; frustrations; and finally death.

True happiness is not material, and money is not its source. And vanity, as Solomon observed, is like a striving after wind. Those people did not realize it, but the 'hunger' they felt was Spiritual...the God-blank. Spiritual hunger is never satisfied with material food or goods.

It seems modern Educational Philosophy does not realize HOW and WHY we were made, or WHAT humans are, and WHY we are here. Of these God seems to say "My people have committed two evils; they have forsaken Me, the fountain of living Waters; and hewed for themselves cisterns; broken cisterns, that can hold no water".

Is there, after all, a PURPOSE to life?

IF we were put here by a Creator, would He have put us here without a REASON? A Creator with the mind and power that would have designed and produced the human mind and body could NOT have failed to make available, for humans, EVERY tool, ingredient, and facility, and faculty needed to fulfill HIS purpose.

Of course, men cut off from God have no knowledge of that PURPOSE because that Knowledge is not material, it is Spiritual knowledge. Spiritual knowledge can only be transmitted by REVELATION, and this country has rejected Revelation. Men that are cut off from their Creator are Spiritually blind and ignorant, groping in the dark. So they fail to seize the proper tools, ingredients, and facilities.

But the Creator has sent an INSTRUCTION BOOK along

with the human mechanism He made. It contains all the REAL answers. That 'Instruction Book', as Bruce Barton aptly said, is "the Book nobody knows". **B**ASIC **I**NSTRUCTIONS **B**EFORE **L**EAVING **E**ARTH.

Almost no one knows that 95% of the contents or that Book is virtually ignored by the professing Christian Clergy. Further compounding and complicating the problem is the utter disarray and disagreements between professing Christian Clergy themselves.

The religious, Bible-believing fundamentalists, generally quote and use not more than approximately 5% of that Book. Almost 1/3 of the contents of that Book is devoted to ADVANCE NEWS REPORTS. Few pay any attention to this 1/3, and most are devoid of understanding it.

Clergy and laymen that I have trained to be Counsellors within the Counselling and Rehabilitation field, have been surprised and shocked to learn that, this ignored, maligned, misrepresented Book contains the answers for the Counselling and Rehabilitation Field. They have found that "it makes sense".

That INSTRUCTION BOOK is the very foundation of the knowledge this Country needs, in ALL areas.

The time when students need 'Divine guidance', enlightenment, and help, is at the very beginning; at the time when the student is trying to choose that RIGHT goal. Without Divine guidance, the WRONG goal is usually set... thanks to Lucifer and his realm.

Life HAS a purpose, and God has set in actual motion, the way that life is to fulfill HIS purpose.

When the student asks the question "what is the PURPOSE of my being here on earth ?", the correct answer is "to know, Love, and serve God. Doing HIS will, allowing HIS will to be done IN your life, WITH your life, and THROUGH your life". In other words, DOING the job He created you to do for him, using the innate talents and aptitudes HE gave you as 'tools'. The students MUST ask God for the wisdom and guidance, to find the path HE created them to walk. The students will be VERY, VERY happy and successful in the end, wanting for nothing.

However, the student must also learn this: we are free moral agents. God will NEVER force us to go His way. The 'key' to the locked door is WILLINGNESS. God not only allows us to choose the wrong way, He compels us to make our own decision. God sets two ways before us; His way in obedience and submission, or our way in rebellion and disobedience. Also, the student must ASK God for the wisdom and guidance needed to find the path the student should walk.

When the number one textbook is the Scriptures, the entire Education and preparation will be different. The Scriptures will provide a sound mental approach in all Education and practice.

God COMMANDS that we do our best. Whatever is worth doing, in worth doing the very best we can. Nine passages Command that we apply ourselves with diligence; ten others

Command us to be diligent; thirty-six others Command or show the example of acting diligently, many of those instruct us to diligently seek God's guidance and help. To our BEST, God adds the rest, if we do not do our best, He adds nothing.

To many, this may seem a foolish or hard saying; "deny yourself, take up your cross, and follow Me". But it will be much harder to hear "depart from Me, I never knew you".

There are gropings and blunders that are inevitable when one enters an unfamiliar environment, without guidance and support. Without the Way, there is no going; without the truth, there is no knowing ; without the Life, there is no growing. The outcome of my life is not in God's hands, it's in my hands; the outcome of my life is not a matter of chance; its a matter of choice. Since by God's Power and Grace I can re-shape myself, I am responsible for the shape I am in. I reap sevenfold what I sow, good or bad. My part God will not do, His part I cannot do.

Many are deaf and hardened to God's voice; things of small or no value are served with eagerness

It seems to me that Educational Philosophy today supposes, erroneously and in ignorance of the facts, that the Bible is merely the book of an ancient race of Jews, striving to devise a concept of some god, in by gone days of ignorance and superstition. They do not examine the Book, as they examine other data, to SEE what it says. They ignore the Bible as something below their pride and intellect to consider.

Did you ever wonder WHY, poor people, possessing

the least knowledge and material goods, appear to be the happiest ? (actually, they are NOT happier, they are merely less discontented). The reason is, that they haven't progressed as far in the WRONG DIRECTION as those who smugly and vainly suppose themselves to be their more intelligent betters!

Parents contribute to this erroneous thinking by their own ignorance and incompetence, today, brought about mainly via the Spock theory on child training which began some fourty years ago. (For which, I might add Dr. Spock apologized, a few months ago, saying he now realizes he was wrong). Further complicating and compounding the problem is PARENTAL INCOMPETENCE, which in turn throws an even larger burden on the Educational System. In my opinion, Educational Philosophy, for the moment, has been FORCED into the position of having to deal with, and correct, parental incompetence...because the Church is not capable of doing so, at this time.

Clergymen, via their own ignorance and incompetence, are further complicating and compounding the problems within our Canadian Society. They have naively accepted the role assigned to them, by an antichristian, anti-religious, consensus in our Society. They have been relegated to a cultural backwater, where they are meant to paddle around, content in the knowledge that they are merely allowed to exist, taking their differences with them.

Clergymen seem to be apologetic for the Christian faith, in spite of the obvious bankruptcy of the human nature.

If Christians do not become profoundly angry very soon, we

will witness the collapse of our Society as history repeats itself. Think of the use of 'labels' to categorize groups of people and individuals. Some 'labels' are used to neutralize the actions of certain groups; others denote being "one of us" or acceptable.

The words 'right wing', 'fundamentalist', 'pro-lifer', 'absolutist', and 'deeply religious', are put-downs more than categories. Conversely, think of the unspoken pat on the back and blessings that the following words convey: 'moderate', 'pluralistic' 'liberal', 'civil libertarian', 'pragmatic', and 'enlightened'. Deceit always deals in stereotypes, and stereotypes perpetuate bigotry.

To Quote Frank Schaeffer, "the myth of neutrality includes the widespread (often deliberate) misunderstanding of SEPARATION OF CHURCH AND STATE. Separation of Church and State was intended to provide freedom FOR religion, not freedom FROM religion. Talk about the division of Church and State is often nothing more than a 'red herring', a convenient excuse for muzzling undesirable Christian opinions and views, rather than a real concern, on the part of the liberal, humanistic consensus. In other words, simple, unadulterated PROPAGANDA, intended to create bigotry and discrimination toward those holding Judeo/Christian views". (The original was SEPARATION OF CHURCH AND EDUCATION, but changed to 'STATE' by the educational elite of the day, (1830)).

IF Educational Philosophy is deliberately committed to destroying ethical commitment to God, then resistance is appropriate, and WILL be forthcoming, providing Educational Philosophy does not destroy our Society, before our Society comes to its senses.

To quote from a paper I wrote in 1982: "what standards do we use?" When we attempt to ascertain whether or not something is right or wrong, good or bad, within a client's response and (or) behaviour patterns, what standard can we use to measure against?

In my opinion, we certainly cannot use the client's own standards because the client, to say the least, is confused, unsure, unstable, and will change standards many times, depending on the moods and feelings of the various times. More often, the client is also quite irrational, irresponsible, insecure, immature and suffering an inferiority complex. Obviously, we cannot use the client's own standards to measure against.

Can we use the Therapists standards? In my opinion, hardly. I know many Therapists that are worse off than any client they will ever see, because they can be manipulated and conned by anyone willing to "suck-up" to them for those purposes. Ego, vanity, power trips, bleeding-heart-do-gooders, etc., to varying degrees, in various combinations, are quite common. Obviously, we cannot use the Therapists own standards to measure against.

The ONLY standards that I have found to be accurate to the point of infallibility, and totally reliable, are the BIBLICAL standards, and these are the standards used within the Nouthetic Counselling and Rehabilitation Technique. I am NOT a 'Bible Thumper', nor a 'religious freak', however, in the areas of Psychology/Psychiatry, Science has given way to human philosophy, gross theosophy, and spurious speculation. I have found the various schools of Psychology just as heavy with dogma as any religion. (end of quote).

Excluding of course a good husband and father, wife and

mother, in my opinion, there is not a higher, more noble calling or profession, than to be a Teacher...a GOOD teacher that is. A BAD teacher is below the integrity and dignity of a 'crooked cop'.

In my opinion, based on my research, we MUST put religious training back into our School system; give God equal time with Freud, Rogers, Darwin, Adler, Skinner, and the other champions of the pseudo sciences. It IS true, God is NOT dead, nor does He sleep; neither is Lucifer dead, nor does he sleep. Once 'wheels' are set in motion, they grind to an inevitable end.

At whose hand the 'blood' will be required is not within the realm of this presentation, however, the Scriptures say the 'blood' will surely be required.

Using Biblical standards will impart subtlety, resourcefulness, wise conduct, knowledge, discretion, etc., even to the simpleton, and teach the student how to convert information into knowledge the way God says to do it.

Educational Philosophy must deal with the problem, and not simply the SYMPTOMS of the problem.

The Manhattan Study claims the incidence of people with emotional problems, in the general population, is one in four (25%). The study also claims this percentage is increasing by leaps and bounds, and that over a long enough span, will reach 100%.

We must not lose sight of this developing problem, that

will prove to be a major additional expense for the Ministry of Human Resources. We must do something about it NOW!

In my opinion, 'modern' Educational Philosophy is further compounding and complicating an already out of control Society.

We are in the midst of a 'knowledge explosion'. As our understanding and insights increase, we will face a growing awareness of the need for a loom on which to weave all this 'knowledge' into a useful 'fabric'. Without conscious planning, the separate parts will have conflicting methodologies and interests, together with great duplication of effort. Great and diverse interests must be brought together in a common working partnership.

In my opinion, based on the established cycle that seems to have engulfed the general population for the past 100 years or so, within the next year or so, a great hue and cry will arise to chastise and condemn the Educational System, for not being of much help...you may even be accused of being ineffective.

You must remember well the wisdom and judicious counsel of Dr. Alexander H. Leighton regarding the "FATAL TRILOGY... underestimation of the problem; inadequate staffing; and insufficient funds", thereby eliminating the chaos, disarray, and harmful effort, together with the ineffectiveness that has entangled, and is binding tighter and tighter, the Educational System.

My opinion, at this time, is that it must fall to the Educational System to correct our present society, due to the fact that at the moment, there is no other institution in a position to do so.

Certainly not the field of Psychology; certainly not the Clergy; certainly not the parents; certainly not the Government.

If the Educational System is not equal to the task, history will repeat itself, and our Society, as we know it, will collapse, along with the Educational System...a cold, hard, stark reality. I ask you neither believe nor contradict, simply weigh and consider my views, as seen from a Social Science point of view.

There is much more to be said, but this presentation may already be too long for some present-day readers.

If I can be of any service, in any way, please do no hesitate to let me know.

Once again, I wish to thank the "Let's Talk About Schools" committee of Fort Nelson, and the Honourable Jack, Heinrich, Minister of Education, for the privilege of making this presentation. THANK YOU.

Respectfully yours.

R. A. Pratt, Ph.D. F.B.F.S.

Susan Viet,   2 JAN 1989
Regional Manager,
Ministry of Social Services and Housing,
Suit 519,
280 Victoria St.,
Prince George, B. C.   V2L 4X3.

Dear Suzanne:

        RE: Recipients being forced into up grading
                or Vocational Skills Programmes.

    Respectfully, I wish to bring to your attention my concerns regarding very real dangers to a certain small percentage of recipients that may be inadvertently harmed by such a general practice without due regard for the individual case. Two examples will be cited.

    XXX, a local recipient, was registered at the Fort Nelson campus of Northern Lights College. After the first morning of classes, XXX stated "I can't do this", and was not coming back to school. XXX was told that if he did not return to class, he would be cut off welfare.

    Every effort was made to browbeat and coerce XXX back into class. The fact of the matter is that XXX is simply not capable of doing so at this time. His mental health condition is the problem. I have attached a copy of his Doctor's assessment of XXX at that time. We have requested a psychiatric assessment for XXX in order to establish Handicapped status for XXX with the Ministry. That assessment is scheduled for 11th January 1989.

    The point is that it was, and still is quite easy to see that

XXX was not capable of such an undertaking at that time, yet he was forced into doing so.

XXX response was to simply take off once again, to another town. We talked XXX out of that by explaining he must stop running and settle down in order to get his life together and stabilized, then to embark on a plan to build himself a future. XXX agreed to do so.

We then applied for Unemployable status for XXX pending the outcome of his psychiatric assessment, which was granted by our Area Manager.

XXX, a local recipient was also registered at Northern Lights College, Fort Nelson campus by the Ministry.

Again, a realistic review of his case would have uncovered the fact this person was also not capable of such a course at this time.

XXX has a history of mental illness. For five months this recipient was left with $17.48 to survive on after he paid his rent and utilities.

The Manager of Westview Manor, where XXX lived, brought XXX to our office. It was quite obvious XXX was in very bad condition.

We immediately had a Doctor examine XXX, that diagnosed XXX as being in a chronic severe malnutrition state. We asked XXX why he did not get food from the food bank, his reply was that he was "too proud for that".

Unfortunately, we got to XXX too late. His Central Nervous System collapsed totally, and he was taken to Riverview Mental Hospital, in a straight jacket, from his Police cell, in Fort Nelson.

XXX was returned to Fort Nelson four months later. However, the damage had been done to both his psyche and his Central Nervous System. In all probability, it will be three to five years before XXX will recover enough to get about building a life for himself.

AGAIN, XXX was coerced into Northern Lights College, Fort Nelson Campus. AGAIN XXX could not handle the class work, naturally, and rather than asking to be excused at this time, (XXX was afraid he would be cut off welfare if he did [his brother Louis can confirm this]), he ran away.

XXX has since phoned, and is coming back to Fort Nelson. (our Group supplied the bus ticket and food money for the trip). We will at that time request Unemployable status for XXX, allowing him room and time to get things under control, with a view of taking the class at N. L. C. when he is ready. This whole experience will set XXX back an estimated six months minimum.

We feel in the cases of XXX and XXX, appropriate considerations were not considered by either the Ministry or Northern Lights College, Fort Nelson campus.

May we reiterate, we have no qualms about coercion as a

tool to get a recipient off his or her butt, if that is appropriate for that recipient. However, in some cases coercion can be outright abuse, and we WOULD object to coercion in such cases.

In most cases whether or not coercion is appropriate will be axiomatic, via reviewing each individual case appropriately.

However, in some cases it will <u>NOT</u> be axiomatic, and coercion will cause harm and may do a lot of damage to recipients.

In order to avoid that scenario, may I suggest the following for your consideration, on the subject of appropriate coercion.

First of all, we must be cognizant of certain unfortunate developments within our sphere of operations.

One such unfortunate development is the FOLDED ARMS "IMPRESS ME" SYNDROME.

This was brought about due to the incompetence of persons or groups that were given a task that was beyond their capabilities, (i.e. to be able to exercise rational and reliable judgments on questions before them), and who were not ethical or honest, open, frank and above board enough to admit to same, and in their ignorance (lack of wisdom), and arrogance, usurped truth.

An example of this is Boards of Directors, sitting with arms folded, waiting to be impressed by a candidate applying for a job. (leaving themselves wide open to the old B.S. baffles brains maxim). As a result, when all of the candidates have been 'interviewed', the candidate selected is rarely the most competent, it is the best showman.

This syndrome is so widely known, and accepted, that schools, as part of the curriculum, are now teaching their students how to do this.

A danger here is that Val Ireland teaches recipients that attend her 'sessions' that they are going to "have to impress the F.A.W. or Social Worker that the course they are asking for should be given them".

At the same time, it's generally accepted as truth, that most recipients, (especially recipients that have been on Social Assistance for any length of time), suffer feelings of anger, shame, fear, guilt, failure, uselessness, unimportance, inadequacy, powerlessness, helplessness, frustration, humiliation, anxiety, depression, isolation, rejection, and a poor self-image. In most cases, they have lost hope, independence, self-respect, purpose, direction, and structure.

Can we REALISTICALLY expect anyone suffering the above to impress an F.A.W., Social Worker, or anyone else in a good, clear, concise, positive manner ? In my opinion, the answer is NO...except in cases where the F.A.W., Social Worker, or anyone else is competent to take 'the above' into consideration, using a totally impersonal approach.

There is a real danger that the person that has learned to con and manipulate others (in the interests of survival) is more likely to be accepted or selected, than the person who genuinely needs and wants help.

Another danger we must be cognizant of (and this one really compounds and complicates the "success ratio'), is the fact that Education is concerned with the development of our capacities as human beings; our capacities for understanding, for appreciation, for interpersonal relationships; for creative participation in the ongoing common life of man.. Job training is concerned with the preparation for some particular kind of employment.

To forget these distinctions, and (or) to think only in terms of the latter, is to render irrelevant a considerable part of what was once typically in any Baccalaureate programme.

It is Education which gives a person a clear conscious view of his own opinions and judgments, a truth in developing them, and a force to urge them on. It teaches him to see things as they are, to go right to the point, to disentangle a skein of thought, to detect what is sophistical or true, and to discard what is irrelevant. It prepares one to fill any post with credit, and to master any subject with facility.

The ideal end product of Education is a person of broad learning and culture, a conscious inheritor of the cultural riches of the past, an expert in the exercise of reason, a master of the art of conversation, a gentleman or lady.

Such a person is at home in any society, and an Educated person. Again, I am sure we can accept the above as a known and accepted truth.......of yesteryear.

Wonderful bloody folly...what do we do now that our whole educational philosophy has gone awry ???   What is there to force us to cut across the artificial barriers of our specialties and compel us to RELATE our little pockets of specialized knowledge (and opinions, and conjecture, and even feelings) in some coherent way ??? To see the recipients life as it really is ???

It is time to concentrate our efforts on attempting to find SOLUTIONS to the Social and Economic problems that plague recipients today, REALISTICALLY.

We have students graduating grade 12 with honours, and upgrading courses, that have not been taught the process necessary to convert information into knowledge; without any idea of where they are going, or what they want to do. (When one doesn't know where he is going, that's where he ends up... nowhere).

It serves no purpose to train a recipient for a job, without first determining for which field the recipient has an innate aptitude and talent. Many times, as a Therapist, I found the job was the major problem, or pre-condition problem; a 'square peg in a round hole'. Yet, we continue to use glorified educational surveys as 'aptitude' tests. We may safely use 'likes' in order to determine a hobby for a person, but not careers (or vocations).

A TRUE aptitude test will disregard COMPLETELY academic standing, (he can get that as necessary). Any aptitude test that is influenced by academic standing in any way whatsoever, is nothing more than a glorified educational survey, NOT a true aptitude test.

If the Ministry does not have access to a true aptitude test,

I will gladly allow the use of the aptitude test I developed many years ago, which is copyrighted by the Nouthetic Counselling and Rehabilitation Corporation.

It is totally non-productive and folly to enrol a recipient into a vocational skills programme, while at the SAME TIME, there is a hand on the middle of his back, pushing him out the door into ANY work he can get. Sure, he may get a job, but rest well assured, he will be back on Social Assistance within a year, if not sooner. Want proof ? Check your records.

There must be REALISTIC vocational training programmes, not only for recipients as of THIS date, but also for those that will end up recipients because there is no longer any work in the field they were working, which in all cases, may prove to be fields for which they had no innate aptitude or talent.

W. P. Gullander warned us over twenty years ago..."profound changes will take place in the kinds of jobs available...some jobs will disappear while new jobs are created". To quote from a submission I presented to the Ministry in August 1982, "Jobs calling for new skills, and the willingness to learn them, and adapt, requires workers to change jobs. It will become the 'NORM' for some workers to have three or four different careers in their lifetime, perhaps requiring them to move with their families to a number of different localities".

The Ministry, in it's wisdom, chose to disregard that 63 page submission; only one thing went wrong...the situations I warned about have come to pass, and to add insult to injury, to this day, the Ministry seems totally oblivious of the necessary solutions, that would have cost a lot less at that time. The Ministry seems to be STILL trying to build a second floor onto a house that doesn't have a first floor.

This quiet, subtle revolution is 'rattling the cages' of many families, and believe me, it's going to get worse. The relationship between a person's work and mental health is basic and axiomatic.

We had better prepare for 'what is coming down the pike" by developing more realistic vocational skills training programmes, geared to the recipient's innate aptitudes and talents.

The employee that has a two or three child family, trying to support his wife at home, (to care for the family as only a wife and mother can), has not got a snowball's chance in hell. The economy is geared to a two-income family, thanks to Mulitnationalism.

Yet, the FAMILY is supposed to be the BACKBONE of the Nation. When poverty comes in the door, love goes out the window (eventually). KNOWING this, we naively ask "how come the percentage of family separations; family break-ups; divorces; mother's with jobs; single parents; children born out of wedlock; crime; violence; rape; unrest and rebellion has more than DOUBLED in the last twenty years ?"

These percentages are ACTIVELY growing more and more each MONTH these days. At the present increase rate, the percentages will MORE than double again, within the next ten years.

We had better return to BUILDING families rather than FORCING them apart.

Another danger we must be cognizant of is the PARENTAL INCOMPETENCE syndrome. We have people raising children today that not only have no idea of WHAT to teach children, they also have no idea as to HOW to teach children. Wait 'til the children of the children with children get into the mainstream...we had better prepare for that syndrome...it will be a 'humdinger'.

Well Suzanne, I did not intend this letter to be this long; it could be much longer. Perhaps next time you are in Fort Nelson I may share the Group's "Ministry" file with you. I am sure it will 'blow your mind'...to reiterate, it seems the Ministry continues to try building a second floor onto a house that doesn't have a first floor; it seems they CANNOT learn, and will NOT listen.

Further, I hope you will not think that I am a negative, pessimistic type; I am not. In fact the opposite is true. Of necessity that must be the case, otherwise I would have given up on the Ministry years ago. Someday they will listen; then, we can begin to solve syndromes rather than treat symptoms with Band-Aids.

Again, to reiterate, as I have said MANY times, if there is anything I can do to help, just let me know and I will.

In the meantime, if Val Ireland remains adamant in "kicking ass" of recipients, let's make sure the recipient is able to withstand coercion, beforehand, by reviewing each case individually, taking an entirely impersonal approach, with the best interests of the recipient uppermost in our minds, without forcing OUR standards or opinions onto the recipient. The

recipient's opinion must be given the same respect that other people's opinions are given.
    Respectfully yours.
    R. A. Pratt,Ph.D.,F.B.F.S.
    Photocopies:

Mr. Cam Millar,	Mr. Aly Kakn
Area Manager.	District Manager

PART 4

11 March 1998

'HOSTILE TO THE CHURCH, FRIENDLY TO JESUS CHRIST.' these words describe large numbers of people, especially young people, today.

They are opposed to ANYTHING that savours of INSTITUTIONALISM. They detest the ESTABLISHMENT and its ENTRENCHED PRIVILEGES. And they reject the Church - not without some justification - because they regard it as impossibly corrupted by many evils.

Yet, what they have rejected is the CONTEMPORARY Church, not Jesus Christ Himself. It is, PRECISELY, because they see a CONTRADICTION between the Founder of Christianity and the current state of the church He founded, they are critical and aloof. The Person and Teachings of Jesus have not lost their appeal, however.

For one thing, He WAS, Himself, an anti-establishment Socialist figure, and some of His words HAD revolutionary overtones. His ideals appear to have been incorruptible. He breathed love and peace wherever He went. And, for another thing, He INVARIABLY practiced what He preached.

But was He TRUE ?

A large number of people throughout the world are still brought up in Christian homes where the truth of Christ and of Christianity is assumed. But when their critical faculties develop, and they begin to think for themselves, they find it easier to discard the religion of their childhood, than to make the effort to investigate its credentials.

Very many others do not grow up in a Christian environment. Instead, they absorb the teaching of Hinduism, Buddhism or Islam, or the ethos of secular humanism, Communism or extentialism. Yet, both groups, if and when they read about Jesus, find that He holds for them, a fascination they cannot easily escape

So our starting point is the historical figure of Jesus of Nazareth. He certainly existed. There is no reasonable doubt about that. His historicity is vouched for by pagan as well as Christian writers. He was also very much a human being, whatever else may be said about Him. He was born, He grew, He worked and sweated, rested and slept, He ate and drank, suffered and died like other men. HE had a real human body, and real human emotions.

But can we really believe that He was also in some Sense 'GOD' ? Is not the DEITY of Jesus a rather Picturesque Christian superstition ? Is there any evidence for the amazing Christian assertion that the carpenter of Nazareth was the unique Son of God ? This question is fundamental. We CANNOT dodge it. We MUST be honest. If Jesus was not God in human flesh,

Christianity is exploded. We are left with just another religion with some beautiful ideas and noble ethics; its unique distinction has gone.

Well, there IS evidence for the deity of Jesus - good, strong, historical, cumulative evidence; evidence to which an honest person can subscribe, WITHOUT committing intellectual suicide.

There are the extravagant claims Jesus made for Himself, so bold, and yet so unassuming. Then there is His uncompromising righteousness and tender compassion. Then there is His incomparable character. His strength and gentleness. His care for children and His love for outcasts. His self-mastery and self-sacrifice have won the admiration of the world. What is more, His cruel death was not the end of Him. It is claimed that He rose again from death, and the evidence for His resurrection is most compelling.

Supposing Jesus was the Son of God, is basic Christianity merely acceptance of this fact ? NO! Once persuaded of the deity of His Person, we must examine the nature of His work. What did He come to do ? The Biblical answer is, He 'came into the world to save sinners'. Jesus of Nazareth is the heaven-sent Saviour we sinners need. We need to be forgiven and restored to fellowship with the ALL-HOLY GOD, FROM WHOM OUR SINS HAVE SEPARATED US. We need to be set free from our selfishness, and given strength to live up to our ideals. We need to learn to love one another, friend and foe alike. This is the meaning of 'salvation'. This is what Christ came to win for us by His death and resurrection.

Then is basic Christianity the belief that Jesus is the Son of God who came to be the Saviour of the world ? NO! It is not even that. To assent to His Divine Person, to acknowledge man's need of salvation, and to believe in Christ's saving work are not enough. Christianity is not just a creed; it involves ACTION. Our intellectual belief may be beyond criticism; but WE have to translate our beliefs into DEEDS.

What must we do then ? We must COMMIT ourselves, heart and mind, soul and will, home and life, personally and unreservedly to Jesus Christ. We must humble ourselves before Him. We must trust in Him as OUR Saviour and submit to Him as OUR Lord; and then go on to take our place as LOYAL members of the Church, and RESPONSIBLE citizens in the Community.

Such is basic Christianity. But before we can come to the evidence for Jesus Christ's deity, an introduction to the right approach is necessary. The Christian claim is that we can find God in Jesus Christ. It should be a help to us in examining this claim if we realize both that God is, Himself, seeking us and that we must, ourselves, seek God.

1. <u>THE RIGHT APPROACH.</u>   'In the beginning God'. The first four words of the Bible are MORE than an introduction to the creation story or to the Book of Genesis. They supply the key which opens our understanding to the Bible as a whole. They tell us that the religion of the Bible is a religion of the initiative of God.

(I) We can never take God by surprise. We can never anticipate Him.

(2) God ALWAYS makes the first move. He is always there 'in the beginning'.

(3) Before man existed, God acted. Before man stirs himself to seek God, God has sought man.

In the Bible we don't see man groping after God; we see God reaching after man.

Many people visualize a God that sits comfortably on a distant throne, remote, aloof, uninterested, and indifferent to the needs of mortals, until, it may be, they can badger Him into taking action on their behalf. Such a view is WHOLLY false. The Bible reveals a God who, (long before it even occurs to man to turn to Him, while man is still lost in darkness and sunk in sin), takes the initiative, rises from His throne, lays aside His Glory, and stoops to seek until He finds man.

This sovereign, anticipating activity of God is seen in many ways. God has taken the initiative in CREATION bringing the universe and its contents into existence; 'In the beginning God created the heavens and the earth'.

He has taken the initiative in REVELATION, MAKING KNOWN TO MANKIND both His nature and will; 'In many and various ways God spoke of old to our fathers by the prophets; but in these last days He has spoken to us by His Son'... HEB 1:1-2. God has taken the initiative in SALVATION, coming in Jesus Christ to set men and women free from their sins: 'God. .. has visited and redeemed His people". Luke 1:68.

God has CREATED. God has SPOKEN. God has ACTED. (CREATION, REVELATION, SALVATION). These statements of

GOD'S INITIATIVE in three different spheres, form a summary of the religion of the Bible. It is with the second and third we deal with, because BASIC CHRISTIANITY, BY DEFINITION, begins with the historical figure of Jesus Christ. If God has spoken, His last and greatest word to the world is Jesus Christ. If God has acted, His noblest act is the redemption of the world through Jesus Christ.

God HAS spoken and ACTED in Jesus Christ.

God has SAID something. God has DONE something. This means that Christianity is NOT just pious talk. It is neither a collection of religious ideas nor a catalogue of rules. It is a GOSPEL' (i.e. GOOD NEWS). In Paul's words 'THE GOSPEL OF GOD...CONCERNING HIS SON...JESUS CHRIST OUR LORD.(ROM 1:1-4). It is NOT primarily an invitation for man to do anything; it is supremely a declaration of what God has DONE, in Christ, for human beings like ourselves.

GOD HAS SPOKEN:
1. Man is an insatiably inquisitive creature.
2. His mind is so made that it cannot rest.
3. It is always prying into the unknown.
4. He pursues knowledge with restless Energy.
5. His life is a voyage of discovery.
6. He is always questioning, exploring, investigating, researching.
7. He never grows out of the child's interminable 'WHY?'

When man's mind begins to concern itself with God, however, IT IS BAFFLED. It gropes in the dark. It flounders helplessly out of its depths. This is NOT surprising, because God, whatever or whoever He may be, is INFINITE, while we are FINITE creatures. God is altogether beyond our comprehension. Therefore our minds, though wonderfully effective instruments in EMPIRICAL sciences and thinking, CANNOT immediately help here, because we CANNOT climb up into the infinite mind of God There is no ladder, only a vast, unmeasured gulf. 'Can you find the deep things of God ?' Job was asked. IT IS IMPOSSIBLE.

And so the situation would have remained if God had not taken the initiative to remedy it. Man would have remained forever AGNOSTIC, asking indeed, with Pontius Pilot, 'WHAT IS TRUTH.?' but never staying around for an answer, because of never daring to hope he would receive one. Man WOULD be a worshipper, such is his nature, but all his altars would be inscribed. like the one in Athens, 'TO AN UNKNOWN GOD'.

But God HAS spoken. He HAS taken the initiative to disclose Himself. The Christian doctrine of revelation is ESSENTIALLY reasonable. God has 'UNVEILED' to our minds what would otherwise have been hidden from them. PART of God's revelation is in NATURE: 'The heavens are telling the Glory of God; and the firmament proclaims His handiwork.'

'What can be known about God is plain to them (men), because God has shown it to them. Ever since the creation of the world His invisible nature, namely, His eternal POWER and DEITY, has been clearly perceived in the things that have been made.' PSALM 19:1 ROM 1:19-20.

But this is not enough. It certainly makes known God's existence, and something of God's Divine Power, Glory and

Faithfulness. But if man is to come to know God personally, to have his sins forgiven and to enter into relationship with God, he needs a more extensive and practical revelation still. God's self-disclosure must include His Holiness, His love and His power to save from sin. This too God has been pleased to give. It is a SPECIAL revelation, because it was made to a special people (Israel) through special messengers (Prophets in the Old Testaments and Apostles in the New).

It is also SUPERNATURAL, because it was given through a process commonly called INSPIRATION, and it found its chief expression in the person and work of Jesus Christ.

The way the Bible explains and describes this revelation is to say that God has 'SPOKEN'. It is by our words that we disclose what is in our minds. This is even more true of God who has desired to reveal His Infinite mind to our finite minds. Since, (as the Prophet Isaiah put it) God's thoughts are as much higher than our thoughts, as the heavens are higher than the earth, we could NEVER have come to know them unless God had clothed them in words. So 'the word of the Lord came' to MANY prophets, until at last Jesus Christ came, and 'THE WORD BECAME FLESH AND DWELT AMONG US'. JOHN 1:1-2 & :14.

Man comes to know God not through his own wisdom, but through GOD'S WORD ('what we preach'), NOT through human reason, but through Divine Revelation. It is because God has made Himself known in Christ that the Christian can BOLDLY go to the agnostic and the superstitious and say to them, as Paul did to the Athenians on the Areopagus, 'What therefore you worship as unknown, this I proclaim to you'.

Much of the controversy between science and religion has arisen through a failure to appreciate this point. The EMPIRICAL method (thinking) is inappropriate in the sphere of religion. Scientific knowledge advances through OBSERVATION and EXPERIMENT. It works on data supplied by the five physical senses.

But when we inquire into the METAPHYSICAL, no data is immediately available. God, today, is neither tangible, visible nor audible. Yet there WAS a time when He chose to speak, and to clothe Himself with a body which COULD be seen and touched. So John began his first Epistle with the claim, 'That which was from the beginning, which we have heard, which we have seen with our eyes, which we have looked upon, and touched with our hands.. .we proclaim also to you'.. .1 JOHN 1:1.

GOD HAS ACTED: The Christian Good News is NOT confined to a declaration that God has SPOKEN. It ALSO affirms that God has ACTED.

We are not only ignorant; (lacking wisdom), we are sinful . It is not sufficient therefore that God should have revealed Himself to us to dispel our ignorance. He must also take action to save us from our sins. Men need to be delivered, not from slavery in Egypt or from exile or from exile in Babylon, but from the exile and the slavery of sin. It was for this PRINCIPALLY that Jesus Christ came; Jesus came as a SAVIOUR;
...'You shall call His name Jesus, for He will save His people from their sins'.

'The saying is sure and worthy of full acceptance, that Christ Jesus came into the world to save sinners'.
'For the Son of man came to seek and to save the lost'.
MATT 1:21   TIM 1:15   LUKE 19:10   LUKE 15:3-7.

Christ was like the Shepherd who missed the only sheep which were lost from the flock, and went out to search until He found it . Christianity is a religion of SALVATION, and there is nothing in the non-Christian religions to compare with this message of a God who loved, and came after, and died for, a world of lost sinners.

The Holy Ghost…Paraclete, leads us to Christ for the initial encounter…"SAVED" scenario; sins forgiven; soul washed clean; reconciled to God via Jesus Christ; we are given the Spirit of Christ. We are now "**BABES IN CHRIST**"…this is GOD'S part.

The next step of <u>OURS</u> to do via REPENTANCE; FAITH; and SELF-DISCIPLINE; TO GROW IN THE KNOWLEDGE OF GOD, i.e. <u>OUR</u> **PART** or response to God's part. And if this is NOT done, (according to God's Natural Law/Covenant), we will <u>NEVER</u> advance beyond the **Babe** in Christ stage, and EVERYBODY loses…GOD, OURSELVES, and   MANKIND. Unfortunately, many Christians never get past the "babe in Christ" stage in their lifetime. We must not allow that to happen to us.

<u>MAN'S RESPONSE:</u> God has SPOKEN, God has ACTED. The record and interpretation of these divine words and deeds are

to be found in the Bible. And THERE, for many people, THEY REMAIN. As far as they are concerned, what God has said and done belongs to past history; it has not yet come out of history into experience, out of the Bible, into life. God HAS spoken; but have we LISTENED to His words? God HAS acted; but have we benefited from what HE has done?

At this stage of this Synthesis, it is necessary to make one point; WE MUST SEEK. God HAS already sought us. God is STILL seeking us. Now WE must seek GOD. God's chief quarrel with man is that man DOES NOT SEEK GOD:

The Lord looks down from heaven upon the children of men, To see it there are any that act wisely, that seek after God. They have all gone astray, they are all alike corrupt; there is none that does good, no, not one. PSALM 14:2-3.

Yet, Jesus PROMISED: 'Seek and you WILL find. If <u>WE</u> do not SEEK, we will NEVER find. The Shepherd searched until he found the lost sheep. The woman searched unit she found her lost coin. WHY should we expect to do less? God DESIRES to be found, but ONLY by those who SEEK Him.

<u>WE MUST SEEK DILIGENTLY:</u> 'Man is as lazy as he dares to be', wrote <u>Emerson</u>. But the matter is so SERIOUS that we MUST overcome our NATURAL laziness and APATHY and give our minds to the quest. God has little patience with 'TRIFLERS'; 'He rewards those who seek Him'. HEB 11:6.

<u>WE MUST SEEK HIM HUMBLY</u>: If apathy is a hindrance to some, PRIDE is an even GREATER and COMMONER hindrance

to others. We must acknowledge that our minds, being finite, are INCAPABLE of discovering God by their OWN efforts, without God's self-revelation via the Holy Ghost. (Which we all receive, but will NOT respond to). I am not saying that we should suspend rational thinking. On the contrary, we are told by the Psalmist not to be like a horse or a mule, which have no understanding. We MUST use our minds; but we must ALSO admit its limitations. Jesus said;

> 'I thank Thee, Father, Lord of heaven, and earth, that Thou hast hidden these things from the wise and learned, and revealed them to the babes.' MATT 11:25.

Jesus loved children. They are TEACHABLE. They are not proud, self-important and critical. We need the OPEN, HUMBLE AND RECEPTIVE mind of a little child.

WE MUST SEEK HONESTLY: We must come to ACT upon the Holy Ghost's urgings, counsels and discernments. . . i.e. our SELF-REVELATIONS, NOT only without PRIDE, but also without PREJUDICE; not only with a HUMBLE mind, but also with an OPEN mind. Any student knows the dangers of approaching his subject with a closed mind and preconceived ideas. Yet, many enquirers' come to the Bible with their minds already made up. But God's promise is addressed only to the EARNEST seeker:

> You will seek Me and find Me; when you seek Me with all your heart'. JER 29:13.
> So we must lay aside our PREJUDICE and OPEN our minds to the possibility that Christianity may, after all, BE TRUE.

WE MUST SEEK OBEDIENTLY: This is the hardest condition of all to fulfill. In SEEKING GOD, we MUST be prepared not only to REVISE OUR IDEAS, but also REFORM OUR LIVES. The Christian message has a moral challenge. If the message is true, the moral challenge MUST be ACCEPTED. So God is not a fit object for man's detached scrutiny. You cannot fix God at the end of a telescope or a microscope and say 'HOW INTERESTING! God is not INTERESTING. God can be deeply upsetting. The same is true of Jesus Christ.

'We had thought intellectually to examine Christ; we find He is spiritually examining us. The roles are reversed between us... we study Aristotle and are intellectually edified thereby; we study Jesus and are, in the profoundest way, spiritually disturbed... we are constrained to take up some inward real moral attitudes of heart and will, in relation to this Jesus... A man may study Jesus with intellectual impartiality, he cannot do it with moral neutrality... we must declare our colours. To this has our unevasive contact with Jesus brought us. We began in the calm of the study; we are called out to the field of moral decision'. Carnegie Simpson, THE FACT OF CHRIST.1930.

This is what Jesus meant when, addressing some unbelieving Jews, He said 'If any man's will is to do His (God's) Will, he shall know whether the teaching is from God or whether I am speaking on My own authority'. The promise is clear; we CAN know whether Jesus Christ was true or false. whether His teaching was human or Divine. But the promise rests on a moral condition: i.e. WE HAVE TO BE READY NOT JUST TO BELIEVE, BUT ALSO TO OBEY; WE MUST BE PREPARED TO DO GOD'S WILL, WHEN HE MAKES IT KNOWN.

I remember a young man coming to see me when he had just left school and began to work. He had given up going to Church, he said, because he could not say the Creed without being a hypocrite. He no longer believed it. When he had finished his explanations, I said to him, 'If I were to answer your problems to your complete intellectual satisfaction, would you be willing to alter your manner of life?' He smiled slightly and blushed... he KNEW his real problem was not intellectual, BUT MORAL.

THIS is the spirit our search must be conducted within: We must cast aside APATHY, PRIDE, PREJUDICE, and SIN, and SEEK GOD IN SCORN (or in spite) OF THE CONSEQUENCE.

Of all these hindrances to an EFFECTIVE search, the last two (SIN and CONSEQUENCES) are the hardest to overcome. INTELLECTUAL PREJUDICE and MORAL SELF-WILL will also be very difficult to overcome. BOTH are expressions of fear, and fear is the greatest enemy of the truth. Fear will paralyse your search. We know that to find God and to accept Jesus Christ would be a very inconvenient experience; It would involve the rethinking of our whole outlook on life. And it is a combination of intellectual and moral COWARDICE that makes us hesitate. We do not find because we do not seek. We do not seek because we do not WANT to find. and we KNOW that the way to be certain of not finding, is NOT TO SEEK.

Be open to the possibility that you may be wrong; Christ may, in fact, BE TRUE. And if you want to be a humble, honest, obedient seeker after God, come to the Book that claims to be God's revelation. Give Jesus Christ a chance to confront you with Himself, and to authenticate Himself to you. Come with the FULL consent of your mind and will, ready to believe and obey if God brings CONVICTION to you. Read through the Sermon on the Mount MATTHEW Chapters 5, 6, and 7, and through the Gospels of Mark and (or) John for your EVENING readings. (Old Testament Didactic Books for the morning readings). See NCRC 6/2.

> 'God, if you exist (and I don't know if You do), and if You can hear this prayer (and I don't know if you can), I want to tell You that I am an honest seeker after the truth.
> Show me if Jesus is Your Son and the Saviour of the world. And if You bring conviction to my mind, I will trust Him as my Saviour and follow Him as my Lord.

NO ONE can pray such a prayer, honestly, and be disappointed. God is no man's debtor. God honours ALL honest and earnest search. He rewards all HONEST seekers. Christ's PROMISE is plain: 'SEEK AND YOU WILL FIND'.

THE CLAIMS OF JESUS CHRIST: We have seen that it is necessary to SEEK if we are to FIND. But where do we begin our search ? The Christian answers, the only place to begin is the historic Person of Jesus of Nazareth; because if God has spoken and acted, it is fully and finally in Jesus Christ that He has done so. The crucial issue is this.' WAS THE CARPENTER OF NAZARETH THE SON OF GOD ?

There are two reasons why our inquiry into Christianity should begin with the Person of Jesus Christ:

1. Essentially, Christianity is Christ. The Person and work of Christ are the ROCK on which the Christian religion is built. If He is not who He said He was, and if He did not do what He said He came to do, the foundation is undermined and the whole superstructure will collapse. Take Christ from Christianity, and you disembowel it; there is practically NOTHING left. Christ IS the centre of Christianity; all else is circumference. We are not primarily concerned to discuss the nature of His philosophy, the value of His system, or the quality of His ethics. Our concern is fundamentally with the character of His Person; WHO WAS HE ?

2. If Jesus Christ can be shown to have been a uniquely Divine Person, many other problems begin naturally to be solved. The existence of God is proven and the character of God revealed, if Jesus was Divine. Questions about man's duty and destiny; life after death; the purpose and authority of the Old testament; and the meaning of the Cross begin to be answered; because Jesus taught about these things, and His teaching must be true if His Person is Divine.

Our investigation MUST, therefore. begin with Jesus Christ and to study Him we must turn to the Gospels; the historical documents they undoubtedly are. It is enough to emphasize that their authors were all Christian men; that Christian men are honest men; and that their contents appear to be both objective and the impressions of eyewitnesses. We will concentrate on what is general and plain.

Our purpose is to marshal the evidence to prove that Jesus WAS the Son of God. We cannot be satisfied with a verdict declaring His vague Divinity; it is His DEITY we mean to establish. We believe Him to possess an eternal and essential relation to God possessed by no other person. We regard Him neither as God in human disguise, nor as a man with divine qualities... but as the GOD /MAN. WE ARE PERSUADED that Jesus was a historic Person possessing two distinct and perfect natures, GODHEAD and MANHOOD. and in this to be absolutely and forever unique. Only so could He be worthy not just of our admiration, but of our Worship.

The evidence is at least threefold. It concerns the claims He made; the character He displayed; and His resurrection from the dead. No one argument is conclusive. but the three converging lines point unfaltering to the same conclusion.

The first witness is that of Christ's own claims. In the words of Archbishop William Temple: 'It is now recognized that the one Christ for whose existence there is any evidence at all is a miraculous figure making stupendous claims'. It is true that claims do not, in themselves, constitute evidence. But here is a phenomenon which demands an explanation for the sake of clarity we will distinguish between four different kinds of claim. <u>CHRIST'S SELF-CENTERED TEACHINGS:</u> The most striking feature of the teaching of Jesus is that He was constantly talking about Himself. It is true that He spoke much about the Fatherhood of God, and the Kingdom of God. But then He added that He was the Father's 'SON', and that He had come to inaugurate the Kingdom. Entry into this Kingdom depended on man's response to Him. He even did not hesitate to call the Kingdom of God 'My Kingdom'.

This self-centeredness of the teachings of Jesus immediately sets Him apart from the other great religious teachers of the world. They were self-effacing. Jesus was self-advancing. They pointed men away from themselves, saying, 'That is the truth, so far as I perceive it; follow that'. Jesus said, 'I am the truth; follow Me'. The founder of none of the ethnic religions ever dared to say such a thing. The personal pronoun forces itself repeatedly on our attention as we read His words. For example:

'I am the bread of life; he who comes to Me shall not hunger, and he who believes in Me shall never thirst'.

'I am the light of the world; he who follows Me will not walk in darkness, but will have the light of life'.

'I am the resurrection and the life; he who believes in Me though he die, yet shall he live, and whoever lives and believes in Me shall never die'.

'I am the way, and the truth, and the life; no one comes to the Father, but by Me'.

'Come to Me, all who labour and are heavy laden and I will give you rest. Take My yoke upon you, and learn from Me'. JOHN 6:35; 8:12; 11:25-26; 14:6 MATT 11:28-29.

The great question that the first part of Christ's teachings led to was, 'Who do you say that I am?' He affirmed that Abraham had rejoiced to see His day; that Moses had written of Him; that the Scriptures bore witness to Him; and that indeed in the three great divisions of the Old Testament - the law, the Prophets and the writings - these were 'things concerning Himself'. MARK 8:29;JOHN 8:56; John 5:39; 5:46; LUKE 24:27 & :44.

Luke describes in some detail the dramatic visit that Jesus paid to the Synagogue of His home village, Nazareth. Christ was given a Scroll of the Old Testament Scriptures and He stood up to read. The passage was Isaiah 61:1-2 'The Spirit of the Lord is upon Me, because He has anointed Me to preach good news to the poor. He has sent Me to proclaim release to the captives and recovering sight to the blind, to set at liberty those who are oppressed, to proclaim the acceptable year of the Lord'. Christ closed the Book, returned it to the Synagogue attendant and sat down, while all the eyes of the congregation were fastened on Him. He then broke the silence with the amazing words, 'Today this Scripture has been fulfilled in your hearing' . In other words, 'Isaiah was writing about Me'.

With such an opinion of Himself, it is not surprising that He called people to Himself. He did more than issue an invitation; He uttered a command. 'Come to Me', He said, and 'Follow Me' If men would only come to Him, He promised to lift the burdens of the weary; to satisfy the hungry; and to quench the thirst of the parched soul. MATT 11:28-30 JOHN 6:35; 7:37. Further. His followers were to obey Him and to confess Him before men. His disciples came to recognize the right of Jesus to make these totalitarian claims, and in their letters, Peter, Paul, James and Jude delight to call themselves His 'SLAVES'.

More than that, He offered Himself to His contemporaries as

the proper object of their faith and love. It is for man to believe in God: Yet Jesus appealed to men to believe in Himself. 'This is the work of God'. He declared, 'that you believe in Him whom He has sent'. 'He who believes in the Son has eternal life'. If to believe in Him was man's first duty, not to believe in Him was man's chief sin. JOHN 6:2; 3:36; 8.24; 16:8-9.

The first and great Commandment is to love God with all the heart and soul and mind and strength. Yet Jesus audaciously claimed a man's supreme love.

Anyone who loved father, mother. son or daughter more than Him was not worthy of Him, He said. In fact, resorting to the vivid Hebrew use of contrasts to convey comparison, Christ added: 'If anyone comes to Me and does not hate his own father and mother and wife and children and brothers and sisters, even his own life, he cannot be My disciple'. MATT 10:37 LUKE 14:26.

So convinced was He of His central place in the purpose of God, that He undertook to send One who would take His place after He had returned to heaven. This was the Holy Ghost. Christ's favourite name for the Holy Ghost was The Comforter; the Paraclete. It would be the Holy Ghost's task to plead the cause of Jesus before the world; to sinners, urging and pointing sinners to Christ for Salvation; to teach the babes in Christ via the Scriptures if they could read, or by urgings, Counsels, discernments, mentors and Sermons, if they were illiterate; to train the 'babes' in Christ through the 'milk', and on up to the Solid Food, i.e. Meat and Potatoes. See NCRC 6/2. 'He will bear witness to Me' and 'He will glorify Me, for He will take what is mine and declare it to you. JOHN 15:26; 16:14. So the Holy Ghost's witness to the world and revelation to the Church, would both concern Jesus Christ.

In one more flash of breath-taking egocentricity, Jesus predicted; 'I, when I am lifted up from this earth, will draw all men to Myself' . He knew that the cross would exert a moral magnetism on men and women. But in drawing them, they would be brought primarily neither to God nor the Church, neither to truth nor to righteousness, but to Himself; they would in fact be brought to those only by being brought to Him. The most remarkable feature of all this self-centered teaching, is that it was uttered by one who insisted on humility in others. Christ rebuked His disciples for their self-seeking and was wearied by their desire to be great.

DID CHRIST NOT PRACTICE WHAT HE PREACHED ?...

CHRIST TOOK A LITTLE CHILD AND SET HIM IN THE MIDST AS THEIR MODEL; HAD HE A DIFFERENT STANDARD FOR HIMSELF ?...

<u>HIS DIRECT CLAIMS</u>: Jesus clearly believed Himself to be the Messiah the Old Testaments predicted. He had come to establish the Kingdom of God, foretold by generations of Prophets.

It is significant that the first recorded word of His public ministry was the word 'FULFILLED' , and His first sentence, 'The time has been fulfilled; the kingdom of God has drawn near'. Christ assumed the title 'Son of man' that was an accepted Messianic title derived originally from one of Daniel's visions.

He accepted the description 'Son of God' when challenged by the high Priest, which was another Messianic taken particularly from Psalm 2:7. He also interpreted His mission in the light of the portrayal of the suffering Servant of Jehovah in the latter part of the Book of Isaias. The first stage of His instruction of the Twelve Apostles culminated in the incident at Caesarea Philippi when Simon Peter confessed his faith in Jesus as the Christ. Others might suppose Christ to be one of the Prophets; but Simon had come to recognize Jesus as the One the Prophets pointed to. He was not just another signpost, but the DESTINATION the signposts would lead to. MARK 1:15; 8:27-29; 14:61-62.

The whole ministry of Jesus is coloured by this sense of fulfillment. 'Blessed are the eyes which see what you see!' Jesus once said privately to His disciples, 'For I tell you that many Prophets and kings desired to see what you see, and did not see it, and to hear what you hear, and did not hear it'. MATT 13:16-17 LUKE 10:23-24.

But the direct claims that we are now concerned with, refer not to His Messiah-ship but to His DEITY. Christ's claim to be the Son of God was more than Messianic; it described the unique and eternal relationship with God He possessed. Three examples follow:

First, there is the close association with God as His 'Father' that Jesus constantly spoke of. Even as a boy of twelve He astonished His human parents by His uncompromising zeal for His Heavenly Father's business. And then He made such statements as:

'My Father is working still, and I am working'.
'I and the Father are one'.
'I am in the Father and the Father in Me'.
JOHN 3:17;   10:30;   14:10-11.

It is true that He taught His Apostles to address God as 'Father' too, but so different is Christ's Sonship from ours that He was obliged to distinguish between them. To Jesus God is 'My Father'. He therefore said to Mary Magdalene, '1 am ascending to My Father and your Father'. It would not have been possible for Jesus to say I ascend to OUR Father.

These verses are all taken from John's Gospel, but the same unique relationship with God is claimed by Jesus in MATT 11:27 where He says:

'All things have been delivered to Me by My Father; and no one knows the Son except the Father , and no one knows the Father except the Son and any one to whom the Son chooses to reveal Him'.

That Jesus did in fact claim this intimate relationship to God is further confirmed by the indignations that Jesus aroused in the Jews. He 'made Himself the Son of God', they said. JOHN 19:7. So close was Christ's identification with God that it was natural for Him to equate His attitude to himself with His attitude to God:

to know Jesus was to know God;
to see Him was to see God;
to believe in Him was to believe in God;
to receive Him was to receive God;

to hate Him was to hate God;
to honour Him was to honour God.
MARK 9:37   JOHN 5:23;   8:19   12:44-45   14:1 & :7 & :9   15:23.

These are SOME of the general claim that Jesus made to a unique relationship to God. He also made two more DIRECT claims. The first is recorded at the end of JOHN 8. In controversy with the Jews, Jesus said: 'Truly, truly. I say to you, if any one keeps My words, he will never see death'. This was too much for His critics. 'Abraham died', they objected, 'as did the prophets.. Are you greater than our father Abraham...? Who do you claim to be?'

Jesus replied 'Your father Abraham rejoiced that he was to see My day'

The Jews were even more perplexed. 'You are not yet 50 years old,. and you have seen Abraham?'

Jesus replied with one of the most far-reaching claims He ever made; 'Truly, truly, I say to you, before Abraham was, I am'.

The Jews took up stones to throw at Jesus.

The Law of Moses made stoning the penalty for blasphemy, and at first, one may wonder what the Jews saw to be blasphemous in Jesus' words. There was the claim to have lived before Abraham. This claim Jesus frequently made. He had 'come down' from Heaven and 'been sent' by the Father. This claim was tolerably innocent. We must look FURTHER. Notice Jesus had not said 'Before Abraham was I was'; but 'I am'.

It WAS therefore a claim to have been existing ETERNALLY before Abraham. But even this is not all. There is MORE in this 'I am' than a claim to eternity; THERE IS A CLAIM TO DEITY. 'I am' is the divine Name by which JEHOVAH had revealed Himself to Moses, at the burning bush. 'I am who I am'...say this to the people of Israel, 'I am has sent me to you'. This divine title Jesus quietly took to Himself. It was because of THIS that the Jews reached out for stones to avenge the blasphemy.

The second example of a DIRECT claim to DEITY took place after the resurrection (we must assume for the moment the resurrection took place... more on this later). JOHN 20:26-29 reports that on the Sunday F0LLOWING Easter Day, doubting Thomas was with the other disciples in the upper room when Jesus appeared. Jesus invited Thomas to feel His wounds, and Thomas, overwhelmed with wonder, cried out 'My Lord and my God!' Jesus ACCEPTED the designation. He rebuked Thomas for his unbelief, not for his worship.

HIS INDIRECT CLAIMS: Christ's claim to DEITY was advanced as forcefully by INDIRECT as by DIRECT means. The implications of Christ's Ministries were as eloquent a testimony to His person as His plain statements. On MANY occasions He exercised functions that belong properly to God. Of these, four will be mentioned.

The first is the claim to FORGIVE SIN. On two separate occasions MARK 2:1-12 LUKE 7:36-50, Jesus forgave sinners. The first time a paralytic was brought to Him by his friends and let him down on his pallet bed through the roof. Jesus saw that his need was spiritual and surprised the crowd by saying to him, 'My son, your sins are forgiven'.

The second declaration of forgiveness was made to a woman known to be immoral. Jesus was taking a meal at a Pharisee's house when she came behind Him as He reclined at table, washed His feet with her tears and wiped them with her hair, kissed them and anointed Him with ointment. Jesus said to her, 'Your sins are forgiven'.

On both occasions the bystanders raised their eyebrows and asked 'Who is this? What blasphemy is this? Who can forgive sins but God only ?' Their questions were correctly worded. We may forgive the injuries that others do to us; but the sins we commit against God only God Himself can forgive.

BESTOW LIFE: Christ's second indirect claim was to BESTOW LIFE: He described Himself as 'the bread of life', 'the life' and 'the resurrection and the life'. He likened his followers' dependence on Him to the sustenance derived from the vine by its branches. Jesus offered a Samaritan woman 'living water' and promised eternal life to the rich young ruler if he would come and follow Him. Jesus called Himself the Good Shepherd who would not only give His life for the sheep but also give life to them. Jesus stated that God had given Him the authority over all flesh, that He should give life to as many as God gave Him, and declared, 'the Son gives life to whom He will'. MARK 10:17-21 JOHN 4:10-15; & 5:21 6:35; 10:28; 11:25; 14:6; 15:4-5; 17:2.

So definite was this claim that His Apostles clearly recognized its truth. It made leaving Him impossible. 'To whom shall we go?' asked Peter. 'You have the words of eternal life'.

Life is an enigma. Whether it be physical life or spiritual, its nature is as baffling as its origin. We can neither define what it is or state where it comes from. We can only call it a divine gift. It is this gift that Jesus claimed to bestow.

<u>TEACH THE TRUTH</u>: Christ's third indirect claim was to TEACH THE TRUTH. It is not so much the truths that He taught as the direct and dogmatic manner that He taught them that calls for notice. His contemporaries were deeply impressed by His wisdom:

>'Where did this man get all this?'
>'What is the wisdom given to him?'
>'Is he not the carpenter?'
>'How is it that this man has learning, when he never studied?'

But they were even more impressed by His authority:
'No man ever spoke like this man'
'His word was with authority'
'When Jesus finished these sayings, the crowds were astonished at His teaching, for He taught them as one who had authority, and not as their scribes'.
MATT 7:28-29   MARK 6:3   LUKE 4:32   JOHN 7:15.

If Christ's authority was not that of the scribes, it was not the authority of the Prophets either. The scribes never taught without quoting their authorities. The Prophets taught with the authority of Jehovah. But Jesus claimed an authority of His own. His formula was not 'Thus says the Lord'. but 'Truly, truly, I say to you'. It is true He described His doctrine as being not His, but the Father's, who had sent Him. Nevertheless, He knew Himself to be such an immediate means of divine revelation as to be able to speak with great personal assurance.

He never hesitated or apologized. He had no need to contradict, withdraw or modify anything He said. He spoke the unequivocal words of God; 'He whom God has sent utters the words of God'. He predicted the future with complete conviction. He issued absolute moral commands like 'Love your enemies', 'Do not be anxious about tomorrow', 'Judge not, that you be not judged'. He made promises of whose fulfillment He had no doubt; 'Ask, and it will be given you'. He asserted that His words were as eternal as the Law, and would never pass away. He warned His listeners that their destiny depended on their response to His teachings, as the destiny of Israel had depended on their response to Jehovah's Word.

JUDGE THE WORLD: Christ's fourth indirect claim was to JUDGE THE WORLD. This is perhaps the most fantastic of all His statements. Several of His parables imply that He will come back at the end of the world, and that the final day of reckoning will be postponed until His return. He Himself will arouse the dead, and all the nations will be gathered before Him. He will sit on the throne of His glory, and the judgment will be committed to Him by the Father. He will then separate men from one another as a shepherd separates His sheep from His goats. Some will be invited to come and inherit the kingdom prepared for them from the foundation of the world. Others will hear the dreadful words 'Depart from me, you cursed into the eternal fire prepared for the devil and his angels. MATT 25:31-46 JOHN 5:22 & :28-29.

Not only will Jesus be the Judge, but the criterion of judgment will be men's attitude to Him as shown in their treatment of His 'brethren' or their response to His word. Those who have acknowledged Him before men He will acknowledge before His Father; those who have denied Him, He will deny. Indeed, for a man to be excluded from heaven on the last day, it will be enough for Jesus to say, 'I never knew you'. (barren gain; bitter loss). MATT 7:23;   10:32-33;   JOHN 12:47-48.

It is difficult to exaggerate the MAGNITUDE of this claim. Imagine a Pastor addressing his congregation in these terms today; 'Listen attentively to my words. Your eternal destiny depends on it. I will return at the end of the world to judge you, and your fate will be settled according to your obedience to me'. Such a Pastor would not escape the attention of the police or the Psychologists/Psychiatrists.

HIS DRAMATIZED CLAIMS: Now we consider the recorded miracles of Jesus, that can be described as His dramatized claims.

There is no reason for a thorough discussion on the possibility and purpose of miracles at this point. It is sufficient to indicate that the value of Christ's miracles lies less in their super-natural character than in their spiritual significance. They were SIGNS as well as 'WONDERS'. They were never performed selfishly or senselessly. Their purpose was not to show off or to compel submission. They were not demonstrations of physical power as illustrations of moral authority. They are in fact the acted parable of Jesus. They EXHIBIT His claims visually. His works dramatize His words.

John saw this clearly. John's Gospel is constructed around six or seven 'signs' via the Holy Ghost, associating them with the great 'I am" declarations of Jesus. The first sign was the changing of water into wine at a wedding reception. It is not in itself a particularly edifying miracle. Its significance lies beneath the surface. John tells us the water pots of stone stood ready 'for the Jewish rites for purification'. This is the clue. The water stood for the old religion, like Jacobs well in Chapter 4. (rich Old Testament associations).

The wine stood for the religion of Jesus. As He changed the water into wine, so the Gospel would supersede the Law. The sign advanced the claim that Jesus was competent to inaugurate the new order. He was the Messiah. Jesus was soon to say to the Samarian woman 'I am He'.

Similarly, Christ's feeding of the five thousand illustrated His claim to satisfy the hunger of the human heart. 'I am the bread of life', He said. A little later, He opened the eyes of a man born blind, having previously said, 'I am the light of the world'. Jesus could open men's eyes to see and to know God.

Jesus brought back to life a man called Lazarus who had been dead four days, and claimed, 'I am the resurrection and the life'. Jesus had resuscitated a dead man. It was a sign. The life of the body symbolized the life of the soul. Jesus could be the life of the believer before death and would be the resurrection of the believer after death. All these miracles are parables, because men are spiritually hungry, blind and dead, and only

Christ can satisfy their hunger, restore their sight and raise them to a new life. JOHN 6:35; 8:12; 11:25.

CONCLUSION: It is not possible to eliminate these claims from the teachings of the carpenter of Nazareth. It cannot be said that they were invented by Apostles. Not even that they were unconsciously exaggerated. They are widely and evenly distributed in the different Gospels and sources of the Gospels, and the portrait is too consistent and too balanced to have been imagined.

The Holy Ghost fits the Soul for the unique (specific) task the soul is intended to accomplish for God during the soul's time on earth. But this is only accomplished within, and according to, God's Natural Law. (modus operendi). See NCRC 99/2.

i.e. Urging, and pointing you to Jesus Christ to 'be transformed in the newness of your mind, that you may discern what is the good and acceptable and perfect will of God' (I urge you)... 'let no one rate himself more than he ought, but let him rate himself according to moderation, and according as God has appointed to each one the measure of faith' ... (according to the dictates of the soul)... 'For just as in one body we have many members, yet all the members have not the same function, so we the many, are one body in Christ, but severally members one of another. But we have gifts differing according to the grace that has been given us!... (according to the work we are to do for God in this life)...'such as prophesy to be used according to the proportion of faith; or ministry, in ministering; or he who teaches, in teaching; he who exhorts, in exhorting.....(making appeals or intercessions etc)...'he who gives, in simplicity; he who presides, with carefulness; he who shows mercy, with cheerfulness'.   ROM 12:2-8.

'To some I speak of ordinary things, to others special things. In the 'Book'...(of the 'Scriptures)'...the same voice and the same words appear, but one will get more out of them than another.. .(according to what is required regarding the dictates of the soul). ..'for it is I who teaches the truth, who searches the hearts. No thoughts are hidden from me. I, the Prime Mover of all holy actions, giving to every man as I see fit'.

I am He who in an instant can so elevate the mind of the humble servant of God that he can grasp the truth more perfectly than another who, lacking humility',... (and not at enmity with his soul) ... 'had studied ten year in school. For I teach without the sound of words, without conflict of opinions, without striving for honours and without obstinate arguments'   Imitation of Christ Book 3, chapter 43.

Unfortunately, within my Church there are Cardinals, Bishops, Theologians, Priests and misguided Lay People at enmity with their souls, 'beguiled by satan,.. (who disguises himself as an angel of light).. .2 COR 11:14, 'sated!..(shorten or alter)...'with the mockery of the arrogant', PSALM 123:4, taking (and being taken) 'captive' (and seducing/being seduced) (secular humanism) (by) 'silly women'...(and men)..., attempting to get God in step with the people (an exercise in futility); for which a heavy penalty will be required (barren gain; bitter loss), (God mocking them to their faces), instead of attempting to get the people in step with God, their rightful duty and obligation. 2 TIM 3:2-6. ('haughty men will not behold wisdom, wisdom is far from the impious') SIR 15:7, 'ever' (attempting) 'learning yet never'...(able to reach)..'attaining knowledge of the truth', 2 TIM 3:7, 'Sons of satan and enemy of all that is right'. ACTS 13:10, denying the Deity of Christ, and teaching the gross theosophy and spurious speculations of their own misguided empirical thinking, as the Doctrine of the Holy See, which it is NOT, earning 'blood guilt'.

They are those who, because of sin, as soon as they have heard, satan comes and takes away the words'...(of God)... 'that had been sown in their hearts', MARK 4:15, 'satan hindered the way'. 1 THES 2:18. 'Some have turned away to follow satan'. 1 TIM 5:15. In some cases, 'the Lord did not choose them, neither did they find the way of knowledge', BAR 3:27, being at enmity with their soul.

'Therefore God sends'...(will allow their wilful rejection of Truth to have its natural results of spiritual blindness, impenitence and damnation) (mocking them to their faces) 'them a misleading influence that they may believe falsehood'. 2 THES 2:11.

We do not understand God's Modus Operendi regarding His Judgments, nor will we ever, this side of our eternity. What we have learned about these Judgments, is that they are Just, and sure to take place. 'All God's deeds are faultless. All God's Judgments proper. God executes proper Judgment. By a proper Judgment God will do this because of their sins'. DAN 3:26-31.

The Canadian/American Council of Bishops (and other

Councils world wide), being held culpable for the coming demise of the Church cast aside by God, in the main, as Israel was, (the chosen of, and established by God), and for the same reasons. But will be re-established by Christ in His Kingdom. UNLESS, OF COURSE, THERE IS A WHOLESALE RETURN TO GOD, AND HE RELENTS. MERCY TRIUMPHS OVER JUDGMENT. JAS 2:13. ('blood guilt').

My Brethren, 'let no one deceive you by persuasive words'. COL 2:4. There are set before you fire and water, to whichever you choose, stretch forth your hand, whichever you choose, shall be given you'. SIR 15:16-17. If we will not ACCEPT the pain of SELF DISCIPLINE, we WILL be GIVEN the pain of REMORSE and REGRET.

Remember my Catholic Brethren, Pope Leo XIII asked we read the Books of the Sacred Scriptures, with the veneration due to the Divine Word, at least a quarter of an hour morning and night, in keeping with the Scriptures. How many of us DO that, or have been TOLD to DO that ? Preces et Pia OPERA. 645.

CONSIDERABLE space has been given to an examination of the evidence for the unique Deity of Jesus of Nazareth. Via the urgings, counsels and discernments of the Holy Ghost... the Teacher/Advocate of God's Realm, we can KNOW and BE CONVINCED that Jesus is Lord; the Son of God; God in the Flesh; very God;... DEITY.

Still MORE space must be given to the subject of the Deity of Jesus Christ, (unfortunately), due to the empirical thinking, and the secular humanism of the 'wise', 'learned', 'educated'

(educated via an educational philosophy that has gone awry), (under the influence of Lucifer, his angels, spirits, saints, instruments and servants), sinners we MUST try to reach for Christ.

Their arguments run something like this: They say, the CLAIMS are there. However, they do not in themselves constitute evidence of Deity. The claims (of Christ) may have been false. Some explanation of those claims must be found.

We cannot any longer regard Jesus as simply a Great Teacher, if He was completely mistaken in one of the chief subjects of his teachings - Himself. There is a certain disturbing 'MEGALOMANIA' (a mania- (excessive or unreasonable enthusiasm) for grandiose performance) (God, forgive them), about Jesus that many (now get this) "SCHOLARS" have recognized.

'These claims in a mere man would be egoism carried even to imperial Megalomania'. P.T. Forsyth. 1947.

'The discrepancy between the depth and sanity, and (let me add) the SHREWDNESS, of his moral teaching, and the rampant Megalomania which must lie behind his theological teachings, unless he IS indeed God, has never been satisfactorily gotten over'. C.S. Lewis. 1947.

Was He (Jesus) then, a deliberate imposter ? (God, forgive them). Did He attempt to gain the adherence of man, to his views, by assuming a divine authority he did not possess ? (this should be very difficult to believe). There is something guileless about Jesus. He hated hypocrisy in others and was transparently sincere Himself).

Was He (Jesus) sincerely mistaken ?
Had Jesus a fixed delusion about himself ?
(This is the end of their arguments/questions)

Jesus does not give the impression of the abnormality one might expect to find in the deluded. His Character supports His claims. It is in that sphere that we must now pursue our investigation.

THE CHARACTER OF CHRIST: Once I received a letter from a young man I knew, 'I have just Made a great discovery', he wrote. 'Almighty God had two sons. Jesus Christ was the first; I am the second'. Glancing at the address at the top of the letter, revealed he was writing from a well-known mental hospital.

There have been many pretenders to greatness and to divinity. Lunatic asylums are full of deluded people who claim to be Julius Caesar, Prime Minister, the Emperor of Japan or Jesus Christ. But no one believes them. No one is deceived except themselves. They have no disciples. except perhaps their fellow patients. They fail to convince other people simply because they do not seem to be what they claim to be. Their character does not support their claims.

The Christian's Conviction about Christ is greatly strengthened by the fact that He does appear to be who He said He was. There is no discrepancy between His words and His deeds. Certainly a very remarkable character would be necessary to authenticate His extravagant claims, but we believe that He displayed just such a character, His character does not prove His claims to be sure, but it strongly confirms them. His claims were exclusive. His character was unique. John Stuart Mill called Him 'A unique figure not more unlike all His predecessors than all His followers'. 1909.

'Instinctively we do not class Him with others. When one reads His name in a list beginning with Confucius and ending with Goethe we feel it is an offence less against orthodoxy than against decency. Jesus is not one of the group of the world's great. Talk about Alexander the Great and Charles the Great and Napoleon the Great if you will.. Jesus is apart. He is not the Great; He is the Only, He is simply Jesus. Nothing could add to that... He is beyond our analyses. He confounds our canons of human nature. He compels our criticism to overleap itself. He awes our spirits. There is a saying of Charles Lamb... that 'If Shakespeare was to come into a room, we would all rise to greet him, but if That Jesus was to come into it, we would all fall down and try to kiss the hem of His garment' '. Carnegie Simpson. 1930. (in humble adoration of our Lord and our God).

We are concerned then to show that Jesus stands in a moral category by Himself. To concede that He was 'the greatest man who ever lived' does not begin to satisfy us. We cannot talk of Jesus in comparative, or even superlative terms. To us it is not a question of comparison, but of contrast. 'Why do you call me good?' He asked the rich young Ruler. 'No one is good but God alone' 'Exactly', we would have replied. 'It is not that You are better than other men, nor even that You are the best of men, but that You are good; good with the absolute goodness of God'.

The importance of this claim should be clear. Sin is a congenital disease among men. We are born with its infection in our nature. It is a universal complaint. Therefore. if Jesus of Nazareth was without sin, He was not just man as we know men. If He was sinless, He was distinct from us. He was supernatural.

> 'His character was more wonderful than the greatest miracle'.
> (Tennyson, quoted by Carnegie Simpson).
> 'The separateness from sinners is not a little, but a stupendous thing; it is the presupposition of redemption; it is that very virtue in Christ without which He would not be qualified to be a Saviour, but would, like us, need to be saved'. James Denny. 1906.

We will summarize the evidence for the sinlessness of Christ under four headings:

<u>WHAT CHRIST HIMSELF THOUGHT</u>: On occasions Jesus stated directly that He was without sin. When a woman was caught in the act of adultery and was dragged before Him, He issued an embarrassing challenge to her accusers, 'Let him who is without sin among you be the first to throw a stone at her'. Gradually they slunk away until there was no one left. A little later, in the same chapter (JOHN 8), it is recorded that Jesus issued another challenge, this time concerning Himself;

'Which of you convicts Me of sin?' No one answered. They slipped away when He accused them. But when He invited them to accuse Him, He could stay and bear their scrutiny. They were all sinners; He was without sin. He lived a life of perfect obedience to His Father's Will. 'I always do', He said, 'what is pleasing to Him'. There was nothing boastful about those words. He spoke naturally, with neither fuss nor pretension.

Similarly, by the very nature of His teachings, He placed Himself in a moral category by Himself. So indeed did the Pharisee in the Temple in his arrogant thanksgiving. 'God, I thank thee that I am not like the rest of men'. But Jesus assumed His uniqueness unselfconsciously. He did not need to draw attention to it. It was a fact so obvious to Him that it hardly required emphasis. It was implied rather than asserted. All other men were lost sheep; He had come as the Good Shepherd to seek and to save them. All other men were sick with the disease of sin; He was the doctor that came to heal them. All other men were plunged in the darkness of sin and ignorance; He was the light of the World. All other men were sinners; He was born to be their Saviour and would shed His Blood in death for the forgiveness of their sins. All other men were hungry; He was the bread of life. All other men were dead in trespasses and sins; He could be their life now and their resurrection here- after. All these metaphors express the moral uniqueness of which He was conscious.

It is not surprising that although we are told of the temptations of Jesus. we hear nothing of His sin. He never confesses sin or asks for forgiveness, although He tells His disciples to do so. He shows no consciousness of moral failure. He appears to have no feelings of guilt and no sense of estrangement from God. His Baptism was indeed John's 'baptism of repentance'. But John demurred before Baptizing Jesus, and Jesus submitted to it not because He was acknowledging Himself to he a sinner, but 'to fulfil all righteousness', and to begin to identify Himself with the sins of others. He Himself lived in unbroken communion with His Father.

This absence of all moral discontent and His sense of unclouded fellowship with God are particularly remarkable for two reasons. Jesus possessed a keen moral judgment. He...'knew what was in the heart of man'. Often it is recorded of Him in the Gospel narratives that He could read the inner questionings and perplexities of the crowd. His clear perception led Him to fearlessly expose the duplicity of the Pharisees. He hated their hypocrisy. He pronounced woes upon them as thunderous as those of the Old Testament Prophets. Ostentation and pretence were an abomination to Him. Yet, His penetrating Eye saw no sin in Himself.

Why Christ's self-conscious purity is astonishing is that it is utterly unlike the experience of all saints and mystics. The Christian, that the nearer he approaches God, the more he becomes aware of his own sin. In this the saint somewhat resembles the scientist. The more the scientist discovers, the more he appreciates the mysteries which await his discovery. So the more the Christian grows in Christ-likeness. the more he perceives the vastness of the distance that still separates him from Christ.

A glance into any Christian biography will satisfy the reader of this fact, (if his own experiences are not sufficient evidence).

Fr. David Brainerd was a young pioneer Missionary among the Indians of Delaware at the beginning of the nineteenth century. His diary and letters reveal the rich quality of his devotion to Christ. Despite great pain and crippling weakness (which led to his death at the age of twenty nine). he gave himself. without reserve, to his work. He traveled on horse back through thick forests, preached and taught without rest, slept in the open, and was content with no settled home or family life. His diary is full of expressions of love to 'my dear Indians' and of prayers and praises to his Saviour.

Here, surely, one would imagine, is a saint of the first order, whose life and work can have been little tainted by sin. Yet, as we turn the pages of his diary, he continually laments his mortal 'corruption'. He complains of lack of prayer and love for Christ. He calls himself 'a poor worm' , 'a dead dog' , and 'an unspeakably worthless wretch' . This is not because he had a morbid conscience. He simply lived near Christ and was painfully aware of his sinfulness. 'And they who would serve Thee best ARE conscious most of wrong within'. Yet, Jesus Christ, who lived more closely to God than anybody else has done. was free from all sense of sin.

<u>WHAT CHRIST'S FRIENDS SAID</u>: It is clear that Jesus believed Himself to be sinless, as He believed Himself to be the Messiah and the Son of God. But may He have been mistaken ? What did His disciples think ? Did they share His opinions of Himself?

It may be thought that the disciples of Christ were poor witnesses. It has (and is) being argued that they were biased, and that they deliberately painted Him in more beautiful colours than He deserved. (God, forgive them). But in this, the apostles are being greatly maligned. The apostles statements cannot be so lightly dismissed. There are several reasons why we may confidently rely on their evidence.

They lived in close contact with Jesus for about three years. They ate and slept together. The experienced the cramped neighbourliness of the same boat. They even had a common purse (a common bank account can be a fruitful cause of dissension!). The disciples got on one another's nerves. They quarreled. But they never found in Jesus the sins they found in themselves. Familiarity normally breeds contempt, but not in this case. Two of the chief witnesses to the sinlessness of Christ are Peter and John, and they belonged to that inner group (consisting of Peter, James and John) to whom Jesus gave special privileges and a yet more intimate revelation.

The testimony of the apostles in this matter is trustworthy because they were Jews whose minds had been soaked since infancy in the doctrines of the Old Testament. And one Old Testament doctrine which they had certainly assimilated is the universality of human sin;

'They have all gone astray. they are all alike corrupt; there is none that does good, no, not one'. 'All we like sheep have gone astray; we have turned every one to his own way'.

In the light of this Biblical teaching, they would not easily have attributed sinlessness to anyone.

The apostolic testimony to the sinlessness of Jesus is the more credible because it is indirect. They do not set out to establish the truth that He was without sin...Their remarks are asides. They are discussing some other subject, and add almost as a parenthesis, a reference to His sinlessness.

This is what they say. Peter first described Jesus as 'a lamb without blemish or spot' and then says that He 'committed no sin; no guile was found on His lips'. John emphatically declares that all men are sinners, and that if we say we have no sin or have not sinned, we are both liars and make God a liar also. But he goes on to say that in Christ, who was manifested to take away our sins, 'there is no sin'.
1 PET 1:19;   2:22   1 JOHN 1:8-10   3:5.

To this testimony of Peter and John we may add the words of Paul and the authors of the Epistles. They describe Jesus as one who 'knew no sin'. but rather was 'holy. blameless, unstained, separated from sinners'. He was indeed 'in every respect...tempted as we are' but 'without sinning'.   2 COR 5:21;   HEB 4:15;   7:26.

<u>WHAT CHRIST'S ENEMIES CONCEDE</u>: We may feel ourselves to be on safer ground when we come to consider what the enemies of Jesus thought of Him. They certainly had no bias - at least not in His favour. We read in the Gospels that 'they watched Him' and tried to 'entrap Him in His talk'. It is well known that when a debate cannot be won by reasoning, controversialists are prone to descend to personal abuse. If arguments are lacking, mud is a good substitute. Even the annals of the Church are smudged by the dirt of personal animosities. So it was with the enemies of Jesus.

Mark assembles four of their criticisms   MARK 2:1 & 3:6. Their first accusation was BLASPHEMY. Jesus had forgiven a man's sins. This was an invasion of divine territory. It was 'blasphemous arrogance', they said. But to say so is to beg the Question: If Jesus were indeed Divine, to forgive sins was His prerogative.

Next, they were horrified by Christ's EVIL ASSOCIATIONS. Jesus fraternized with sinners; He ate with publicans; He allowed harlots to approach Him. No Pharisee would dream of this behaviour. The Pharisee would gather his skirt around him and recoil from contact with such scum. He would have thought himself righteous for doing so. He would not appreciate the grace and tenderness of Jesus who, though 'separate from sinners', yet earned the honoured title 'friend of sinners'.

The third accusation was that CHRIST'S RELIGION WAS FRIVOLOUS. He did not fast like the Pharisees, or even like the disciples of John the Baptist. He was 'a glutton and a drunkard' who came 'eating and drinking'. Such an attack on Jesus hardly deserves a serious refutation. That Jesus was full of joy is true, but there can be no doubt that He took religion seriously.

Fourth. they were incensed by HIS SABBATH-BREAKING. He healed sick people on the Sabbath day. And His disciples even walked through the cornfields on the Sabbath, plucking, rubbing and eating corn, which the scribes and Pharisees forbade as tantamount to reaping and threshing. Yet, no one can doubt that Jesus was submissive to the Law of God. HE obeyed it Himself, and in controversy He referred His opponents to it as the arbiter. He also affirmed that God made the Sabbath, and that He made. it for man's benefit. But being, Himself, 'Lord of the Sabbath'. He claimed the right to set aside the false traditions of men and to give God's Law its true interpretation.

All these accusations are either trivial or question begging. So when Jesus was on trial for His life, His detractors had to hire false witnesses against Him. But even then they did not agree with one another. In fact. the only charge they could manufacture against Him was not moral. but political. And as the Stately prisoner came before men for a verdict. again and again He was pronounced righteous. Pilate, after several cowardly attempts to evade the issue, publicly washed his hands and declared himself 'innocent of this Man's Blood' - Herod could find no fault in Jesus. Judas the traitor, filled with remorse, returned the thirty pieces of silver to the priests with the words 'I have sinned in betraying innocent Blood'. The penitent thief on the Cross rebuked his confederate for his abuse and added. 'this Man has done nothing wrong'. Finally, the centurion, having watched Jesus Suffer and Die, said 'certainly this man was innocent!' MATT 27:3-4 & :24; LUKE 23:15 &:41-47.

<u>WHAT WE CAN SEE FOR OURSELVES</u>: In assessing the Character of Jesus Christ, we do not need to rely only on the testimony of others; we can make our own estimates. The moral perfection that was quietly claimed by Him, confidently asserted by His friends, and reluctantly acknowledged by His enemies. is clearly exhibited in the Gospels.

We are given ample opportunity to form our own judgment. The picture of Jesus painted by the evangelists is a comprehensive one. True, it depicts largely His public Ministry of barely three years. But we are given a glimpse of His boyhood, and LUKE twice repeats that during Christ's hidden years at Nazareth, He was developing naturally in Body, Mind and Spirit, and was growing in favour with God and man.

We see Christ withdrawn into privacy with His disciples, and we watch Him in the noisy bustle of the crowd. He is brought before us in the Galilean Ministry, hero-worshipped by the mob who wanted to take Him by force and make Him a King. And we follow Him into the cloisters of the Jerusalem Temple where Sadducees and Pharisees united in their subtle inquisition. But whether scaling the dizzy heights of success or plunged into the depths of bitter rejection, He is the same Jesus. He is consistent. He has no moods. He does not change.

Again, the portrait is balanced. There is in Him no trace of the crank. He believes ardently in what He teaches, but He is not a fanatic. His doctrine is unpopular, but it is not eccentric. There is as much evidence for His Humanity as for His Divinity. He gets tired. He needs to sleep, eat and drink like other men. He experiences the human emotions of Love and Anger, Joy and Sorrow. He is fully human. Yet He is not mere man.

Above all, He was unselfish. Nothing is more striking than this. Although believing Himself to be Divine, He did not put on airs or stand on His dignity. He was never pompous. There was no touch of self-importance about Jesus. He was humble.

It is this paradox that is so baffling, this combination of the self-centredness of His teaching and the unself-centredness of His behaviour. In thought He put Himself first; in deed last. He exhibited both the greatest self-esteem and the greatest self-sacrifice. He knew Himself to be the Lord of all, but He became the servant. He said He was going to judge the world, but He washed His apostles' feet.

Never has anyone given up so much. It is claimed (by Him as well as by us) that He renounced the joys of Heaven for the sorrows of earth, exchanging an eternal immunity to the approach of sin for painful contact with the evil in this world. He was born of a lowly Hebrew Mother in a dirty stable in the insignificant village of Bethlehem. He became a refuge baby in Egypt. He was brought up in the obscure hamlet of Nazareth, and toiled at a carpenter's bench to support His family. In due time He became an itinerate preacher, with few possessions, small comforts and no home. He made friends with simple fishermen and publicans. He touched lepers and allowed harlots to touch Him. He gave Himself away in a Ministry of healing, helping, teaching and preaching.

He was misunderstood, misrepresented, maligned and ridiculed, and became the victim of men's prejudice and vested interests. He was despised and rejected by His own people, and deserted by His own friends. He gave His back to be flogged, His face to be slapped and spat upon, His head to be crowned with thorns, His hands and feet to be nailed to a common Roman gallows. And as the cruel spikes were being driven home, He kept praying for His tormentors, 'Father, forgive them; for they know not what they do'.

Such a man is altogether beyond our reach. He succeeded just where we invariably fail. He had complete self-mastery. He never retaliated. He never grew resentful or irritable. He had such control of Himself that, whatever men might think or say or do, He would deny Himself and abandon Himself to the Will of God and the welfare of mankind. 'I seek not My Own Will', He said, and 'I do not seek My Own Glory'. As Paul wrote, 'For Christ did not please Himself'.

The utter disregard of Self in the service of God and man is what the Bible calls love. There is no self-interest in love. 1 COR 13:4-8. See NCRC 44/2. The essence of love is self-sacrifice. The worst of men is adorned by an occasional flash of such nobility, but the life of Jesus irradiated love with a never-fading incandescent glow.

Jesus was sinless because He was selfless. Such selflessness is love. And God is love.

THE RESURRECTION OF CHRIST: We have considered the extravagant claims that Jesus made, and the selfless character that He displayed. We will now examine the evidence for His historical Resurrection from the dead.

If it is true, the resurrection has great significance. If Jesus rose from the dead. then He was beyond dispute, a unique figure. It is not a question of His spiritual survival, nor of His physical Resurrection, but of His conquest of death, and His Resurrection to a new plane of existence altogether. Some modern scholars and theologians are as scornful as the Athenian philosophers that heard Paul preach on the Areopagus; 'When they heard of the resurrection of the dead, some mocked'.

The argument is not that the Resurrection establishes Christ's Deity, but that it is consistent with it. It is only to be expected that a supernatural person should come and to leave the earth in a supernatural way. This is in fact, what the New Testament teaches and what, in consequence, the Church has always believed. His birth was natural, but His conception was supernatural. His death was natural, but His Resurrection was supernatural. His miraculous conception and Resurrection don't prove His Deity, but they are congruous with it.

We are not concerned here with the Virgin Birth of Jesus, because it is not used in the New Testament to demonstrate His Messiahship or Deity, as is the Resurrection. The case for the Virgin Birth is well argued and proven in THE VIRGIN BIRTH OF CHRIST by James Orr, Hodder, and Stoughton. 1907. And THE VIRGIN BIRTH by J. Gresham Machen, Marshall, Morgan, and Scott. 1936.

Jesus Himself never predicted His death without adding that He would rise, and described His coming Resurrection as a 'sign'. Paul, at the beginning of His letter to the Romans, wrote that Jesus was 'designated Son of God in power... by His Resurrection from the dead', and the earliest sermons of the apostles recorded in the ACTS repeatedly assert that by the Resurrection, God has reversed man's sentence and vindicated His Son.

Of this resurrection, Luke, who is known to have been a painstaking and accurate historian says there are 'many proofs'. We may not be able to go as far as Thomas Arnold who called the Resurrection 'the best attested fact in history', but certainly many impartial students have judged the evidence to be extremely good. For instance: "As a lawyer I have made a prolonged study of the evidence for the events of the first

Easter Day. To me the evidence is conclusive, and over and over again in the High Court I have secured the verdict on evidence not nearly so compelling. Inference follows on evidence, and a truthful witness is always artless and disdains effect. The Gospel evidence for the Resurrection is of this class. and as a lawyer I accept it unreservedly as the testimony of truthful men, to facts they were able to substantiate". Sir Edward Clarke. K.C.

What is this evidence ? An attempt may be made to summarize it by four statements:
<u>THE BODY GONE</u>: The resurrection narrative in the four Gospels begin with the visit of certain women early on Easter Sunday morning to the tomb. On arrival, they were dumbfounded to discover that the body of the Lord has disappeared.

Not many days later the apostles began to preach that Jesus had risen. It was the main thrust of their message. But they could have hardly have expected men to believe them if a few minutes walk could have taken them to Joseph's tomb where the body of Jesus still lay! No. The tomb was empty. The body was gone. There can be no doubt about this fact. The question is how to explain it.

First there is the objection that THE WOMEN WENT TO THE WRONG TOMB. They were dazed with sorrow. They could have easily (it is claimed), have made a mistake.

This sounds plausible on the surface, but it hardly bears examination. To begin with, it cannot have been completely dark. It is true that John says the women came 'while it was still dark' . But in MATT 28.1 it is 'toward dawn', while Luke says it was 'at early dawn', and Mark distinctly states that 'the Sun had risen'.

Further, these women were no fools. At least two of them had seen for themselves where Joseph and Nicodemus had laid the body. They had even watched the whole process of burial, 'sitting opposite the sepulchre'. The same two (Mary Magdalene and Mary the mother of James) returned at dawn, bringing with them Salome, Joanna and 'the other women'. so that if one mistook the path to the tomb, she is likely to have been corrected by the others. And if Mary Magdalene went to the wrong place the first time, she can hardly have repeated her error when she returned in the full light of morning and lingered in the garden till Jesus met her.

Besides, no mere sentiment brought them so early to the tomb.

They had come on a practical mission. They had brought spices and were going to complete the anointing of their Lord's body, since the approach of the Sabbath had made the work so hasty two days previously. These devoted and business-like women were not the kind to be easily deceived or to give up the task they had come to do. Again, even if THEY mistook the tomb, would Peter and John, who ran to verify their story, make the same mistake, (and others who doubtless came later, including Joseph and Nicodemus) themselves?

The second objection of the empty tomb is THE SWOON THEORY. Those who maintain this view would have us believe that Jesus did not die on the cross, but only fainted. He then revived In the tomb, left it, and subsequently made Himself known to the disciples.

This theory simply bristles with problems. It is thoroughly

perverse. The evidence entirely contradicts it. Pilate was surprised that Jesus was already dead, but he was sufficiently convinced by the centurion's assurance, to give Joseph permission to remove the body from the cross. The centurion was certain because he must have been present when 'one of the soldiers pierced His side with a spear, and at once there came out blood and water'. So Joseph and Nicodemus took down His body, wound it in the grave-clothes. and laid it in Joseph's new tomb.

Are we to seriously believe that Jesus was all this time only in a SWOON ? That after the rigors and pains of trial, mockery, flogging and crucifiction, He could survive thirty-six hours in a sepulchre with neither warmth nor food nor medical aid ? That He could then rally sufficiently to perform the superhuman feat of shifting the boulder that secured the mouth of the tomb, and this without disturbing the Roman guard ? That when, weak and sickly and hungry, He could appear to the disciples in such a way as to give them the impression that He had vanquished death ? That He could go on to claim that He had died and risen, could send them into all the world and promise to be with them unto the end of time ? That He could live somewhere in hiding for forty days, making occasional surprise appearances, and then finally disappear without any explanation ? Such credulity is more incredible than Thomas' unbelief.

The third objection is the idea that THIEVES STOLE THE BODY. There is no shred of evidence for this objection. Nor is it explained how thieves could have hoodwinked the Roman guard. Nor can one imagine why thieves should have taken the body and left the grave-clothes, nor what possible motive they could have had for their actions. (Save carrying out a plan of the Scribes and Pharisees).

The fourth objection that has been argued is that the DISCIPLES REMOVED THE BODY. This, Matthew tells us, is the rumour the Jews spread from the earliest days. He describes how Pilate, having given permission to Joseph to remove Christ's body, received a deputation of chief priests and Pharisees, who said:

'Sir, we remember how that impostor said, while He was still alive, 'after three days I will rise again'. Therefore order the sepulchre to be made secure until the third day. lest his disciples go and steal him away, and tell the people, 'He has risen from the dead', and the last fraud will be worse than the first'.

Pilate concurred. 'Make it as secure as you can', he said, and the Jews 'made the sepulchre secure by sealing the stone and setting a guard'. Matthew goes on to describe how the stone, the seal and the guard could not prevent the Resurrection, and how the guard went into the city to report to the chief priests what had happened. After consultation they bribed the soldiers and said: 'Tell the people, 'His disciples came by night and stole Him away while we were asleep'. And if this comes to the Governor's ears, we will satisfy him and keep you out of trouble'. So they took the money and did as they were directed; and this story has been spread among the Jews to this day'.

But the story does not hold water. Is it unlikely that a picked guard, whether Roman or Jewish, would all sleep on duty when detailed to watch ? And if they did remain awake, how did the women get past them, and roll back the stone ?

Even supposing the disciples could have succeeded in removing the Lord's Body, there is a psychological consideration which is enough to discredit the whole theory. We learn from the first part of ACTS that in their early preaching, the apostles concentrated on the Resurrection. 'You killed Him, but God raised Him, and we are witnesses'... they kept saying. Are we then to believe that they were proclaiming what they knew to be a deliberate lie ? If they themselves had taken the body of Jesus, to preach the Resurrection was to spread a known planned falsehood. They not only preached it; they suffered for it. They were prepared to go to prison, to the flogging post and to death, for a fairy-tale ?

This simply does not ring true. It is so unlikely as to be virtually impossible. If anything is clear from the Gospels and the ACTS, it is that the Apostles were sincere. They may have been deceived, if you like, but they were not deceivers. Hypocrites and Martyrs are not made of the same stuff.

The fifth and least unreasonable (though still hypothetical) objection to the disappearance of Christ's body is that THE ROMAN OR JEWISH AUTHORITIES TOOK IT INTO THEIR OWN CUSTODY. They would certainly have had motive enough for doing so. They had heard that Jesus had talked of Resurrection, and were afraid of hanky-panky. So (the argument runs). in order to forestall trickery, they took the precaution of confiscating the corpse.

But when it is examined, this conjectural reconstruction of what happened falls to pieces. We have already seen that within a few weeks of Jesus' death the Christians were BOLDLY proclaiming His resurrection. The news spread rapidly. The new Nazarene movement threatened to undermine the bulwarks of Judaism and to disturb the peace of Jerusalem. The Jews feared conversions; the Romans riots. The authorities had before them one course of action; they could produce the remains of the body and publish a statement of explanation.

Instead, they were silent and resorted to violence. They arrested the apostles, threatened them, flogged them, imprisoned them, vilified them, plotted against them, and killed them. But all this was entirely unnecessary if they had in their possession of the corpse. The Church was founded on the Resurrection. Disprove the Resurrection, and the Church would have collapsed. But they could not; the body was not in their possession. The authorities silence is as eloquent a proof of the Resurrection as the Apostles witness.

These are the theories Academics, Scholars and Theologians have invented to try to explain the emptiness of the tomb and the disappearance of the body, (among many other topics and subjects of their misguided empirical thinking), and, as is the 'norm' for those at enmity with their souls, none of them are satisfactory, and for none of them is there any historical evidence. Christians prefer the simple and sober narrative of the Gospels, as the writers wrote ,under the inspiration and guidance of the Holy Ghost, (as it is with ALL Scripture), describing the events of the first Easter Sunday. THE BODY OF JESUS WAS NOT REMOVED BY MEN; IT WAS RAISED BY GOD.

THE GRAVE CLOTHES WERE UNDISTURBED: It is a remarkable fact that the narratives that say that the body of Jesus has gone, also tells us that the grave clothes had not gone. It Is John who lays particular emphasis on this fact, he accompanied Peter on that dramatic early morning race to the tomb. The account John gives of this incident (JOHN 20;I-10) bears the unmistakable marks of first-hand experience. He outran Peter, but on arrival at the tomb he did no more than look in, until Peter came and entered it. 'Then the other disciple, who reached the tomb first, also went in, and he saw and believed'. The question is: What did he see that made him Believe ? The story suggests that it was not just the absence of the body, but the presence of the grave clothes and, in particular, their undisturbed condition.

We will reconstruct the story as per the narrative of HENRY LATHAM 1904: ' John tells us (JOHN 19:38-42) that while Joseph begged Pilate for the body of Jesus, Nicodemus 'came bringing a mixture of myrrh and aloes, about a hundred pounds weight'. Then together 'they took the body of Jesus, and bound it in linen clothes with the spices, as is the burial custom of the Jews'. That is to say, as they wound the 'bandages' round Christ's body, they sprinkled the powdered spices into the folds. A separate cloth will have been used for His head. This is clear from John's account of the burial clothes of Lazarus. When Jesus resuscitated him, 'The dead man came out his hands and feet bound with bandages, and his face wrapped with a cloth'. JOHN 11:44. Henry Latham. 1904. They thus enswathed His body and head, leaving the face and neck bare, according to oriental custom. They laid the body on a stone slab that had been hewn out of the side of the cave-tomb.

Supposing we had been present in the sepulchre when the resurrection of Jesus actually took place. What should we have seen ? Would we have seen Jesus begin to move, then yawn & stretch and get up ? No! Christians do not believe that Jesus returned to this life. He did not recover from a swoon. Jesus had died, and He rose again. His was a resurrection, not a resuscitation. Christians believe that Jesus passed miraculously from death into an altogether new sphere of existence. What then should we have seen had we been there ? We would suddenly have noticed that the body had disappeared. It would have 'vaporized' , being transmuted into something new and different and wonderful. The body would have passed THROUGH the grave clothes, as it was to later pass through closed doors. leaving the grave clothes untouched and almost undisturbed. Almost but not quite. The body cloths, under the weight of 100 lbs. of spices. once the support of the body had been removed, would have subsided or collapsed, and would be lying flat. A gap would have appeared between the body cloths and the head napkin, where Christ's face and neck had been. And the napkin itself, because of the complicated criss-cross pattern of the bandages. would have retained its concave shape. a crumpled turban. but with no head inside it.

A careful study of the text of John's narrative suggests that it is just these three characteristics of the discarded grave clothes that John saw. First, he saw the cloths LYING. The word is repeated twice, and the first time it is placed in an emphatic position in the Greek sentence. We might translate. 'He saw, as they were lying (or collapsed), the linen cloths. Next, the head napkin was 'NOT...WITH THE LINEN CLOTHS BUT...IN A PLACE BY ITSELF'. This is unlikely to mean that it had been bundled up and tossed into a corner. It lay on the stone slab, but was separated from the body cloths by a noticeable space. Third. this same napkin was 'NOT LYING...BUT WRAPPED TOGETHER'...This last word has been translated 'twirled'. The Authorized Version 'wrapped together' and the Revised Standard Version 'rolled up' are both unfortunate translations. The word aptly describes the rounded shape which the empty napkin still preserved.

It is not hard to imagine the sight that greeted the eyes of the Apostles when they reached the tomb; the stone slab, the collapsed grave clothes. the shell of the head-cloth and the gap between the two. No wonder they 'saw and believed'. A glance at these grave clothes proved the reality, and indicated the nature, of the Resurrection. They had been neither touched nor folded nor manipulated by any human being. They were like a discarded chrysalis from which the butterfly has emerged.

That the state of the grave clothes was intended to be visible, corroborative evidence for the Resurrection is further suggested by the fact Mary Magdalene (who had returned to the tomb after bringing the news to Peter and John), 'stooped to look into the tomb; and saw two angels in white, sitting where the body of Jesus had lain, 'one at the head and one at the feet'. Presumably this means that they sat on the slab with the grave clothes between them. Both Matthew and Mark add that one of the angels said 'He is not here; for He has risen as He said. Come. see the place where he lay'. MATT 28:6 MARK 16:6 John 20:11.

Whether or not one believes in angels, these allusions to the place where Jesus had lain, emphasized by both the position and the words of the angels, at least confirm what the understanding of the evangelists was: THE POSITION OF THE GRAVE CLOTHES AND THE ABSENCE OF THE BODY WERE CONCURRENT WITNESSES TO CHRIST'S RESURRECTION.

THE LORD WAS RISEN: Every reader of the Gospels knows that they include some extraordinary stories of how Jesus appeared to His disciples after His resurrection. We are told of ten separate appearances of the Lord to what Peter calls 'chosen witnesses'. It is said that He appeared to Mary Magdalene; to the woman returning from the sepulchre; to Peter; to two disciple on the road to Emmaus; to ten gathered in the upper room; to the eleven including Thomas a week later; to 'more than five hundred brethren at one time'; probably on the mountainside in Galilee, to James, to some disciples including Peter, Thomas, Nathanael, James and John by the Galilee lakeside; and to many on the Mount of Olives near Bethany at the time of the Ascension. Paul adds himself at the end of this catalogue in 1 COR 15:, of those who saw the risen Jesus, referring to his experience on the Damascus Road. And since LUKE tells us at the beginning of the ACTS that Jesus 'presented Himself alive after His passion by many proofs, appearing to them (the Apostles) during forty days', there may well have been other appearances, of which no record has survived.

We cannot dismiss this body of living testimony to the Resurrection. We must find some explanation of these narratives. Only 3 seem possible. One is that they were inventions; second they were hallucinations; three they were true.

INVENTIONS ? There is no need to devote much space to the

refutation of THIS suggestion. That the resurrection appearance stories are not deliberate inventions is as plain as could be. For one thing the narratives are sober and unadorned; for another, they are graphic, and enlivened by the detailed touches that sound like the work of an eyewitness. The stories of the race to the tomb, and of the walk to Emmaus are too vivid and real to have been invented.

Besides, no one could call them good inventions. If we had wanted to invent the Resurrection. we would have done much better ourselves. We would have been careful to avoid the complicated jigsaw puzzle of events the four Gospels together produce. We would have eliminated, or at least watered down, the doubts and fear of the Apostles. We would have included a dramatic account of the resurrection itself, describing the power and glory of the Son of God as He broke the bonds of death, and burst from the tomb in triumph. But no one saw it happen, and we have no description of it. Again. we should scarcely have chosen Mary Magdalene as the first witness, if only to avoid Renan's sneer that 'la passion d'une hallucinee donne au monde un monde un dieu ressuscite', (the passion of one who saw a hallucination gives the world a God Resurrected).

There is an objection to the theory of invention greater than the naivety of the narratives. It is the obvious fact, to which we have already had occasion to refer, that the Apostles. (evangelists), and the early Church, were sublimely convinced that Jesus had risen. The whole new Testament breathes an atmosphere of certainty and conquests. Its writers may have been tragically misled; they were definitely not deliberately misleading.

If these accounts were not inventions, were the appearances themselves HALLUCINATIONS ? This opinion has been widely held and confidently expressed; and of course, hallucinations are not an uncommon phenomenon. A hallucination is the 'apparent perception of an external object when no such object is present', and is associated most frequently with someone who is at least neurotic, it not actually psychotic'. Most of us have known people who see things and hear voices, and live sometimes or always in an imaginary world of their own. It is not possible to say that the Apostles were unbalanced people of this type. Mary Magdalene may have been. but hardly blustering Peter and doubting Thomas.

Hallucinations have also been known to occur in quite ordinary and normal people. and in such cases two characteristics may usually be discerned. First, they happen as the climax to a period of exaggerated wishful thinking. Second, the circumstances of time, place and mood are favourable. There must be the strong inward desire and the predisposing outward setting.

When we turn to the Gospel narratives of the resurrection. however, BOTH these factors are missing. Far from wishful thinking. it was just the opposite. When the women first found the tomb empty, they fled in 'trembling and astonishment' and were 'afraid'. When Mary Magdalene and the other women reported that Jesus was alive, the apostles 'would not believe it', and their words 'seemed to them an idle tale'. When Jesus Himself came and stood in their midst 'they were startled and frightened, and supposed that they saw a spirit', so that Jesus' upbraided them for their unbelief and hardness of heart'. Thomas was adamant in his refusal to believe unless he could actually see and feel the nail-wounds. When later Christ met the eleven and others by appointment, on a mountain in Galilee, 'they worshipped Him; but some doubted'. Here was no wishful thinking, no naive credulity. no blind acceptance. The disciples were not gullible, but rather cautious, skeptical and 'slow of heart to believe'. They were not susceptible to hallucinations. Nor would strange visions have satisfied them. Their faith was grounded on the hard facts of verifiable experience.

The outwardly favourable circumstances were missing too. If the appearances had all taken place in one or two particularly sacred places, that had been hallowed by memories of Jesus, and their mood had been expectant, our suspicions might well be aroused. If we had only the story of the appearances in the upper room, we would have cause to doubt and question. If the eleven had been gathered in that special place where Jesus had spent with them some of His last earthly hours, and they had kept His place vacant, and were sentimentalizing over the magic days of the past, and had remembered His promises to return, and had begun to wonder if he might return and to hope that He would, until the ardour of their expectation was consummated by His sudden appearances, we might Indeed fear that they had been mocked by a cruel delusion.

But this was not the case. An investigation of the ten appearances reveals an almost studied variety in the circumstances of person, place and mood in which they occurred. Jesus was seen by individuals alone (Mary Magdalene, Peter and James); by small groups and by more than five hundred people together. He appeared in the garden of the tomb; near Jerusalem; in the upper room; on the road to Emmaus; by the lake of Galilee; on a Galilee mountain and on the Mount of Olives.

There was variety in person and place; there was variety in mood also. Mary Magdalene was weeping; the women were afraid and astonished; Peter was full of remorse, and Thomas of unbelief and doubt. The Emmaus pair were distracted by the events of the week and the disciples in Galilee by their fishing. Yet, through their doubts and fears; their unbelief and preoccupation, the risen Lord made Himself known to them.

It is impossible to dismiss these revelations of the Divine Lord as the hallucinations of deranged minds. So, if they were neither inventions nor hallucinations, the only alternative left is that they actually happened; TRUE. The Risen Lord WAS seen.

<u>THE DISCIPLES WERE CHANGED</u>: The TRANSFORMATION of the disciples of Jesus is the greatest evidence of all for the resurrection, because it is entirely artless. They do not invite us to look at themselves, as they invite us to look at the empty tomb and the collapsed grave clothes and the Lord whom they had seen. We can see the change in them without being asked to look. The men who figure in the pages of the Gospels are new and different men in the ACTS. The death of their Master left them despondent, disillusioned, and near to despair. But in the ACTS they emerge as men that hazard their lives for the name of the Lord Jesus Christ. and they turn the world upside down.

What made the change ? What accounts for their new faith and power, joy and love ? Partly, no doubt, Pentecost and the coming of The Holy Ghost; The Holy Ghost came only when Jesus had risen and ascended. It is as if resurrection let loose mighty moral and spiritual forces. Two examples stand out:

The first is Simon Peter. During the telling of the Passion story, Peter has suffered a tragic eclipse. He had denied Christ three times. He has cursed and sworn as if he had never known the restraining influence of Jesus In his life. He has gone out into the night to weep bitterly. When Jesus is dead, he joins the others in the upper room, behind barred doors 'for fear of the Jews', and is utterly dejected.

But when we turn over a couple of pages in the Bible, we see Peter standing, preaching so boldly and so powerfully, to a vast crowd. that three thousand people believe in Christ, and are Baptized. We turn on to the next chapters of the ACTS, and we watch Peter defying the very Sanhedrin that had condemned Jesus to death, REJOICING that he is counted worthy to suffer shame for His name, and later, sleeping in his cell on the night of his expected execution.

Simon Peter is a new man. The shifting sands have been blown away; true to his nickname, he is a REAL Rock now. What has made the difference ?

Or take James, who later assumed a position of leadership in the Jerusalem Church. He is one of the 'brethren' of The Lord. James is evidently a believer now. What has made the difference ? What convinced him ? Perhaps the clue we are seeking is in 1 COR 15:7 where Paul, cataloguing those that had seen the risen Jesus. adds 'He Appeared to James'. It was the RESURRECTION that transformed Peter's fear into courage, and James' doubt into faith. It was the RESURRECTION that changed the Sabbath into Sunday, and the Jewish remnant into the Christian Church. It was the RESURRECTION that changed Saul the Pharisee into Paul the Apostle, the fanatical persecutor into a preacher of the vary faith he previously tried to destroy. 'Last of all', Paul wrote... 'He appeared also to me'.

These are the evidences for the Resurrection:

The body had disappeared;

The grave clothes remained undisturbed;

The Lord was seen;

The disciples were changed.

There is no other adequate explanation of these phenomena, other than the great Christian affirmation IT IS TRUE; 'The Lord is risen indeed'.

We have been occupied in a critical investigation of the most absorbing Personality of history, a modest carpenter from Nazareth, that became a peasant preacher, and died a criminal's death.

His claims were stupendous;

He was morally perfect;

He rose from the dead;

The cumulative weight of the evidence is conclusive.

It makes it eminently reasonable, that the last step of faith will bring us before Him. on our knees, with the words of doubting Thomas on our lips... 'MY LORD AND MY GOD'.

MAN'S NEED.

THE FACT AND NATURE OF SIN: Considerable space has been given to a examination of the evidence for the Resurrection, and the unique Deity of Jesus of Nazareth; and Christians are convinced that Jesus is the Lord, the Son of God.

Yet, the preoccupation of the New Testament is not just with WHO Jesus was, but also with WHAT He came to do. Christ is presented as the Lord from heaven; but also as the Saviour of sinners. The two CANNOT be separated. The validity of His work depends on the Divinity of His Person.

In order to appreciate the work that Jesus accomplished, we must understand who WE are, as well as who HE was. Christ's work was done for us. It was the work of a PERSON for PERSONS; a mission undertaken for needy persons, by the ONLY Person competent to meet their needs. His competence lies in His DEITY; our need lies in OUR SIN. We have tested His competence; we must now expose our NEED.

God does not give Grace to play at Worship, or to silly, pseudo, or falsidical babes or hypocrites. Hidden, unfelt, unconfessed sin is leprosy to the soul.

God gives them (by permitting them, in punishment for their pride and hypocrisy, to be blinded to the truth of the Christian revelation) a spirit of stupor until this present day, eyes that they may not see, and ears that they may not hear. ROM 11:8 & :20; ISA 29:10; DEUT 29:4; MATT 13:14.

See, then, the goodness and the severity of God; His severity towards those who sin, but the goodness of God towards us if we abide in His goodness; otherwise, we also will be cut off. ROM 11:22.

Learning, undigested by thought (meditation), is labour lost; thought (meditation), undigested by learning, is perilous.

So we turn from Christ to man, from the sinlessness and Glory that are in Him, to the sins and shames that are in man. Only then, after we have CLEARLY grasped what we truly are, can we be in a position to perceive the wonder of what He has done for us, and offers us. Only when we have had our malady accurately diagnosed, will we be willing to take the medicine prescribed by God.

Sin is an unpopular subject, especially by those at enmity with their souls. True Christians are often criticized for speaking of sin, (It is only because true Christians are realists, that they do so). Sin is not a convenient invention of Clergymen, to keep them in their job; sin is a FACT of human experience and nature.

The history of the past hundred years or so has convinced many people that the problem of evil, is sin located in man himself, not merely in his society. In the nineteenth century, a liberal, humanistic optimism flourished. It was widely believed that human nature was good; that evil was caused by ignorance and bad housing; and that education and social reform would enable men to live together in happiness and goodwill. But this illusion has been shattered by the hard facts of our present day and history. (Via an educational philosophy that has gone awry, presented by scholars trapped well within their own empirical thinking and misguided rejection of religion). Educational opportunities have spread rapidly in the western world, and many welfare states have been created.

Yet, the atrocities that accompanied both world wars, the subsequent international conflicts, the continuance of political oppression and racial discriminations, and the general increase of violence and crime, broken homes and families, have forced Christian people to acknowledge the existence, in every man, a hard core of sin. i.e. selfishness, greed, sensuality and violation of God's Precepts, Oracles and Commandments, regarding UNITY within God's Natural Law.

It should be axiomatic, much that we take for granted in a 'civilized' society is BASED on the assumption of human SIN. Nearly all legislation has grown up because human beings cannot be trusted to settle their own disputes with justice, and without self-interest. A promise is not enough; we need a contract. Doors are not enough; we have to lock and bolt them. The payment of fares is not enough; tickets have to be issued, inspected and collected. Law and order are not enough; we need police to enforce them. ALL this is due to man's SIN. We cannot trust each other. We need protection against one another. It is a terrible INDICTMENT of a SINFUL HUMAN NATURE.

<u>THE UNIVERSALITY OF SIN:</u> The Biblical writers are quite clear that sin is universal. 'There is no man that does not sin', says Solomon in an aside during his great prayer at the dedication of the Temple. 'Surely there is not a righteous man on earth who does good and never sins' adds the Preacher in the Book of

Ecclesiastes. Several Psalms lament the universality of human sin. PSALM 14: describes the godless 'fool', and gives a very pessimistic description of human wickedness:

'They are corrupt, they do abominable deeds, there is none that does good. The Lord looks down from Heaven upon the children of men, to see if there are any that act wisely, that seek after God. They have all gone astry, they are all alike corrupt; there is none that does good, no, not one'.

Then all of a sudden, individual judgments are handed down by God. (at times, via the soul), and He mocks us to our faces. 'when distress and anguish befall you'... 'they spurned all My reproof'... 'with their own devices be glutted'... 'the smugness of fools destroys them'...PROV 1:22-33.

The Prophets are as insistent as the Psalmists on the fact that all men are sinners, and no statement is more definite than the two that are to be found in the second half of the Book of ISAIAH.

Nor is this a fancy of the Old Testament writers. Paul opens his Epistle to the Romans with a closely reasoned argument, that extends over the first three chapters, that all men indiscriminately, Jews and Gentiles, are sinners in God's sight. Paul depicts the degraded morals of the pagan world and then adds that the Jew is no better, since, possessing God's Holy Law himself, and teaching it to others, he is yet guilty of breaking it. Paul then quotes from the Psalms and Isaiah to illustrate this theme, and concludes, 'there is no distinction; since all have sinned and fall short of the glory of God'. John is, if anything, even more explicit when John declares that 'If we say that we have no sin, we deceive ourselves', and 'If we say we have not sinned. we make God a liar'.   ROM 3:22-23   1 JOHN 1:8-10.

BUT WHAT IS SIN ?   Its universal extent is clear; what is its NATURE ? Several words are used in the Bible to describe it. They group themselves into two categories, according to whether wrongdoing is regarded negatively or positively. NEGATIVELY, it is shortcoming. One word represents as a LAPSE, a SLIP, a BLUNDER. Another pictures it as THE FAILURE TO HIT A MARK, as when shooting at a target. Yet another shows it to be an INWARD BADNESS, a disposition which falls short of what is good, i.e. playing at worship or God's Precepts, Oracles or Commandments.

POSITIVELY, sin is TRANSGRESSION (of Worship, Precepts, Oracles or Commandments). One word makes sin the TRESPASS OF A   BOUNDRY. Another reveals it as LAWLESSNESS, and another as an act that VIOLATES JUSTICE.

Both of these groups of words imply the existence of a MORAL STANDARD. It is either an IDEAL that we fail to reach, or a LAW that we break. 'Whoever knows what is right to do and fails to do it, for him it is sin', says JAMES. That is the NEGATIVE aspect. 'Every one who commits sin is guilty of lawlessness; sin is lawlessness', says JOHN. That is the POSITIVE aspect.

The Bible accepts the fact that men have different standards. The Jews have the Law of Moses (so do we). The Gentiles have the Law of conscience (so do they). But all men have broken the Law they know, and have fallen short of their own standards.

What is our ETHICAL CODE ? It may be the Law of Moses or the Law of Jesus Christ. It may be the DECENT thing, or the DONE thing, Or the CONVENTIONS OF SOCIETY. But whatever it is, we have not succeeded in observing it. We all stand self-condemned.

To some GOOD-LIVING people this comes as a genuine surprise. They have their IDEALS and think they attain them, more or less. They do not indulge in much introspection. They are not unduly self-critical. They KNOW they have had occasional LAPSES. They ARE aware of certain CHARACTER DEFICIENCIES. (but make no attempt to correct them). But they are not particularly alarmed by them, and they consider themselves no worse than other men. All this is understandable enough, UNTIL we remember two things: First, our sense of failure depends on how high OUR standards are. It is quite easy to consider oneself good at high jumping if the bar is never raised more than waist high. Second, GOD concerns Himself with the THOUGHT behind the deed and with the MOTIVE behind the action. Jesus clearly taught this in the Sermon on the Mount. With these two principles in mind, it would prove a healthy exercise to take the Ten Commandments in EXODUS 20; as OUR standard, and see how very far short of it we fall.

THE TEN COMMANDMENTS: 1. YOU SHALL HAVE NO OTHER GODS BEFORE ME. YOU SHALL NOT MAKE FOR YOURSELVES A GRAVEN IMAGE. This is God's DEMAND for man's EXCLUSIVE WORSHIP. It is not necessary to worship the sun, the moon, or the stars etc, to break this Law. We break it whenever we give to something or someone, OTHER than God Himself, the first place in our thoughts or our affections.

It may be some engrossing sport, absorbing hobby or selfish ambition. Or it may be that we idolize. We may worship a god of gold and silver, in the form of safe investments and a healthy bank balance, or a god of wood and stone in the form of property and possessions. None of these things are necessarily wrong in itself. They only becomes wrong when we give to it, the place in our lives that belongs only to God. Sin is fundamentally the EXALTATION of self at the expense of God. i.e. He is 'a self-made man who worships his creator.. himself'.

For I, The Lord, your God am a jealous God, inflicting punishment for their father's wickedness on the children of those who hate Me, down to the third and forth generation; but bestowing mercy down to the thousandth generation, on the children of those who love Me and keep My Commandments.

We may have never manufactured some gruesome mental image with our hands, but what hideous MENTAL IMAGE do we hold in our minds? Further, although this Commandment does NOT forbid the use of all external forms of Worship. (i.e. statues or pictures as an aid to MEDITATION or MENTAL ATTITUDE; but not, statues to be kissed and deemed an icon or a person actually present), but it implies that they are useless unless there is an INWARD REALITY as well. We may have attended Church; have we REALLY worshipped God? We may have said Prayers, have we REALLY prayed? We may have READ THE BIBLE, have we ALLOWED THE PARACLETE TO TEACH US? Or LET GOD SPEAK TO US THROUGH IT or DONE WHAT IT SAID? It is useless to approach God with our LIPS if our HEART is far from Him. To do so is sheer FOLLY and HYPOCRICY. ISA 29:13   MARK 7:6

For us to keep this Commandment would be, as Jesus said, to love the Lord our God with all our heart, and with all our soul and with all our mind; to make GOD'S will our guide and HIS glory our goal; to put God first in thought, word and deed; in business and leisure; in friendships and career; in the use of our money, time and talents; at work and at home.

The first Commandment concerns the OBJECT of our worship, the second concerns it's MANNER. In the 1st God DEMANDS our EXCULSIVE worship, and the 2nd our SINCERE and SPIRITUAL worship. For "God is Spirit, and those who worship Him, must worship in Spirit and Truth." JOHN 4:24

2. YOU SHALL NOT TAKE THE NAME OF THE LORD YOUR GOD IN VAIN. The Name of God represents the Nature of God. There is much in the Bible that Commands us to reverence His Name, and in The Lord's Prayer, we are taught to pray that His Name may be Hallowed. God's Holy Name can be profaned by swearing, and our loose language, and most of us could do worse than revise our vocabulary from time to time. To take God's Name in vain is not just a matter of words, but also of thoughts and deeds. Whenever our behaviour is inconsistent with our belief, or our practice contradicts our preaching, we take God's Name in vain. To call God 'Father' and be filled with doubts, anxiety and depression, is to deny His Name. To take God's Name in vain is to TALK one way, and ACT another... This is hypocrisy.

3. REMEMBER THE SABBATH DAY, TO KEEP IT HOLY. The Jew's Sabbath and the Christian's Sunday are a DIVINE INSTITUTION. To set one day in seven apart is not just a human

arrangement or a social convenience. It is God's plan. He made the Sabbath for man (for whom He made the Sabbath). He adapted it to Man's need. MARK 2:27. Man's body and mind needs rest, and man's spirit needs the opportunity for Worship. The Sabbath day, therefore, is a day of REST and WORSHIP.

Not only are we to keep it as such OURSELVES, for our own good, but we are to do all we can for the COMMON good; to ensure that others do not have to work UNNECESSARILY ON THIS DAY. Sunday is a 'HOLY' day, set apart FOR GOD, and HIS purposes. It is THE LORD'S day; for GOD'S Worship and service, and not for OUR selfish pleasure.

4. HONOUR YOUR FATHER AND YOUR MOTHER, THAT YOU MAY HAVE A LONG LIFE. This Commandment belongs to the first half of the Law that concerns OUR duty to God. It is also the only Commandment that carries with it a PROMISE of God. Our parents, while we are children, stand 'IN LOCO DEI'; they REPRESENT GOD'S AUTHORITY (whether the parents/children like and/or believe it or not, does not matter a whit to God). Yet, it is in their homes that people, (young people especially), are at their most SELFISH and INCONSIDERATE. It is all too easy to be UNGRATEFUL, and NEGLECTFUL, and to fail to' show our parents DUE respect and affection. How often do we write them or visit them ? Or. do they need financial support that we COULD give, but DENY them ? DEUT 21:18-21

5. YOU SHALL NOT KILL. This is not just a forbidding murder. If LOOKS could kill, many would kill with a LOOK. If murder can be committed by CUTTING WORDS, many are guilty. Jesus said that to be ANGRY with someone, and to be INSULTING, are just

as serious, JOHN writes, 'Any one who HATES HIS BROTHER is a murderer'. Every LOSS OF TEMPER, every OUTBURST OF UNCONTROLLED PASSION, every STIRRING OF SULLEN RAGE, every BITTER RESENTMENT and THIRSTING FOR REVENGE; all these things are murder. We can kill by MALICIOUS GOSSIP. We can kill by STUDIED NEGLECT and CRUELTY. We can kill by SPITE and JEALOUSY. We have probably all done so.

6. YOU SHALL NOT COMMIT ADULTERY. Again, this Commandment has a far wider application than just to unfaithfulness in marriage. It includes ANY SORT OF SEX outside of the marriage relationship (for which sex was designed, by God). It includes FLIRTING, EXPERIMENTING and SOLITARY SEXUAL EXPERIENCE (masturbation), FORNICATION and ADULTERY . It also includes SEXUAL PERVERSIONS, and PERVERTED INSTINCT. (remember. satan has angel, spirits, saints, instruments and servants as well). It includes SELFISH DEMANDS within wedlock, and many (it not all) DIVORCES. It includes the DELIBERATE READING of pornographic literature, and GIVING IN to impure fantasies. Jesus made this clear when He said... 'every one who looks at a woman LUSTFULLY has ALREADY committed adultery with her in his heart'. Just as to entertain murderous thoughts in the heart is to commit murder, so to entertain adulterous thoughts in the heart is to commit adultery. This Commandment in fact embraces every abuse of a sacred and beautiful gift of God.

7. YOU SHALL NOT STEAL. To steal is to rob a person of anything that belongs to him, or is due to him. The theft of money or property is not the only infringement of this

Commandment. TAX EVASION also. So is DODGING CUSTOMS. So is WORKING SHORT HOURS. SCROUNGING God calls stealing, to OVERWORK and/or UNDER PAY is to break this Commandment. There must be a few of us who have not have been CONSISTENTLY and SCRUPULOUSLY honest in PERSONAL AFFAIRS. Not to TITHE is to ROB GOD. As ARTHUR HUGH CLOUGH wrote:

> 'Thou shalt not kill', but need'st not strive officiously to keep (another) alive; 'Thou shalt not steal'- an empty feat when it's more lucrative to cheat.

These negative commandments also imply a positive counterpart. In order to truly abstain from killing, one must do all In one's power to foster the health, and preserve the life of others. To refrain from the act of adultery is insufficient; the right, healthy and honourable attitude of each sex towards the other is also required. Similarly, to avoid stealing is no particular virtue, if one is miserly or mean. Paul was not satisfied that a thief stop stealing; he had to start working; he had to continue in honest labour until he found himself in a position to TITHE, and give to those in need.

8. YOU SHALL NOT BEAR FALSE WITNESS AGAINST YOUR NEIGHBOUR. The last 5 Commandments express that the respect for the rights of others that is implicit in true love. To break these Commandments is to rob a man of the things most precious to him. his LIFE ('you shall not kill), his HOME and HONOUR ('you shall not commit adultery). his PROPERTY ('you shall not steal'), and now, his REPUTATION ('you shall not bear false witness against your neighbour').

This Commandment is not only applicable to the LAW COURTS. It DOES include PERJURY. But it also includes all FORMS OF SCANDAL, SLANDER, IDLE TALK and TITTLE-TATTLE, all LIES and DELIBERATE EXAGGERATIONS or DISTORTIONS of the truth. We can bear false witness by LISTENING TO UNKIND RUMOURS, as well as by PASSING THEM ON, by MAKING JOKES AT SOMEBODY ELSE'S EXPENSE, by CREATING FALSE IMPRESSIONS, by NOT CORRECTING UNTRUE STATEMENTS, and by our SILENCE as well as by our SPEECH. "A PERSON WITH A FROWARD MOUTH WILL NEVER MATURE AS LONG AS HE LIVES". PROV. 8:13 SIR 23:15.

Generally speaking, Lucifer's servants and instruments are BRANDED or MARKED with the characteristics of a TALE BEARER'S for the benefit of GOD'S Servants and Instruments; allowing them to identify Lucifer's instruments and servants.

9. YOU SHALL NOT COVET THY NEIGHBOUR'S WIFE. See SIR 9: 8-9. We will group Commandments 9 & 10 together re COVETOUSNESS (via "author's licence).

10. THOU SHALT NOT COVET THY NEIGHBOUR'S GOODS. The 9th and 10th Commandments are, in some ways, THE MOST REVEALING OF ALL. they turn the decalogue from an OUTWARD LEGAL CODE. into an INWARD MORAL STANDARD. The civil law can't touch us for COVETOUSNESS, but only for THEFT; Covetousness belongs to the INNER LIFE. It lurks in the heart and the mind. What lust is to adultery and temper is to murder, THAT covetousness is to theft.

The particular things that we are not to covet, and that are mentioned in the Commandments, are surprisingly MODERN. The Divorce Courts would not be so full if men did not covet their neighbour's wife. In a housing shortage, there is MUCH coveting of our neighbour's house. "Covetousness...is idolatry" wrote Paul, and by contrast, "There is great gain in Godliness with contentment". COL 3:5 1 TIM 6:6.

Listing these Commandments has brought to light an UGLY CATALOGUE OF SINS. So much takes place beneath the surface of our lives, in the secret places of our hearts and minds, that other people don't see, and that we manage even to conceal from ourselves, and/or others., via deceit; deception; malicious cunning; secret guilt; and unfaithfulness.

But God sees these things. His eye penetrates into the deep recesses of our hearts; 'Before Him no creature is hidden, but all is open and laid bare to the eyes of Him to whom we must give an account re our actions and deeds. God sees us as we REALLY are, and His Law (Precepts, Oracles and Commandments), shows up our sins for what they REALLY ARE. In fact, it is the PURPOSE of the Law (Precepts. Oracles and Commandments), to EXPOSE SIN, for 'through the Law comes knowledge of sin'.

In our case too, nothing can convince us of our sinfulness and EVIL cowardice, compromise and tolerance, like the lofty, righteous Law of God (Precepts. Oracles and Commandments), who judges via the THOUGHT behind the DEED; the MOTIVE behind the ACTION.

I shall stand CONDEMNED if I
HEAR your Word, but do not KEEP it
KNOW it, but do not LOVE it;
BELIEVE it, but do not OBEY it.
Lucifer ALSO can say 'my sheep hear my voice, and I know them, and they follow ME.
There is no such thing as INSTANT Godliness; Godliness develops and grows in PRECISE ratio to our SINCERITY.
When C. H. Spurgeon, the famous 19th century Preacher, was only fourteen, he experienced a tremendous sense of his own sinfulness. Two truths came home to him as never before; 'God's Majesty and my sinfulness'. He experienced a crushing sense of his unworthiness. 'I do not hesitate to say that those who examined my life would not have seen any extraordinary sin. Yet as I looked upon MYSELF, I saw outrageous sin against God. I was not like other boys, untruthful, dishonest, swearing and so on. But of a sudden, I met Moses carrying the Law...God's ten words.. and as I read them, they all seemed to Join in condemning me in the sight of the thrice Holy Jehovah'. No wonder God was able to use him so mightily. What an example of Godly repentance.

THE CONSEQUENCES OF SIN: We have seen something of the NATURE and the UNIVERSALITY of human sin. We will leave these distasteful subjects and pass on to the good news of Christ's Salvation, but we are not ready to do so. We need to grasp what the RESULTS of sin are, before we can appreciate what God has done for us, and is OFFERING us, in Christ.

IS sin really so very serious ? Its evil CONSEQUENCES can be best understood when its EFFECTS are seen, ON GOD, ON US, AND ON OUR FELLOW MEN.

ALIENATION FROM GOD: Even if we don't realize the fact now, the most terrible result of sin, is that IT CUTS US OFF FROM GOD. Man's highest destiny is to KNOW GOD; to be in PERSONAL RELATIONSHIP WITH HIM. Our chief claim to nobility as human beings, is that we were made in the image of God, and ARE, therefore, capable of knowing Him. But this God, whom we are meant to know, and whom we OUGHT to know, is a RIGHTEOUS BEING, infinite in His MORAL PERFECTION. Scripture lays much stress on this TRUTH:

'For thus says the high and lofty One who inhabits eternity. whose name is Holy; "I dwell in the high and holy place..."

'The King of Kings and the Lord of lords, who.. dwells in unapproachable light'.

'God is light and in Him is no darkness at all. If we say we have fellowship with Him while we walk in darkness, we lie and do not live according to truth'.

'Our God is a consuming fire'.

'Who among us can dwell with the devouring fire ? Who among us can dwell with everlasting burning ?

'Thou who art of purer eyes than to behold evil and canst not look on wrong'.

DEUT 4:24;   ISA 33:14 and 57:15;   HAB 1:13; and 12:29; 1 TIM6:15;

1 JOHN 1:5-6.

All those men of God who HAVE caught a glimpse of God's Glory, have shrunk from the sight in an overwhelming consciousness of their own sins. MOSES, to whom God appeared in the bush that burned, but was not consumed, 'hid his face, for he was afraid to look at God'. JOB, to whom God spoke 'out of the whirlwind' in words that exalted His transcendent Majesty, cried out, 'I have heard of Thee by the hearing of the ear. but now my eyes see Thee; therefore I despise myself, and repent in the dust and ashes'.

ISAIAH, a young man at the threshold of his career, had a vision of God as the King of Israel 'sitting upon a throne, high and lifted up', surrounded by worshipping angels who sang of His holiness and Glory, and said, 'Woe is me! For I am lost; for I am a man of unclean lips, and I dwell in the midst of a people of unclean lips; for my eyes have seen the King, the Lord of hosts!'.

When EZEKIEL received his strange vision of living winged creatures and whirring wheels, and above them a throne, and on the throne One like a man, enveloped in the brightness of fire and of the rainbow, EZEKIEL recognized it as 'the appearance of the likeness of the Glory of the Lord', and he added, 'When I saw it, I fell upon my face'. SAUL OF TARSUS, travelling to Damascus, mad with rage against the Christians, was struck to the ground and blinded by a brilliant light that flashed from heaven more brightly than the noonday sun, and wrote later of his vision of the Risen Christ, 'He appeared also to me'.

The aged JOHN, exiled on the Island of Patmos, described

in detail his vision of the Risen and Glorified Jesus, whose 'eyes were like a flame of fire' and whose 'face was like the sun shinning in full strength', and JOHN tells us. 'When I saw Him, I fell at His feet as though dead'. EXODUS 3:1-6; JOB 42:5-6; ISA 6:1-5; EZEK 1:26-28; ACTS 9:1-9; 1 COR 15:8; REV 1:9-17.

If the curtain that veils the unspeakable Majesty of God could be drawn aside but for a moment, we too would not be able to bear the sight. As it is, we only dimly perceive how pure and brilliant must be the Glory of Almighty God. However. we know enough to realize that sinful man, while still in his sins, can NEVER approach this Holy God. A GREAT chasm yawns between God in His Righteousness, and man in his sin. 'What partnership have righteousness and iniquity ? Or what fellowship has light with darkness' ? asks Paul.

That sin cuts us off from God was brought home dramatically in the Old Testament, in the construction of the Tabernacle and the Temple. Both were made in two compartments, the first and larger being called the Holy Place, while the further and smaller was known as the Most Holy Place or the Holy of Hollies. In this inner sanctuary was the Shekinah Glory, the visible symbol of God's presence. Between the two was the 'veil', a thick curtain that barred access into the Holy of Hollies. NO ONE was allowed to pass through into God's presence except the high priest, and he only on the annual Day of Atonement, and then only if he took with him the blood of a sacrifice for sins.

What was VISIBLY demonstrated to the Israelites is taught by Old and New Testament writers. SIN BRINGS INEVITABLE

SEPARATION and this separation is spiritual death, the severance of a person from God, the ONLY source of true spiritual life. 'The wages of sin is death'.

Further, if in this world we deliberately reject Jesus Christ, (through whom ALONE we may find eternal life), we will die eternally in the next world. Hell is a GRIM and DREADFUL REALITY. Let no man deceive you. Jesus Himself spoke of it. Jesus called it 'OUTER DARKNESS because it is an INFINITE separation from God, who is light. It is also called, in the Bible. 'THE SECOND DEATH' , and 'the lake of fire' terms that describes symbolically the FORFEITURE of eternal life, and the ghastly thirst of the soul, that is involved in irrevocable banishment from God's presence. MATT 25:30   LUKE 16:19-31   Rev 20:14-15.

This separation from God that is caused by sin, is not only taught in the Bible; it is CONFIRMED by human experience. I can still remember my own bewilderment when I was a boy, as I said my prayers and tried to penetrate into God's presence. I could not understand why God seemed shrouded in mists, and I could not get near Him. God seemed remote and aloof. ISAIAH gave me the answer:

> 'Behold, the Lord's hand is not shortened. that it cannot save, or His ear dull. that it cannot hear; but your iniquities have made a separation between you and your God. and your sins have hid His face from you so that He does not hear'. ISA 59:1-2.

We are tempted to say to God, as in the Book of Lamentations, 'Thou hast wrapped thyself with a cloud so that no prayer can pass through'. But, in FACT, God is NOT responsible for the cloud. WE ARE. Our sins blot out God's face from us, as effectively as the clouds do the sun.

Sometimes, in emergencies, in danger, in joy or in the contemplation of beauty, God seems to us to be near, but more often than not, we are aware of an inexplicable AWAYNESS from God, and we feel abandoned. This is not just a feeling; IT IS A FACT. Until our sins are forgiven, we are exiles, far from our true home. We have no communion with God. In Biblical terms, we are LOST, or 'DEAD through the trespasses and sins' that we have committed.

It is THIS that accounts for the RESTLESSNESS of men and women today. There is a hunger in the heart of man that none but God can satisfy; a vacuum that only God can fill. The extravagant love or crime stories in the movies; pools and pubs; the dirt track and the dog track; the current epidemic of drugs, sex and violence - all these things are SYMPTOMS of man's search for SATISFACTION. They betray his 'thirst', and separate from God. St. Augustine was correct when he said; 'Thou hast made us for Thyself, and (therefore) our hearts are restless till they rest in Thee'. This situation is TRAGIC beyond words. Man IS missing the destiny for which God made him. See NCRC 99/2.

BONDAGE TO SELF; Sin does not only ESTRANGE; it also ENSLAVES. If it alienates us from God, it ALSO brings us into CAPTIVITY.

We must now consider the 'INWARDNESS' of sin. It is

more than an unfortunate outward act or habit; it is a deep-seated inward corruption. In fact, the sins we commit are merely outward and visible manifestations of the INWARD and INVISIBLE MALADY, the SYMPTOMS OF A MORAL DISEASE. The metaphor Jesus used, however, is that of a tree and its fruit. The kind of fruit a tree bears, He said (whether figs or grapes, for example), and their condition (whether good or bad), depend on the nature of the tree itself. Just so, 'out of the abundance of the heart the mouth speaks'.

In this respect, Jesus IS at odds with MANY 'modern' SOCIAL REFORMERS and REVOLUTIONARIES. We are all influenced for good or evil by our EDUCATION and ENVIRONMENT,. and by the POLITICAL and ECONOMIC SYSTEM under which we live. We SHOULD seek JUSTICE, FREEDOM and WELL BEING for ALL men. Yet, it was not to a lack of these that Jesus attributed the EVILS OF HUMAN SOCIETY, but to MAN'S VERY NATURE, what Jesus called our 'HEART'. Here are Christ's exact words:

> 'For from within, out of the heart of man, come evil thoughts, fornication, theft, murder, adultery, coveting, wickedness, deceit, licentiousness, envy, slander, pride, foolishness. All these evil things come from within, and they defile a man. MARK 7:21-23.

The Old Testament had already taught this truth. As JEREMIAH put It, 'THE HEART IS DECEITFUL ABOVE ALL THINGS, AND DESPERATELY CORRUPT; WHO CAN UNDERSTAND IT ? JER 17:9. The Bible is full of references to this INFECTION of human nature, or 'ORIGINAL SIN'. It is a tendency or bias of self-centredness, that we inherit, that is rooted deeply in our human personality/character, and that manifests itself in a thousand UGLY ways. Paul called it 'THE FLESH', and gives an inventory of its 'WORKS', or products:

"Now the works of the flesh are plain: IMMORALITY, IMPURITY, LICENTIOUSNESS, IDOLATRY, SORCERY, ENMITY, STRIFE. JEALOUSY, ANGER, SELFISHNESS, DISSENSION, PARTY SPIRIT, ENVY, DRUNKENNESS, CAROUSING, AND THE LIKE". GAL 5:19-21.

Because sin is an inward corruption of human nature, we are in BONDAGE. It is not so much certain ACTS or HABITS that enslave us, but rather the EVIL INFECTION from which these spring. So many times in the New Testament we are described as 'SLAVES'. We resent it because it is TRUE. Jesus aroused the indignation of certain Pharisees when He said to them, 'If you continue in My word, you are truly My disciples, and you will know the truth, and the truth will make you free.' They retorted, 'We are descendants of Abraham, and have never been in bondage to anyone. How is it that You say, 'you will be made free ?' Jesus answered them, 'Truly, truly, I say to you, every one who commits sin is a slave to sin'.

Paul several times in his Epistles describes the HUMILIATING SERVITUDE into which sin brings us:

'you..... were once slaves of sin'.
'We all once lived in the passions of our flesh,
following the desires of body and mind'.
'we ourselves were once foolish,
disobedient, led astray,

slaves to various passions and pleasures'.
ROM 6:17   EPH 2:3   TITUS 3:3.

The example of our LACK OF SELF-MASTERY that JAMES gives, is the DIFFICULTY WE HAVE CONTROLLING OUR TONGUE. In a well-known Chapter FULL of graphic metaphor, he says that if a man 'makes no mistakes in what he says he is a perfect man, able to bridle the whole body also'. He points out that 'the tongue is a little member and boasts of great things'. Its influence spreads like fire: it 'is a restless evil' and is 'full of deadly poison'. We can tame all kinds of beasts and birds, he adds, 'but no human being can tame the tongue'.   JAS 3:1-12.

We KNOW this, all too well. We have HIGH IDEALS, but WEAK WILLS, We WANT to live a good life, but we are CHAINED in the prison of our SELF-CENTREDNESS. However much we may boast of being FREE, we are, in reality, SLAVES. We need to come in TEARS to God and say:
'It is not finished Lord, There is not one thing done,
there is no battle of my life that I have really won.
And now I come to tell Thee how I fought to fail,
my human, all too human tale of weakness and futility'.
(Studdert Kennedy)

It is no use giving us rules of conduct: we can't keep them. Let God go on saying 'Thou shalt not', yet we shall to the end of time. A lecture will not solve our problem; we need a Saviour. The education of the mind is not enough without a CHANGE OF HEART. Man has found the secret of physical power, the power of nuclear reaction. Now man needs SPIRITUAL POWER, to

SET HIM FREE FROM HIMSELF, to CONQUER and CONTROL himself, the power to give him MORAL CHARACTER to match his scientific achievement.

CONFLICT WITH OTHERS: Our list of the TERRIBLE CONSEQUENCES of sin is not complete...There is one more to consider, ITS EFFECT ON OUR RELATIONSHIPS WITH OTHERS.

We have seen that sin is a deep-seated INFECTION OF NATURE. It lies at the root of our personality/character. It controls our ego. In fact, SIN IS SELF. And all the sins we commit are assertions of the self, against either God or others. The Ten Commandments, although a series of negative prohibitions, set out our duty to God and to others. This is even more clear in the positive summary of the Law that Jesus made by joining a verse from LEVITICUS 19:18, to a verse from DEUTERONOMY 6:5: 'You shall love the Lord your God with all your heart, and with all your soul, and with all your mind. This is the great and first Commandment. And a second is like it, you shall love your neighbour as yourself. On these two Commandments depend all the Law and the prophets'.

It is important to observe that the first Commandment concerns our duty to God, and not our duty to our neighbour. We are to love God first; and then we are to love our neighbour as ourselves. So God's order is that we put Him first; others next; ourselves last. Jesus first;+ Others second; +Yourself last = JOY. Sin is a reversal of the order. It is to put ourselves first, our neighbour next, and God somewhere in the background.

The man who wrote his autobiography and entitled it DEAR ME was only giving expression to what we all think of ourselves when the ice cream is brought into the children's party, the cry goes up 'ME FIRST!' As we grow up we learn not to say that kind of thing; but we still think it. Archbishop William Temple's definition of Original Sin perfectly describes this truth:

'I am the centre of the world I see; where the horizon is depends on where I stand... Education may make my self-centredness less disastrous by widening my horizon of interests; so far, it is like climbing a tower, that widens the horizon for physical vision, while leaving me still the centre and standard of reference'.
CHRISTIANITY AND SOCIAL ORDER. 1942.

This basic self-centredness affects all of our behaviour. We don't find it easy to adjust to other people. We tend either to despise them or to envy them, to have either superiority or inferiority feelings. We seldom think of ourselves with that 'sober judgment' that Paul urged on his readers. Sometimes we are full of self-pity, at other times, self-esteem, self-will or self-love.

All the relationships of life are complicated - parents and children; husband and wife; employer and employees. Juvenile delinquency has MANY causes. MUCH is due to lack of security at home; but the FACT is that delinquents are, (for whatever reason), asserting themselves AGAINST SOCIETY.

Hundreds of divorces could be prevented if people were humble enough to blame THEMSELVES more than their partner.

Whenever couples have come to myself because their marriage was threatened, it has been noticed that each tells a different story - a story so different, that one would not guess they were describing the same situation, unless one knew.

Most quarrels are due to MISUNDERSTANDING, and the misunderstanding is due to THEIR failure to appreciate the other point of view. It is more natural for man to talk, rather than LISTEN; more natural to ARGUE rather than to SUBMIT. This is also true in Industrial disputes, as much as in domestic quarrels. Many management/labour conflicts would be resolved if BOTH sides first examined THEMSELVES, critically, and then examined the other side CHARITABLY. Instead, we are ALWAYS charitable to OURSELVES, and CRITICAL of others. The same could be said of complex INTERNATIONAL unrest.

The tensions of today are due largely to FEAR and FOLLY. Our outlook is ONE-SIDED. We exaggerate our own VIRTUE and the other man's VICE.

It is easy to write this CONDEMNATION of SOCIAL RELATIONSHIPS today. The only reason for doing so is to show how HUMAN SIN or SELF-CENTREDNESS is the CAUSE of all our troubles. It brings us into CONFLICT with each other. If only the spirit of SELF ASSERTION could be replaced by the spirit of SELF-SACRIFICE, our conflicts would CEASE. And SELF-SACRIFICE is what the Bible means by 'LOVE'. While sin is POSSESSIVE, love is EXPANSIVE. Sin's characteristic is the desire TO GET; love's characteristic is the desire TO GIVE.

'Love ever gives, forgives, outlives, and ever stands

with open hands, and while It lives, it gives. For this is love's prerogative; to give.. and give... and give"... Prof. H.M.GWATKIN

What man needs is a RADICAL change of nature. What Prof. Gwatkin has called 'A CHANGE FROM SELF TO UNSELF'.

Man cannot work it within himself. Man cannot operate on himself. Again, MAN NEEDS A SAVIOUR.

This exposure of our sinful human nature, and our incompetence and gross inability to deal with it ourselves, has only one purpose. It is to: CONVINCE US OF OUR NEED FOR JESUS CHRIST; and to PREPARE US FOR AN UNDERSTANDING AND AN ACCEPTANCE OF WHAT JESUS CHRIST OFFERS.

Faith is born of need. We will NEVER put our trust in Jesus Christ until we have FIRST despaired of ourselves. Jesus Christ HIMSELF said; 'Those who are well have no need of a physician, but those who are sick; I came not to call the righteous, but sinners'. ONLY when we have REALIZED and FACED UP TO the seriousness of our illness, will we ADMIT our urgent need for a cure.

CHRIST'S WORK

<u>THE DEATH OF CHRIST;</u>   Christianity is a RESCUE religion. It declares that God has taken THE INITIATIVE in Jesus Christ, to deliver US from OUR SINS. This is the MAIN theme of the Bible:

'You shall call His name Jesus. For He will save His people from their sins'.

'The Son of man came to seek and to save the lost'.

'The saying is sure and worthy of full acceptance, that Christ Jesus came into the world to save sinners'.

'We have seen and testify that the Father has sent His Son as the Saviour of the world'.

MATT 1:21   LUKE 19:10   1 TIM 1:15   1 JOHN 4:14.

1. ALIENATION FROM GOD;
2. BONDAGE TO SELF;
3. CONFLICT WITH OTHERS.

Since sin has three principal CONSEQUENCES, as we have seen, 'SALVATION' includes man's liberation from them ALL. Through Jesus Christ the Saviour, we can be brought out of exile, and reconciled to God; "SAVED". We can be 'BORN AGAIN'; receive a new nature, and be set free from our moral bondage. And we can have the old discords replaced by a fellowship of love.

The FIRST aspect of Salvation Christ made possible by His suffering and death. The SECOND by the Gift of the Holy Spirit of Christ. And the THIRD by the building of Christ's Church.

PAUL described Christ's work as a 'MINISTRY OF RECONCILIATION', and PAUL'S Gospel as a 'MESSAGE OF RECONCILIATION' Paul also made it quite clear where this reconciliation comes from; God is its author, Paul says, and Christ its agent. 'All this is from God, who through Christ reconciled US to HIMSELF'. 'God was in Christ reconciling the world to Himself'. 2 COR 5:19.

All that was achieved through the death of Jesus on the Cross, had its origin in the Mind and Heart of the Eternal God. No explanation of Christ's death or man's salvation that fails to do justice to this FACT, is loyal to the teachings of the Bible. 'God so loved the world that He gave His only Son, that whoever believes in Him shall not perish. but have eternal life'. JOHN 3:16. Again, 'in Him (Christ) all the fullness of God was pleased to dwell, and through Him (Christ) to reconcile to Himself (God) all things, whether on earth or in heaven, making peace by the blood of His (Christ's) cross.
COL 1:19-20.

But what does this 'RECONCILIATION' mean ? The same word is translated 'ATONEMENT' in ROMANS 5:11. and an 'ATONEMENT' denotes either an action by which two conflicting parts are made 'AT ONE', or the state in which their oneness is enjoyed and expressed. This 'ATONEMENT', Paul says, we have 'RECEIVED' through our Lord and Saviour Jesus Christ. We have not, ourselves, achieved it by our own effort; we have received it from Christ as a gift. Sin caused an estrangement; the Cross, the Crucifixion of Christ, has accomplished an ATONEMENT.

Sin bred ENMITY; the Cross has brought PEACE. Sin created a gulf between man and God; the Cross has bridged it. Sin broke the fellowship; the Cross has restored it. To state the same truth in different words, as Paul did to the ROMANS. 'the wages of sin is death, but the free gift of God is eternal life in Christ Jesus our Lord'. ROM 6:23.

But why was the Cross necessary for our Salvation ? Is it REALLY vital to Christianity ? What exactly did it achieve ? The centrality and meaning of the Cross are what we must now go on to consider.

THE CENTRALITY OF THE CROSS: In order to grasp the Death of Jesus as a SACRIFICE for sin (that is central to the message of the Bible), we must go back to the Old Testament. Old Testament religion was sacrificial from the beginning. Ever since Abel brought lambs from his flock and 'the Lord had regard for Abel and his offering' worshippers of Jehovah brought sacrifices to God. Altars were built, animals were killed and blood was shed long before the Law of Moses. But under Moses, after the covenant had been ratified between God and the people at Mount Sinai, what had been somewhat haphazard was regularized by Divine Ordinance.

The great Prophets of the eighth and seventh centuries BC protested against the formalism and immorality of the worshippers, but the sacrificial system continued without interruption until the destruction of the Temple In 70 AD. Every Jew was familiar with the ritual attached to burnt offering, trespass offering and their appropriate drink offerings, as well with the special occasions. daily; weekly; monthly; and yearly, when they had to be offered. No Jew could have failed to learn the fundamental lessons of all this educative process that 'the life of the flesh is in the blood' , and that 'without the shedding of blood. there is no forgiveness of sins. LEV 17:11   HEB 9:22.

The Old Testament sacrifices foreshadowed the sacrifice of

Christ in visible symbol; the Prophets and Psalmists foretold it in words. We can see Christ in the persecuted but innocent victim described in certain Psalms that were later applied to Jesus. We detect Jesus in Zechariah's shepherd who is smitten and whose sheep are scattered abroad, and in Daniel's Prince or 'anointed one' who is 'cut off'. Above all, we can find Christ in the noble figure who appears in the Servant Songs towards the end of the prophecy of Isiah, the suffering servant of Jehovah, the despised 'man of sorrows', who is wounded for the transgressions of others, is led like a lamb to the slaughter and bears the sins of many. Truly, 'thus it is written. that the Christ should suffer. ZECH 13:7; DAN 9:25; ISA 53: MARK 14:27 LUKE 24:46.

When Jesus came, He knew Himself to be a Son of destiny. He knew the Scriptures were bearing witness to him; that it was in Him that their expectations were to be fulfilled. This is particularly clear in references to His coming sufferings. The turning point of Christ's Ministry came at Caesarea Philippi when, immediately after Simon Peter had confessed Him to be the Christ. 'He began to teach them that the Son of man must suffer many things'. Mark 8:31 Luke 17:25

It is this 'MUST', this sense of COMPULSION laid upon Christ via the Father's Will, that continually recurs in Christ's teaching. Christ had 'a Baptism to be Baptized with', and felt Himself constrained until it was accomplished. Christ kept moving steadily towards what He called His 'hour', that, in the Gospel narrative, is said several times. At last, shortly before His arrest. with the Cross in sight. He could say, 'Father, the hour has come'. JOHN 17:1.

When at last the moment of Christ's arrest arrived, and Simon Peter lunged out with a sword to protect Him. slashing the ear of the High Priest's servant, Jesus rebuked Peter, 'Put your sword into its sheath; shall I not drink the cup that the Father has given Me ?' According to Matthew, Jesus added, 'Do you think that I cannot appeal to My Father, and He will at once send Me more than twelve legions of angels ? But how then should the Scriptures be fulfilled, that it must be done ?' MATT 26:53; MARK 8:31; LUKE 12:50; JOHN 12:27 & 17:1 & 18:11.

The supreme importance of the cross that the Old Testament foretold, and Jesus taught, is fully recognized by the New Testament writers. The writers of the four Gospels devote a disportionate amount of space to Christ's last week and death in comparison to the rest of His life and Ministry. Two-fifths of the first Gospel; three-fifths of the second; one-third of the third; and almost one-half of the fourth, are given to an account of the events between Christ's triumphal entry into Jerusalem. and His triumphant ascension into heaven. It is particularly striking in the case of John, whose Gospel has sometimes been divided into two equal halves, that have been entitled 'The Book of the Signs' and 'The Book of the Passion'.

What is implied in the Gospels is stated EXPLICITLY in the Epistles. Paul never, never grew tired of reminding us of the Cross. Paul had a vivid sense of INDEBTEDNESS TO OUR SAVIOUR who had died for us. 'The Son of God... loved me', he could write, 'and gave Himself for me', and therefore, 'far be it from me to glory except in the Cross of our Lord Jesus Christ'.

To the Corinthians, who were in danger of being entangled in the subtleties of Greek philosophy, Paul wrote, 'Jews demand signs and Greeks seek wisdom, but we preach Christ crucified, a stumbling block to Jews and folly to Gentiles, but to those who are called, both Jews and Greeks, Christ the power of God and the wisdom of God'. This is what Paul had in fact proclaimed when he first came to Corinth from Athens on his second missionary journey. 'I decided to know nothing among you except Jesus Christ and Him crucified', and again, 'I delivered to you as of first importance what I also received, that Christ died for our sins in accordance with the Scriptures'.
1 COR 1:22 & 2:2 & 15:3;
GAL 2:20 & 6:14.

The same emphasis on the Cross can be found in the rest of the New Testament. In the Epistle to the Hebrews comes the UNEQUIVOCAL STATEMENT that Christ 'has appeared once for all at the end of the age to put away sin by the Sacrifice of Himself' When we read the mysterious and wonderful Book of the REVELATION, we catch a glimpse of the Glorious Jesus in Heaven, not only as 'the Lion of the tribe of Judah' but also as 'a Lamb standing, as though it had been slain', and we hear the countless multitude of the Saints and Angels singing His Praise. 'worthy is the Lamb who was slain, to receive power and wealth and wisdom and might and honour and Glory and Blessing!' HEB 9:26: Rev 5:5 & 6:12.

From the early chapters of Genesis to the final chapters of the Revelation, we can trace what some writers have called a SCARLET THREAD. It is, in fact, like the thread of Thesaurus that enables us to find our way through the labyrinth of Scripture.

What the Bible teaches concerning the CENTRALITY of the Cross, the true Christian Church has recognized. Many Churches mark us with the sign of the Cross at our Baptism, and erect a Cross over our grave when we are dead. Some Christians wear a Cross on lapel, necklace or chain. None of this is accidental. The Cross is the symbol of our Faith. The Christian faith is 'the faith of Christ crucified'. What the Emperor of Constantine is said to have seen in the sky, we can see ourselves in the pages of the Bible; 'In hoc signo vinces'; (in this sign you shall conquer). There is no conquest without the Cross; There is no Christianity without the Cross. But WHY ? WHAT does it mean ?

THE MEANING OF THE CROSS: We CANNOT begin to unfold the meaning of the death of Christ. without first confessing that MUCH remains a Mystery. Christians believe that the Cross is the PIVOTAL event in history; no wonder that our puny minds cannot fully take it in! One day the veil will be altogether removed; all the riddles will be solved. We will see Christ as He is, and worship Him through eternity for what He has done. 'Now we see in a mirror dimly, but then face to face. Now I know in part; then I shall understand fully, even as I have been fully understood'. So said the great apostle PAUL, with his massive Intellect, and his many revelations; and if Paul said it, how much MORE should we ?   1 COR 13:12.

We will confine ourselves to what Simon Peter wrote about the death of Jesus in his first Epistle. I turn to his writings on purpose. I have three reasons:

The FIRST reason is that Peter was one of the INNER and INTIMATE group of three apostles, 'Peter, James and John' form a trio who enjoyed a closer fellowship with Jesus, than the rest of the Twelve. Peter is as likely as anyone to have grasped what Jesus THOUGHT and TAUGHT concerning His death. In fact, we find, in his first letter, several clear reminiscences of his MASTER'S teaching.

SECOND. I turn to Peter with confidence, because at the beginning, he was, himself, very reluctant to accept the necessity of Christ's sufferings. He had been the first to acknowledge the UNIQUENESS of Christ's person, but he was also the first to deny the NEED for Christ's death; Peter had declared, 'Thou art the Christ', shouted 'No, Lord' when Jesus began to teach that the Christ must suffer. Throughout the remaining days of Jesus' ministry, Peter retained his dogged hostility to the idea of a Christ who would die. He tried to defend Christ in the garden, and when Christ's arrest was a fait accompli, followed Christ at a distance. In sullen disillusionment, he denied Christ three times in the courtyard, and the tears he wept were not only of REMORSE, but also of DESPAIR.

Only after the resurrection, when Jesus taught the apostles from the Scripture that it WAS necessary that the Christ should suffer these things and enter into His Glory, did Peter at last, begin to understand and believe. Within a few weeks Peter had laid hold of the truth so firmly, that he could address the crowd in the Temple cloisters with the words, 'what God foretold by the mouth of all the prophets, that His Christ should suffer, He thus fulfilled', and Peter's first letter contains several references to 'the sufferings and Glory of the Christ'. We too may at first be reluctant to admit the NECESSITY of the Cross, and slow to fathom its meaning, but if anyone can persuade and teach us, it will be Simon Peter.   ACTS 13: 32-33

THIRD, the references to the Cross in Peter's first Epistle are aside. (apart/digression). If Peter were deliberately marshalling arguments to prove that the death of Jesus was indispensable, we might suspect him of having some 'axe to grind'. But his allusions are more ethical than doctrinal. He simply urges his readers to live their Christian lives consistently, and to bear their suffering patiently, and then refers them to the Cross for their inspiration.

<u>CHRIST DIED FOR OUR EXAMPLE:</u> PERSECUTION is the background to this Epistle. The Emperor Nero was known to be hostile to the Christian Church, and the hearts of many Christians were failing them out of fear. Already spasmodic outbreaks of violence had occurred. It seemed that worse was to come.

The advice Peter gives is straightforward.   1 PET 2:18-25. If Christian servants are ill-treated by pagan masters, let them be SURE that they are not receiving a punishment that they deserve. It is no credit to them to accept a beating for wrongdoing. Let them rather suffer for righteousness' sake, and welcome reproach for the name of Christ. They are not to resist, still less to retaliate. They must submit. To bear unjust suffering patiently has God's approval. Then at once, Peter's mind flies to the Cross. Undeserved suffering is part of the Christian's calling, he asserts, 'because Christ also suffered for you, leaving you an example, that you should follow His steps'.

Christ was sinless and guileless. Yet, when He was insulted,

He took no revenge; when He suffered, He uttered no threats. He simply committed Himself, or as the text may rather read He committed them (His tormentors) into the hands of the Just Judge of all mankind.

Christ has left us an example. The Greek word is unique here in the New Testament, it denotes a teacher's copybook, the perfect alphabet on which a pupil models his script as he learns to write. So if we would master the A B C's of Christian love, we must trace out our lives according to the pattern of Jesus. We must 'follow in His steps'. The verb is eloquent, as used by The Holy Ghost through Peter. Peter had boasted he would follow Jesus to prison and to death, but during the 'event', he 'followed afar off'. On the shore of Galilee Jesus renewed His call and commission to Peter, in His familiar terms 'Follow Me'. So Peter was urging his readers to join him, as he tried NOW to follow more obediently in the Master's steps.

The challenge of the Cross is as uncomfortable in this twentieth century, as it was in the first century; and is as relevant today, as it was then. Perhaps nothing is more completely opposed to our natural instincts, than this Command not to resist, but to bear unjust suffering, and overcome evil with good. Yet the Cross bids us to accept injury; love our enemies; and leave the outcome to God.

The death of Jesus is more than an inspiring example however. If it were NOT more than this, much in the story of the Gospels would be inexplicable. There are those strange sayings, for instance, in which Christ said He would 'give His life as a ransom for many', and shed His blood - 'blood of the covenant', He called it - 'for the forgiveness of sins'. MATT

26:28   Mark 10:45. There is no redemption in an example. A pattern cannot secure our pardon.

Besides, why was Jesus burdened with such heavy and anxious foreboding as the Cross approached ? How can we explain the dreadful agony in the garden, Christ's tears and cries, and bloody sweat ? 'My Father, if it be possible, let this cup pass from Me; nevertheless, not as I will, but as Thou wilt'. Again, 'My Father, if this cannot pass unless I drink it, Thy will be done'.   MATT 26:39   MARK 14:36

Was the cup that Jesus shrank from, the symbol of death by crucifixion ? Was Jesus then, afraid of pain and death ? If so, His example may have been one of SUBMISSION and PATIENCE, but it was hardly one of COURAGE. Socrates, Plato tells us, drank his cup of hemlock, in the prison cell in Athens 'quite readily and cheerfully'. Was Socrates braver than Jesus ? Or were their cups filled with different poison ? And what is the meaning of the darkness, and the cry of dereliction, and the rending from top to bottom of the Temple curtain before the Holy of Hollies ? These things have no explanation if Jesus died only as an example; they seem to make His example less exemplary. Christ's death was an ATONEMENT.

Much in the Scriptures remain mysterious if Christ's death were purely an example, but our human need would remain unsatisfied. We need MORE than AN EXAMPLE: we need a SAVIOUR. An example can stir our imagination; kindle our idealism; and strengthen our resolve. but it cannot cleanse the defilement of our sins; bring peace to our troubled conscience; or reconcile us to God.

In any case, the apostles leave us in no doubt about the matter. They regularly associate Christ's coming and death, WITH OUR SINS:

'Christ died for our sins in accordance with the Scriptures'.
'Christ also died for sins once for all'
'You know that He appeared to take away sins'.
1 COR 15:3   1 PET 3:18   1 JOHN 3:5.

Here are the three GREAT apostolic writers of the New Testament, PETER, JOHN and PAUL, UNANIMOUS in linking Christ's death with our sins.

<u>CHRIST DIED AS OUR SAVIOUR:</u> The relationship between Christ's death, and our sins is this: 'He Himself bore our sins in His body on the tree'. 1 PET 2:24. The expression to 'bear sin' is rather a foreign sound in our ears, and we need to go back to the Old Testament to understand it. The idea occurs FREQUENTLY in the Books of LEVITICUS and NUMBERS. Many times it is written of an offender that breaks God's revealed laws that, 'he shall bear his iniquity' (the offender), or 'he shall bear his sin'. For instance, 'If anyone sins, doing any of the things which the Lord God has Commanded not to be done... he is guilty and shall bear his iniquity'. The expression can only mean one thing. To 'bear sin' is to suffer the consequences of one's sin,; TO BEAR ITS PENALTY. LEV 5:17.

But at times it is implied that SOMEBODY ELSE can assume responsibility for the sinner, (i.e. Intercessory Prayer). In the thirtieth chapter of the Book of NUMBERS, that deals with the VALIDITY OF VOWS, Moses explains that a Vow taken by a man or a widow MUST STAND. A vow, however, taken by an unmarried girl, or by a married woman, MUST BE VALIDATED by her father (unmarried), or by her husband (married) respectively. IF. on the day that the man (husband/father) hears of the woman's vow, he does NOT INVALIDATE IT, and it later proves to be foolish, it is said, 'HE shall bear HER iniquity'. Another example comes toward the end of the Book of LAMENTATIONS, in which, after the destruction of Jerusalem, the Israelites cry; 'Our fathers sinned, and are no more; and WE bear THEIR iniquities'.

This POSSIBILITY of somebody else ACCEPTING the responsibility for, and bearing the CONSEQUENCES OF, OUR SINS WAS FURTHER taught by those Old Testament BLOOD SACRIFICES in the Mosaic legislation that seems so strange to us today. EXODUS 20:5-6 EZEK 4:4-6.

Of the sin offering, it was said that God had given it to 'bear the iniquity of the congregation; to make atonement FOR them, before the Lord'. Similarly, on the annual Day of Atonement, Aaron was instructed to lay his hands on the head of the SCAPEGOAT, thereby identifying himself, and his people, with it: he was then to confess the nations sins, SYMBOLICALLY transferring them to the goat, that was then driven out into the wilderness; then we read, 'The goat shall bear all their iniquities upon him to a solitary land'.   LEV 10:17 & 16:22. It is PLAIN from this, that to 'BEAR' somebody else's sin, is to become his SUBSTITUTE, to bear the PENALTY of his sin, in his place.

Despite this remarkable TEMPORARY provision, 'it is IMPOSSIBLE that the blood of bulls and lambs should take away sins', as the Holy Ghost says via the writer of HEBREWS. So in the longest Servant Song of Isaiah (chapter 53:), the innocent suffer (that foreshadows Jesus), is described in terms that are INTENTIONALLY sacrificial. Jesus was 'like a lamb that is led to the slaughter', because 'He opened not His mouth' and because 'the Lord has laid on Him the iniquity of us all', so that Christ's soul was made 'an offering for sin'. WE ALL 'like sheep have gone astray', but Jesus also, 'like a sheep' 'was wounded for our transgressions, He was bruised for our iniquities; upon Him was the chastisement that made us whole, and with His stripes we are healed'. ALL THIS CLEAR LANGUAGE OF SUBSTITUTION, describing Jesus as 'stricken for the transgressions of My people', is summed up in the chapter, in the two phrases with which we have been made aware of by LEVITICUS, 'He shall bear their iniquities' and 'He bore the sins of many'.

When at last, after centuries of preparation, Jesus Christ Himself arrived. John the Baptist greeted Him publicly, with the extraordinary words: 'behold, the Lamb of God, who takes away the sins of the world!' Similarly, when the New Testament came to be written by The Holy Ghost, via various authors, had no difficulty in recognizing the death of Jesus as the FINAL sacrifice, in which ALL the Old Testament sacrifices WERE fulfilled. This TRUTH is an important part of the message of HEBREWS. The old sacrifices were of bulls, lambs and goats: CHRIST OFFERED HIMSELF. The old sacrifices were interminably repeated: CHRIST DIED ONCE AND FOR ALL. Christ was 'offered once to bear the sins of many'.

The last words are via PAUL; these are among the most STARTLING in the whole Biblical teaching about the ATONEMENT. And we CANNOT escape their SIGNIFICANCE.

In previous verses (2 COR 5:), Paul has AFFIRMED that God refused to impute our sins to us, or count them against us, THAT is God's utterly UNDESERVED love for us. Then, WHAT did God Do ??? 'For our sake He made Him (Jesus) to be sin who knew no sin, so that in Him we might become the righteousness of God'. Jesus Christ had NO SINS of His own; He was made sin with our sins, on the cross.

As we look at the Cross, we can BEGIN to understand the TERRIBLE IMPLICATIONS of these words. At twelve noon 'there was darkness over the whole land', that continued for three hours, until Jesus died. With the darkness came silence, for no eye should see, and no lips could tell, THE AGONY OF SOUL THAT THE SPOTLESS LAMB OF GOD NOW ENDURED. The ACCUMULATED sins of ALL HUMAN HISTORY, WERE LAID UPON JESUS. VOLUNTARILY Jesus bore all this sin in His OWN BODY. Jesus MADE them HIS OWN. Jesus SHOULDERED FULL RESPONSIBILITY FOR THEM.

And then, in DESOLATE spiritual abandonment, that cry was WRUNG from His lips, 'MY GOD, MY GOD, WHY HAST THOU FORSAKEN ME ? (it was a quotation from the first verse of PSALM 22). But why did He quote THAT verse ??? Why not one of the TRIUMPHANT verses at the end ? Why not, 'You who fear the Lord, praise Him!' Or ' Dominion belongs to the Lord ? Are we to believe it was a cry of human weakness and despair ? Or that the Son of God was imagining things ?

NO! These words must be taken at their face value. Jesus quoted this verse of Scripture, (as He quoted all others), because

He KNEW He Himself was FULFILLING it... Jesus WAS bearing our sins, and the STARK REALITY, was being "driven home", GOD, who is 'of purer eyes than to behold evil' and CANNOT/ WILL NOT 'look on sin' TURNED AWAY HIS FACE. (as He does to this day (and forever)). OUR SINS came between the Father and the Son. The Lord Jesus Christ who was eternally with the Father; who enjoyed UNBROKEN communion with the Father, throughout His life on earth, WAS MOMENTARILY ABANDONED. Our sins sent Christ to hell. Jesus tasted the TORMENT of a soul estranged from God. Bearing our sins, Jesus died OUR death. Jesus endured, instead of us, the PENALTY of SEPARATION FROM GOD, that WE deserved.   HAB 1:13

Then, EMERGING from that outer utter darkness, Jesus cried, IN TRIUMPH, 'IT IS FINISHED', and finally, 'FATHER, INTO THY HANDS I COMMIT MY SPIRIT'. And then Jesus died. The work He had come to do was completed. The Salvation He had come to win was accomplished. The sins of the world were borne. Reconciliation to God was now AVAILABLE to ALL who would trust Jesus, FOR THEMSELVES, and RECEIVE Him AS THEIR OWN.

IMMEDIATELY, as if to demonstrate this TRUTH publicly, the unseen hand of God tore down the curtain of the Temple, and hurled it aside; it was needed no longer. The way into God's Holy presence was NO LONGER barred. Christ had 'opened the gate of heaven' to ALL BELIEVERS. ANYBODY can access God THROUGH JESUS CHRIST, from that day forward; but ONLY through Jesus Christ. And thirty six hours later, Christ was raised from death, to PROVE He had not died in vain.

This SIMPLE and WONDERFUL fact of the SIN BEARING of the Son of God...is strangely UNPOPULAR today. That Jesus should have borne OUR sins, and taken OUR penalty, is said to be IMMORAL or UNWORTHY, or UNJUST of our Heavenly Father, by MANY unthinking (trapped within their OWN empirical thinking, (God mocking them to their faces)). 'Scholars'(?) and 'Theologians'(?), and like-minded Pastors and lay people, as well as MANY 'Educators'(?) of these, the final days. They CANNOT see their PRIDE and ARROGANCE and HYPOCRISY, for the reasons already stated above. MATT 11:25 & 13:14; ROM 11:8 & :20; DEUT 29:3; ISA 29:10, AT ENMITY WITH THEIR SOULS. The exaltation of SELF, at the expense of GOD. Within satan's realm, truth can EASILY be travestied.

It is NOT suggested there is nothing left for sinners to do; they must turn 'to the Shepherd and Guardian of our souls', dying to sin and living to righteousness, as Peter went on to say. Above all, we don't forget that 'all this is from God', issuing from His UNIMAGINABLE MERCY. We are NOT to think of Jesus Christ as a third party, wresting Salvation for us from a God unwilling to save.

The initiative was with God Himself. 'God was in Christ reconciling the world unto Himself'. Precisely HOW God could have been in Christ, while He made Christ to be sin for us, I can't explain, but the same apostle states BOTH truths in the same paragraph. And we MUST accept this paradox, along with the equally baffling paradox that Jesus of Nazareth WAS both God and man, and yet one Person. If there WAS a paradox in His Person, it is NOT surprising that we find one in His work as well. 2 COR 5:19.

But even if we CANNOT resolve the paradox, or fathom the 'mystery', we should believe the direct statement of Christ, and His apostles, that He bore our sins, understanding the phrase in its Biblical meaning, that Christ underwent the penalty of our sins for us.

That Peter meant this is clear from three considerations;
1. Peter says that it was on the 'tree' that Christ bore our sins. There can be no doubt the word was used deliberately, just as he did in his early sermons recorded in ACTS, he said, 'The God of our fathers raised Jesus whom you killed by hanging Him on a tree'. His Jewish listeners would have had no difficulty in grasping his implied reference to DEUT 21:23, 'Cursed be every one who hangs on a tree'. The fact that Jesus ended His life hanging on a 'tree' (the Jews regarded nailing to a cross and hanging on a tree as equivalents) , meant that Jesus was under the Divine curse.

Instead of repudiating this idea; the apostles ACCEPTED it, and Paul explained it in GAL 3:13. Paul pointed out that it was also written in DEUTERONOMY: 'cursed be every one who does not abide by all things written in the Book of the Law, and do them'. But then Christ redeemed us from the curse of the Law, having become a curse for us for it is written, 'cursed be every one who hangs on a tree'. The meaning of these verses in the context is plain and INESCAPABLE. It is this: the righteous curse of the broken Law which rests on the transgressors, was transferred to Jesus on the Cross. Jesus HAS freed us from the curse, by taking it upon Himself when He died.

2. 1 PETER 2: contains no fewer than five CLEAR verbal reminiscences of ISAIAH 53:

1 PET 2:	ISAIAS 53:
:22 He committed no sin; no guile was found on His lips.	:9 He had done no violence, and there was no deceit in His mouth.
:23 He was reviled.	:3 He was despised and rejected by men.
:24 He Himself bore our sins.	:12 He bore the sins of many.
By His wounds you have been healed	:5 With His stripes we are healed.
:25 You were straying like sheep	:6 All we like sheep have gone astray.

We have already seen that this chapter portrays an innocent sufferer who, in a Sacrificial death, is wounded for the transgressions of others. It Is beyond question that Jesus Himself interpreted His mission and death in the light of this chapter, as did His followers after Him. When the Ethiopian eunuch asked the evangelist Philip to whom the prophet was referring in this passage (that he was reading in his chariot) Philip immediately 'told him the good news of Jesus'. ACTS 8:35.

3. Peter has other references to the Cross in his letter, that confirm our interpretation of his words in the second chapter (1 PET), He describes his readers as having been 'ransomed with the precious blood of Christ, like that of a lamb without blemish

or spot', and even as having been 'sprinkled' with His blood'.1 PET 1:2 & :18-19.

Both expressions allude to the original Passover sacrifice at the time of the Exodus. EACH Israelite family took a lamb, killed it, and sprinkled its blood on the lintel and side posts of the house. ONLY in this way, were they safe from the judgment of God, and only so, did they escape from the slavery of Egypt. Peter BOLDLY applies the Passover symbolism to Christ (as does Paul also, 'Christ our paschal lamb, has been sacrificed' 1COR5:7). Christ's blood was shed to redeem us from the judgment of God, and the BONDAGE of sin. IF we are to benefit from it, it must be sprinkled on our hearts, that is, applied to each one of us INDIVIDUALLY.

Peter's other significant reference to the Cross Is in 1 PET 3:18; 'Christ also died for sins once for all, the righteous for the unrighteous, that He might bring us to God...' Sin had separated us FROM God; but Christ desired to bring us BACK to God. So He suffered for our sins, an innocent Saviour dying for guilty sinners. And He did it 'once for all', DECISIVELY, so that what Jesus did CANNOT be REPEATED or IMPROVED upon, or even supplemented.

WE MUST NOT MISS THE IMPLICATION OF THIS! It means that no religious observances or good deeds of ours could EVER EARN OUR FORGIVENESS. Yet, a great many people in the post Christian west have fallen into this CARICATURE of Christianity. They, then, (understandably) see no fundamental difference between the Christian Gospel and the eastern religions. Because they regard all religion as a system of HUMAN MERIT.

'God helps those who help themselves', they say. But there is no POSSIBILITY of RECONCILING that notion with the Cross of Christ. Christ died to atone for our sins, for the simple reason, that we cannot atone for them ourselves. If we could, Christ's atoning death would be redundant. To claim that we can secure God's favour by our own efforts, is to insult Jesus Christ: it is tantamount to saying that we can manage without Christ; Christ really need not have bothered to die. As Paul put it, 'if justification (i.e. acceptance with God) were through the law i.e. (through our obedience), then Christ died to no purpose. GAL 2:21.

The message of the Cross REMAINS, in our day, as in Paul's; folly to the wise, and a stumbling block to the self-righteous, but it has brought PEACE to the conscience of MILLIONS. As RICHARD HOOKER wrote:
> let it be accounted folly, or frenzy, or fury, or
> whatever. It is our wisdom and our comfort; we care
> for no knowledge in the world but this, that man has
> sinned and God has suffered; that God has made Himself
> the sin of men, and that men are made in the
> righteousness of God. RICHARD HOOKER. 1585.

EVERY Christian can echo these words. There is HEALING through His wounds, life through His death; pardon through His pain; Salvation through His suffering.

<u>THE SALVATION OF CHRIST:</u> 'SALVATION' is a wonderful comprehensive term. It is a GREAT MISTAKE to suppose it is merely a synonym for FORGIVENESS. God is as much concerned with our present and future, as with our past. God's plan is to:

RECONCILE US TO HIMSELF;
LIBERATE US FROM OUR SELF-CENTREDNESS,
SELFISHNESS and SIN; and to
BRING US INTO HARMONY WITH OUR FELLOW MAN

We owe our forgiveness and reconciliation mainly to THE DEATH OF CHRIST, but it is by HIS SPIRIT, that we can be set free from ourselves; and In HIS CHURCH, that we can be united in a FELLOWSHIP OF LOVE. These are the aspects of Christ's Salvation that we will consider.

THE SPIRIT OF CHRIST: Our sins should NOT be seen as a series of UNRELATED INCIDENTS, but as SYMPTOMS of an INWARD MORAL DISEASE. To illustrate this, Jesus several times used the similie of the TREE and the FRUIT. The QUALITY of the fruits, He taught, depends on the quality of the tree that bears them:

> 'Every sound tree bears good fruit, but the bad tree bears evil fruit. A sound tree cannot bear evil fruit, nor can a bad tree bear good fruit'.
> LUKE 6:43-45

The CAUSE of our sins, is OUR SIN; our INHERITED NATURE, which is PERVERTED, SELF-CENTRED, and SELFISH (inherited from Adam and Eve, via Original Sin). As Jesus put it, our sins come from WITHIN, out of our 'HEART'. An improvement in response and behaviour patterns, depends on a CHANGE of nature... (a change in response and behaviour patterns; OUR effort). 'Make the tree good', said Jesus, 'and its fruit will be good.

But can human nature be changed ? Is it possible to make a SOUR person SWEET ? a PROUD person HUMBLE ? or a selfish person UNSELFISH ? The Bible declares EMPHATICALLY that these miracles CAN take place. It is part of the Glory of the Gospel. Jesus offers to change not only our standing before God, but also our very nature. Jesus spoke to Nicodemus of the indispensable necessity of a NEW BIRTH, and His words are STILL APPLICABLE TO US: 'Truly truly, I say to you, unless one is born anew, he cannot see the kingdom of God. Do not marvel that I said to you', 'you must be born anew'   JOHN 3:

Paul's statement is even more dramatic; Paul blurts out, a sentence that has no verbs: 'If anyone in Christ - new creation!' 2 COR 5:17. Here is the possibility the New Testament speaks of: A NEW HEART, A NEW NATURE, A NEW BIRTH, A NEW CREATION. This TREMENDOUS inward change, is the work of the Holy Spirit of Christ; this new birth 'from above'. To be born again is to be 'born of the spirit' of Christ.

If Christ's Holy Spirit has not taken up residence within us, we are NOT REAL CHRISTIANS at all. 'Any one who does not have the (Holy) Spirit of Christ does not belong to Him'. ACTS 2:4 ROM 8:9   EPHA 5:18. This is what the New Testament teaches. ACTS 16:7 ROM 8:9-11 ROM 15:5-6 GAL 4:6 PHIL 1:19.

When we put our trust in Jesus Christ, surrender our ALL (12 apostles) to Him, and commit ourselves to Him, the Holy Spirit of Christ is sent by God, 'into our hearts'. He makes our bodies His temple. 1 COR 6:19   GAL 4:6.

This does NOT MEAN THAT, FROM NOW ON, WE ARE EXEMPT. from the possibility of sinning. On the contrary, in some ways, the conflict is INTENSIFIED; but on the other hand, a way of victory HAS been opened for us. PAUL gives a VIVID description of the BATTLE in GAL 5:19-26   ROM 7:15-25. The COMBATANTS are the FLESH, (PAUL'S name for our INHERITED self-centred and sinful human nature), and the Holy Spirit of Christ. 'The desires of the flesh', he explains, 'are AGAINST the Spirit, and the desires of the Spirit are against the flesh; for these are opposed to each other'.

This is NOT arid 'theological theorizing'; it is FACT, it is the DAILY experience of every Christian. We continue to be conscious of sinful desires, that are tugging us down; but we NOW also have, a COUNTERACTING FORCE, pulling us upward to Holiness. If 'the flesh' were given free rein, it would stampede us into the jungle of immoral and selfish vices Paul lists. GAL 5:19-21. If, on the other hand, the Holy Spirit of Christ is allowed His way, the result will be 'love, joy, peace, patience, kindness, goodness, faithfulness, gentleness, self-control'. These virtues Paul names 'the fruit of the Spirit'. Our human nature is likened to an orchard, that the Holy Spirit of Christ is cultivating.   Let Christ make the tree good, and the fruit will be good also.

HOW, then, can 'the flesh' be subdued, so that 'the fruit of the Spirit' may grow and ripen ? The answer lies in the INNER ATTITUDE that WE adopt towards each. 'Those who belong to Christ Jesus, have crucified the flesh with its passions and desirers'. 'Walk by (or in) the Spirit of Christ, and DO NOT (or you will not) gratify the desires of the flesh'. GEN   17:2.

(Come out of the Garden; take up your Cross; go on to your Calvary.

Towards 'the flesh', WE must take up such an ATTITUDE of FIERCE RESISTANCE and RUTHLESS REJECTION, that only the word 'CRUCIFIED' can describe it; but to the indwelling Spirit of Christ, we must TRUSTFULLY SURRENDER the undisputed dominion of Christ over our lives. The more we make a HABIT of DENYING the flesh, and OBEYING the Spirit of Jesus, the more the ugly works of the flesh will disappear, and the lovely fruit of the Spirit of Christ WILL take their place, in PRECISE ratio to our SINCERITY. If WE do not DO this, via self-discipline, it does not get done, and we stay on 'square one', (babe in Christ), advancing no further, then sliding back. (slack abiding produces backsliding).

2 COR 3:18: 'We all, with unveiled faces, beholding the glory of the Lord, (Jesus), are being changed into His likeness from one degree of glory to another; (milk - meat & potatoes) for this comes from the Lord Jesus who is the Spirit'. It is by the Spirit of Christ that we CAN be TRANSFORMED into the image of Christ, as we keep looking steadfastly towards Him, IMITATING Him. WE have OUR part to play, via REPENTANCE, FAITH, and DISCIPLINE. And if this is NOT done, we will NEVER advance beyond the 'babe in Christ' stage, where, unfortunately, many 'SAVED AND STUCK' Christians remain, their entire lifetime, and EVERYONE loses; God, themselves, and mankind.

Archbishop William Temple illustrated the point this way: 'It is no good giving me a play like Hamlet or King Lear, and telling me to write a play like that. Shakespeare could do it; I can't.

And it is no good showing me a life like the life of Jesus, and telling me to live a life like that. Jesus could do it; I can't. But if the genius of Shakespeare could come and live in me, then I could write plays like that. And if the Spirit of Jesus could come and live in me, then I could live a life like that. This is the secret of Christian Sanctity. It is not that we should strive to live like Jesus, but that Jesus by His Holy Spirit, should come and live in us. To have Jesus as our example is not enough; we need Him as our Saviour. It is thus through His atoning death that the penalty of our sins may be forgiven; it is through His indwelling Holy Spirit that the power of our sins may be broken'. ARCHBISHOP WILLIAM TEMPLE 1942.

It is hardly relevant here, to discuss the mysterious doctrine of The Trinity. For our present purpose, it is sufficient to consider what the apostles wrote about the Holy Ghost as their teaching was illuminated by their experience.

First, however, it is important to realize that The Holy Ghost neither came into existence, nor began to be active, at Pentecost. The Holy Ghost is God. He is, therefore, eternal and has been at work in the world since creation. The Old Testament contains many references to the Holy Ghost, and the prophets looked forward to the time when The Holy Ghost's activity would increase and spread; when God would put His Holy Ghost's Spirit within His people, dispatched by God, to solid, standing, mature, instruments and servants of God, at the MEAT/SOLID FOOD level of Spiritual Development, replacing the Holy Spirit of Christ. which will have done its work. (milk to junior food).

What the Old Testament prophets foretold, Christ promised as an immediate expectation. A few hours before Jesus died, secluded in the upper room with the apostles, Jesus spoke of 'the Comforter', 'the Spirit of Truth', who would come and take Jesus' place.   JOHN 14:26   & 16:13-15.

The presence of the Holy Ghost's Spirit would be better for them , than Christ's earthly presence had been. 'It is to your advantage that I go away', Jesus said, 'for if I do not go away, the Counsellor will not come to you; but if I go, I will send Him to you'.   JOHN 14:17   & 16:7.

Some skeptical scholars (?) and theologians (?) think that the teaching Ministry of Jesus had proved a failure. Several times Jesus had urged His disciples to humble themselves like a child, but Simon Peter remained proud and self-confident. Often Jesus had told them to love one another, but even John seems to have deserved his nickname 'son of thunder' to the end. However, may I remind them, when you read Peter's first letter, you cannot fail to notice its references to humility, and John's letters are full of love.

WHAT made the difference ? The Spirit of The Holy Ghost. Jesus taught them to be humble and loving; but neither quality appeared in their lives until the Spirit of The Holy Ghost entered in, and began to change them from within.

On the day of Pentecost 'they were filled with the Holy Ghost'. Do not imagine that this was a freak experience for apostles and other eminent saints, although, doubtless, we are NOT to expect a repetition of the outward phenomena like the rushing wind and tongues of fire. However, 'Be filled with the Spirit' is a command addressed to ALL Christians. The inner presence of the Spirit of The Holy Ghost is the spiritual birthright of EVERY Christian that grows and develops spiritually, to the MEAT/SOLID FOOD level of the solid, standing, mature, instrument and servant of God. (See NCRC 6/2 & WANSS 307/2). But NOT for the 'babes in Christ' until their spiritual development has grown to the MEAT/SOLID FOOD level.

<u>THE CHURCH OF CHRIST:</u> The tendency of sin is CENTRIFUGAL. It pulls us out of harmony with our neighbours. It estranges us not only from our Creator, but from our fellow-creatures too. We all know from experience, how a Community, whether college, hospital, factory, or an office or home, or Church, can become a hotbed of jealousy and animosity. We find it VERY difficult 'TO DWELL TOGETHER IN UNITY'.

But GOD'S plan is to RECONCILE us to each other, as well as to HIMSELF. So GOD doesn't save Independent and unconnected individuals, in isolation, from one another; He is calling out 'A PEOPLE' for HIS OWN POSSESSION. (a function of Jesus Christ; to save individuals).

In the early chapters of Genesis this is made clear. God called Abraham to leave his home and relations in Mesopotamia, and promised to give him both a land for his inheritance and descendants, as numerous as the stars in the sky and the sand on the seashore. This pledge to multiply Abraham's posterity and through them, to bless all the nations of the earth was renewed to his son Isaac and his grandson Jacob.

Jacob, however, died in exile in Egypt. But his twelve sons survived him, and became the fathers of the twelve tribes of 'ISRAEL', the name God had given to Jacob. With these 'children of Israel', rescued years later from their Egyptian slavery, God renewed His covenant.

But how were ALL the families of the earth to be blessed ? Century followed century, as the fortunes of Israel unfolded, and still the nation seemed, to the rest of the world, more of a curse than a blessing. Surrounded by high walls of their own building, God's people protected themselves from defiling contact with the unclean Gentiles. It seemed as if they would miss their destiny as benefactors of the WORLD. Was God's promise to Abraham to prove a LIE ? NO! MANY of the prophets KNEW, by the Word of the Lord, that when the Messiah came, GOD'S OWN APPOINTED PRINCE, pilgrims would come from every point of the compass to enter the Kingdom of God.

At last the Christ came. Jesus of Nazareth announced the arrival of the long-awaited Kingdom. MANY would come, He said, from north, south, east and west, and sit down with Abraham, Isaac and Jacob. God's people would no longer be a nation apart, but a society whose members would be drawn from EVERY race, kindred and language. 'GO'... the Risen Lord COMMANDED His followers, 'and make disciples of all nations'... The sum total of these disciples He called "MY CHURCH". MATT 16:18 & 28:19. (HALLELUJAH)

So God's pledge to Abraham, repeated several times to him, and renewed to his sons, IS being FULFILLED in the growth of the WORLD WIDE Church of Jesus Christ today. 'If you are Christ's', Paul wrote, 'THEN YOU ARE ABRAHAM'S OFFSPRING, HEIRS ACCORDING TO PROMISE'. GAL 3: 29.

One of the most striking pictures that Paul uses to convey the UNITY of believers in Christ, is that of the human body. The Church, He says, is THE BODY OF CHRIST. Every Christian is a MEMBER or ORGAN of the body, while Christ HIMSELF is the HEAD, controlling the body's activities. Not every organ has the same function, but EACH is NECESSARY for the maximum HEALTH and USEFULLNESS of the body.

The whole body Is also animated by a COMMON LIFE. This is The Holy Ghost, whose presence makes the body ONE. The Church owes its COHERENT UNITY to that PRESENCE, 'there is one body and one Spirit', EMPHASIZES Paul. Even the outward, organizational divisions of the Church (regrettable as they are), do NOT destroy its INWARD and SPIRITUAL UNITY. THIS IS INDISSOLUBLE, for it is 'THE UNITY OF THE SPIRIT' or 'THE FELLOWSHIP OF THE SPIRIT'. 2 COR 13:13; EPH 4:3-4; PHIL 2:1-2. Our common share in the Holy Ghost makes us DEEPLY and PERMANENTLY ONE.

It is, of course, NONSENSE to claim membership of a great WORLD-WIDE BODY, THE CHURCH UNIVERSAL, without in PRACTICE, sharing in one of its LOCAL MANIFESTATIONS. It is HERE, as MEMBERS OF A LOCAL CHURCH, that we SHALL find OPPORTUNITY to worship God, to enjoy fellowship with one another, and to SERVE THE WIDER COMMUNITY i.e. MENTORS. Again,
H A L L E L U L A H!

MANY today, react AGAINST the Church as an organization, and some entirely REJECT it. Unfortunately, this is often

UNDERSTANDABLE, because the Church can certainly be ARCHAIC, INWARD-LOOKING, and REACTIONARY. However, we must remember, that the Church is PEOPLE - SINFUL and FALLIBLE people. This is NO REASON to shun it, because we are also SINFUL and FALLIBLE OURSELVES.

We must ALSO remember, that not all members of the visible Church are necessarily OF THE REAL CHURCH OF JESUS CHRIST. Some, whose names are inscribed on Church rolls and registers, have NEVER had their names, as Jesus put it, 'WRITTEN IN HEAVEN'. Although this is a FACT to which the Bible often refers, IT IS NOT FOR US TO JUDGE: 'the Lord knows those who are His'. The Pastor, via Baptism, welcomes into the visible Church those who PROFESS faith in Christ. But only God KNOWS, those who actually EXERCISE faith, for only God sees THE HEART. No doubt, the two groups largely overlap. They are NOT, however, IDENTICAL. These things ought NOT TO BE SO.

The Holy Ghost is not only the Author of the common life of the Church, but the CREATOR of its common love as well. The first fruit of The Spirit is love, whose VERY NATURE is love, imparts it to those indwelt. All Christians have known the remarkable experience of being drawn to other Christians that they hardly know, and whose background may be very different than their own. The relationship that EXISTS and GROWS between the children of God, is DEEPER and SWEETER than blood relationships. It is the KINSHIP of the FAMILY OF GOD. Truly, 'we know that we have passed out of death into life, because we love the brethren', as John says. This love is not sentimental. It is not even fundamentally emotional. Its

ESSENCE is self-sacrifice; it MANIFESTS itself in the desire to SERVE, HELP and ENRICH OTHERS, (an interjection...we need MENTORS and INTERCESSORY PRAYER WARRIORS desperately). It is by LOVE that the CENTRIFUGAL FORCE OF SIN is COUNTERACTED, for sin DIVIDES, while love RECONCILES.

The pages of the Church's history have often been smudged by STUPIDITY and SELFISHNESS, even by OPEN DISOBEDIENCE or REBELLION, to the TEACHINGS OF CHRIST. Today, some Churches appear to be DEAD or DYING, rather than VIBRANT WITH LIFE; and others are torn by FACTIONS and BLIGHTED by LOVELESSNESS toward Almighty God and the brethren. Unfortunately, we have to admit, that not all those who PROFESS and call themselves CHRISTIANS exhibit either the LOVE or LIFE OF JESUS CHRIST. i.e. Many SCHOLARS(?) and THEOLOGIANS(?), as well as MISGUIDED LAYPEOPLE, at enmity with their souls, and The Holy Trinity of God.

NEVERTHELESS, The Christian's place is in the LOCAL CHRISTIAN COMMUNITY, HOWEVER IMPERFECT IT MAY BE, there to SEEK the new quality of relationship that the HOLY GHOST gives CHRIST'S people, and in that fellowship, to SHARE in the Church's WORSHIP, WITNESS and SERVICE TO ALL MANKIND.

<u>MAN'S RESPONSE.</u>

<u>COUNTING THE COST:</u> We have considered man's NEED as a SINNER, ESTRANGED FROM GOD, imprisoned in himself, and out of harmony with his fellows; and the main aspects of

the Salvation that Christ has WON for us, and OFFERS to us. It is now time for us to ask the personal question put to Jesus by Saul of Tarsus, on the road to Damascus, 'WHAT SHALL I DO, LORD ?' or the similar question asked by the Philippian jailer, 'WHAT MUST I DO TO BE SAVED ?'

CLEARLY, we must do SOMETHING. Christianity is no mere passive ACQUIESCENCE in a series of PROPOSITIONS, however true. We may believe in the DEITY and the SALVATION of Christ, and ACKNOWLEDGE ourselves to be SINNERS in need of Christ's SALVATION; but this does NOT make us Christians. We MUST make a PERSONAL RESPONSE TO JESUS CHRIST, COMMITTING ourselves UNRESERVEDLY to Christ, as OUR SAVIOUR and LORD

Jesus NEVER concealed the fact that His religion included a DEMAND as well as an OFFER. In fact, the DEMAND was as total as the OFFER was free. If Christ OFFERED men His Salvation, He also DEMANDED their SUBMISSION. Christ gave no encouragement whatever to THOUGHTLESS applicants for discipleship. He brought no PRESSURE to bear, on ANY inquirer. Christ sent IRRESPONSIBLE ENTHUSIASTS away empty. Luke tells us of three men who either VOLUNTEERED, or were INVITED, to follow Jesus; but not one passed THE LORD'S tests. The rich young ruler; moral, earnest and attractive, who wanted eternal life on HIS OWN terms, went away SORROWFUL, with his riches intact, but with NEITHER life nor Christ as his possession.

On another occasion, great crowds were following Jesus. Perhaps shouting their slogans of allegiance and giving an

IMPRESSIVE outward demonstration of their loyalty. But Jesus KNEW how SUPERFICIAL their attachment to Him was. Stopping, and turning around to speak to them, Jesus told a pointed parable in the form of a question:

> "Which of you, desiring to build a tower, does not first sit down and count the cost, whether he has enough to complete it ? Otherwise, when he has laid a foundation, and is not able to finish, all who see it begin to mock him, saying, this man began to build, and was not able to finish".
> LUKE 14:25-30.

The Christian landscape is STREWN with the WRECKAGE of DERELICT, HALF-BUILT TOWERS.. the RUINS of those who began to build, and were UNABLE to finish. THOUSANDS of people STILL ignore Christ's warning, and undertake to follow Him, without first pausing to REFLECT on the COST of doing so. The result is the GREAT SCANDAL of Christendom today, so called 'NOMINAL CHRISTIANITY'. Worldwide, large numbers of people have covered themselves with a decent, BUT THIN, veneer of Christianity.

They have allowed themselves to become 'somewhat' involved; enough to be respectable, but not enough to be UNCOMFORTABLE. Their religion is a GREAT SOFT CUSHION. It protects them from the hard UNPLEASANTNESS of life, while changing its place and shape, to SUIT THEIR CONVENIENCES. No wonder the cynics speak of HYPOCRITES in the Church, and dismiss religion as ESCAPISM.

The message of Jesus was VERY different. Jesus NEVER lowered HIS standards or modified His CONDITIONS, to make His call more readily ACCEPTABLE. Jesus asked His first disciples, and He has asked EVERY disciple since, to give Him their THOUGHTFUL and TOTAL COMMITMENT. NOTHING LESS THAN THIS WILL DO.

Lets discuss PRECISELY what Jesus said:
'He called to Him the multitude with His disciples, and said to them, "If any man would come after Me, let him deny himself and take up his cross and follow Me. For whoever would save his life will lose it; and whoever loses his life for My sake and the Gospel's will save it. For what does it profit a man, to gain the whole world and forfeit his life ? For what can a man give in return for his life? For whoever is ashamed of Me and My words in this adulterous and sinful generation, of him will the Son of man also be ashamed, when He comes in the Glory of His Father with the holy angels". MARK 8:34-38.

THE CALL TO FOLLOW CHRIST: At its simplest, Christ's call was to 'FOLLOW ME'. He asked men and women for their PERSONAL ALLEGIANCE. He invited them to LEARN from Him, to OBEY his words, and to IDENTIFY THEMSELVES with HIS CAUSE.

There can be no FOLLOWING without a previous FORSAKING. To follow Christ, is to RENOUNCE all lesser loyalties. In the days when He lived among men on earth, this meant a LITERAL abandonment of HOME and WORK. Simon and Andrew 'left their nets and followed Him'. James and John 'left their father Zebedee in the boat, with the hired servants, and followed Him'. Matthew, who heard Christ's call while he was 'sitting at the tax office... left everything, and rose and followed Him'.

Today, the call of the Lord Jesus HAS NOT CHANGED. He STILL says 'FOLLOW ME', and adds, 'whoever of you does not renounce all that he has cannot be My disciple'. In practice, however, this does NOT mean, for the majority of Christians, a PHYSICAL departure from their home or job. It implies, rather, an INNER SURRENDER of both, and a refusal to ALLOW either family or ambition to occupy the FIRST PLACE in our lives. Let me be more EXPLICIT about the forsaking that CANNOT be separated from the following of Christ.

There must be A RENUNCIATION OF SIN. This, in a word, is REPENTANCE. It is the FIRST PART of a Christian CONVERSION. Under NO CIRCUMSTANCES to be BYPASSED. REPENTANCE and FAITH belong TOGETHER. We CANNOT follow Christ without FORSAKING SIN.

REPENTANCE is a DEFINITE turning from every THOUGHT, WORD, DEED and HABIT that is known to be wrong. It is NOT sufficient to feel pangs of REMORSE, or to make some kind of APOLOGY to God. Fundamentally, repentance is a matter neither of EMOTION nor of SPEECH. It is an INWARD change of MIND and ATTITUDE towards SIN, that leads to a change of BEHAVIOUR and RESPONSE patterns.

There can be NO COMPROMISE here. There may be sin in our lives that we don't think we EVER could renounce; but we must be WILLING to let them go, as we cry to God for deliverance FROM them. If you are in doubt regarding what is right and what is wrong; what must go, and what may be retained, don't be too greatly influenced by the CUSTOMS and CONVENTIONS of Christians you know. Go to the CLEAR teaching of THE BIBLE (Basic Instructions Before Leaving Earth), and by the prompting of your soul and conscience, and CHRIST will gradually (in PRECISE ratio to your sincerity), lead you further along the path of righteousness. When Christ puts His finger on anything, GIVE IT UP. It may be some ASSOCIATION or RECREATION; some LITERATURE we read, or some ATTITUDE OF PRIDE, JEALOUSY or RESENTMENT, or AN UNFORGIVING SPIRIT.

Jesus told His followers to pluck out their eye and cut off their hand or foot if these caused them to sin. We are not to obey this with dead literalism, of course, and mutilate our bodies. It is a VIVID figure of speech for dealing RUTHLESSLY with the avenues along which TEMPTATION comes to us.

Sometimes, TRUE repentance includes 'RESTITUTION' . This means putting things right with other people whom we may have injured. ALL our sins WOUND GOD, and nothing we can do can heal the wound. ONLY the atoning death of our Saviour, Jesus Christ, can do this. But when our sins have damaged other people, we can sometimes help repair the damage, where we CAN, WE MUST. Zacchaeus, the dishonest tax-collector, more than repaid the money he had stolen from his clients, and promised to give away half of his capital to the poor to compensate (no doubt) for thefts he could not make good. We must follow his example. There may be money or time for us to pay back, rumours to be contradicted, property to return, apologies to be made, or broken relationships to be mended.

We should not be EXCESSIVELY over-scrupulous in this matter however. It would be foolish to rummage through past years, and make an issue of insignificant words or deeds long ago forgotten by the offended person. NEVERTHELESS, we MUST be REALISTIC about this duty. If we REALLY repent, we will want to do EVERYTHING in our power to redress the past. We CANNOT continue to enjoy the fruits of the sins we want to be forgiven.

There must be A RENUNCIATION OF SELF. In order to follow Christ, we must not only forsake isolated sins, but RENOUNCE the very principle of SELF-WILL, that lies at the root of every act of sin. To follow Christ is to SURRENDER to Him, the rights over our own lives. It is to ABDICATE the throne of our heart, and surrender our heart to Christ, and do homage to Him as our King. This RENUNCIATION of self, is VIVIDLY described by Jesus in three phrases.

1. It is to DENY OURSELVES: 'If any man would come after Me, let him deny himself'. We are to DISOWN ourselves, as COMPLETELY as Peter disowned Christ when he said 'I do not know the man'. SELF-DENIAL is not just giving up candy and cigarettes, either for good or for a period of VOLUNTARY ABSTINENCE. It is not to deny things to myself, but to DENY MYSELF TO MYSELF. It is not easy to say NO to self, and yes to Christ; to repudiate self, and acknowledge Christ.

2. The next phrase Jesus used is to TAKE UP THE CROSS: 'If any man would come after Me, let him deny himself and take up his cross and follow Me'. If we lived in Palestine, and seen a man carrying his cross, we would at once, recognize him as

a convicted prisoner, being led out to pay the supreme penalty. Palestine was an occupied country, and this is what the Romans compelled their convicted criminals to do. Prof. H. B. Swete put it this way; 'to put oneself into the position of a condemned man on his way to execution' . In other words, the ATTITUDE to self that we are to adopt is that of CRUCIFIXION. Paul uses the same metaphor when he declares that 'those who belong to Christ Jesus have crucified the flesh (i.e. their fallen nature) with its passions and desires'.

Luke added the adverb 'DAILY'. EVERY DAY, THE CHRISTIAN IS TO DIE TO SELF. Every day, he renounces the sovereignty of HIS OWN WILL. Every day he renews his unconditional surrender to JESUS CHRIST.

3. The 'FOLLOW ME' expression that Jesus used to describe the renunciation of SELF, is to LOSE OUR LIFE: 'Whoever loses his life...will save it'. The word for 'LIFE' here, denotes neither our PHYSICAL existence, nor our SOUL, but OUR SELF. The PSYCHE is the EGO, the human personality that THINKS, FEELS, PLANS and CHOOSES. According to a similar saying preserved by Luke, Jesus simply used the reflexive pronoun, and talked about a man FORFEITING 'HIMSELF'. The man who commits himself to Christ, LOSES HIMSELF. This does NOT mean that he loses his INDIVIDUALITY. His WILL is indeed submitted to Christ's WILL, but his PERSONALITY/CHARACTER is not absorbed into Christ's Personality. On the contrary, when the Christian loses himself, he FINDS himself; he discovers his TRUE identity.. his SOUL.

In order to follow Christ, we MUST DENY ourselves, CRUCIFY ourselves, and LOSE ourselves. The FULL, inexorable DEMAND of Jesus Christ is NOW LAID BARE. Christ does NOT call us to a SLOPPY, HALF-HEARTEDNESS, but to a VIGOROUS, ABSOLUTE COMMITMENT. JESUS CALLS US TO MAKE HIM OUR LORD.

The ASTONISHING idea that is current with some scholars (?), theologians (?) and misguided lay people today, is that we CAN enjoy the benefits of Christ's Salvation WITHOUT accepting the CHALLENGE of HIS LORDSHIP. Such an UNBALANCED NOTION is not found in the BIBLE. 'JESUS IS LORD', is the earliest KNOWN formulation of the Creed of TRUE CHRISTIANS.

In the days when Imperial Rome was pressing its citizens to say 'CAESAR IS LORD', these words had a DANGEROUS flavour. But Christians did not flinch. They could NOT give Caesar their first allegiance, because they had ALREADY given it to the Emperor JESUS. GOD had exalted His Son FAR above ALL PRINCIPALITY and POWER, and INVESTED Jesus, with a rank SUPERIOR TO EVERY RANK; that before Christ, 'EVERY KNEE SHALL BOW.. and EVERY TONGUE CONFESS THAT JESUS CHRIST IS LORD'. PHIL 2:10-11.

To make Christ LORD, is to bring EVERY department of our PUBLIC and PRIVATE lives under HIS control. This includes our CAREER, GOD HAS A PURPOSE FOR EVERY LIFE. OUR business is to DISCOVER it, and DO IT, in cooperation with our SOUL. God's plan will probably be different from OUR plan, or our PARENTS' plan, (thanks to satan, and his angels, spirits, saints, instruments and servants, who will do all in their power to keep us out of the path God created us to walk, for HIM).

If he is wise, the Christian will do nothing Rash or RECKLESS. He may already be engaged in, or preparing for, the work God has for him to do. BUT HE MAY NOT. If Christ is our Lord, we must OPEN OUR MINDS to the possibility of a change. See NCRC 99/2.

What IS certain, is that God calls EVERY Christian to 'MINISTER', (MENTOR, INTERCESSORY PRAYER WARRIOR ETC.), that is, to SERVICE, to be the servant of other people, for the sake of Christ. No Christian can live for HIMSELF any longer. What is NOT certain, is WHAT form this 'SERVICE' will take. It MIGHT be the Ordained Ministry of the Church, or some other kind of full-time Church work, at home or overseas. But it is a GREAT MISTAKE, to SUPPOSE that EVERY committed Christian is called to this.

There ARE other forms of service that are EQUALLY deserving of the job description 'CHRISTIAN MINISTRY' For example, the calling of women to be wife, mother, and home maker is in the FULLEST sense, CHRISTIAN MINISTRY', since she IS serving CHRIST, HER FAMILY, and THE COMMUNITY. So is EVERY form of work.. MEDICINE, RESEARCH, LAW, EDUCATION, SOCIAL SERVICE, CENTRAL and LOCAL GOVERNMENT, INDUSTRY, BUSINESS and TRADE... where the worker is cooperating with God., in the SERVICE OF MAN.

If you are surrendered to Christ, waiting on God to disclose it, He WILL make it KNOWN to you, in His own time.(i.e. when He sees that YOU ARE READY). WHATEVER it is, the Christian CANNOT be IDLE. Whether he is an EMPLOYER, EMPLOYEE or SELF-EMPLOYED, he HAS a Heavenly Master. He learns to grasp God's purpose in his work, and labours at it with ALL HIS HEART, 'as serving the Lord and not men'. (Do the most productive thing possible, with every GIVEN moment).

ANOTHER department of life that is under Jesus Christ, is our MARRIAGE and our HOME. Jesus once said, 'Do not think that I have come to bring peace on earth; I have not come to bring peace, but a sword'. He went on to speak of the CLASH of loyalties that sometimes arises within a family, when one of its members begins to follow HIM. Such family conflicts STILL take place today. The Christian must NEVER SEEK such conflicts. He has a DEFINATE DUTY to LOVE and HONOUR his parents, and OTHER members of his family. Since he is CALLED to be a PEACEMAKER, he will make as many CONCESSIONS as he can, WITHOUT COMPROMISING HIS DUTY TO GOD. Yet, he can NEVER forget Christ's words: 'He who loves father or mother.. son or daughter more than Me is not worthy of Me'. MATT 10:34-37.

Further, a Christian is at liberty to marry ONLY A CHRISTIAN. The Bible is DEFINITE here: 'do not be mis-mated with unbelievers'. 2 COR 6:14. This COMMAND can bring great DISTRESS to somebody who is already engaged, or NEARLY so, BUT, the FACT must be HONESTLY faced. And we MUST remember, GOD FORBIDS FORNICATION and ADULTERY.

Marriage is NOT merely a CONVENIENT social custom. It is a DIVINE INSTITUTION. And the married relationship is the DEEPEST, into which human beings can enter. GOD DESIGNED IT to be an INTIMATE UNION, not only PHYSICAL, EMOTIONAL. INTELLECTUAL and SOCIAL, but SPIRITUAL.

For a Christian to marry someone with whom he or she CANNOT be SPIRITUALLY ONE, is not only to DISOBEY GOD, but also to miss the FULLNESS of the UNION HE INTENDED. It also puts the children of the marriage at risk; DEUT 5:9-10, for it INTRODUCES the children to RELIGIOUS CONFLICT, in their OWN HOME, and makes IMPOSSIBLE, the Christian EDUCATION they should receive from both parents. BUT remember WELL, the HUSBAND/FATHER is responsible, before God, for the SPIRITUAL and MATERIAL well-being of the WIFE and CHILDREN, and WILL be held RESPONSIBLE, BY GOD, to give an account, TO GOD, FOR THE END RESULT REGARDING HIS WIFE AND CHILDREN. And, whether or not the husband/father LIKES, BELIEVES or ACCEPTS this FACT, will make no difference WHATSOEVER to GOD. 1 SAM 3:13-14 & :18.

Indeed, so RADICAL is Christian CONVERSION, that our whole attitude to MARRIAGE, and to RELATIONS BETWEEN THE SEXES, will change. We begin to see sexuality... the fundamental distinction between man and woman, and the need of each for the other.. as itself, the CREATION of God. And sex...the physical expression of sexuality... is no longer DEBASED by selfish IRRESPONSIBILITY, into something casual and essentially impersonal, but becomes what GOD MEANT IT TO BE; something good and right, the expression of love, a fulfillment of the DIVINE purpose, and the human personality.

Other formerly private affairs over which Jesus Christ becomes Master, when we commit our lives to HIM, are our MONEY and our TIME. Jesus often spoke about money, and about the DANGER of riches. MUCH of Christ's teaching on the subject is VERY DISTURBING. It sometimes seems as if He was recommending His disciples to realize their capital, and give it all away. No doubt, Christ STILL calls some of His followers to DO this, TODAY. But for most, His command is to an INNER DETACHMENT rather than to a LITERAL RENUNCIATION. The New Testament does NOT imply that possessions are sinful in themselves. However, the RULE OF THUMB, is that we tithe ten percent, off the top, of our gross income.(FIRST FRUITS; before we pay or use any of the money).

Christ CERTAINLY meant us to put HIM above material wealth, just as we are to put HIM above family ties. We CANNOT serve GOD and MAMMON. However, we ARE to be conscientious in the use of our money. It is NO LONGER OURS. We hold it in STEWARDSHIP from GOD. And in an era where the gap between AFFLUENCE and POVERTY is WIDENING throughout the world, and in which the Christian Missionary enterprise is SEVERELY hampered by lack of funds, we should be GENEROUS and DISCIPLINED in what we give away. But remember, WOE to those that take given money from charitable people, given in good faith, in obedience to God, then FRAUDULENTLY or carelessly use it; they WILL repay ten fold, guaranteed by GOD, and the blood of those that should have been helped, and were NOT, will ALSO be required of those same dirty hands. And the SAME RECOMPENSE WILL BE ALLOTTED to those that COULD have, or SHOULD have given, but DID NOT, for WHATEVER reason. God is VERY concerned about these matters. It is difficult to fathom ANY ONE robbing God.

TIME is EVERY MAN'S PROBLEM THESE DAYS; and the newly converted Christian will UNDOUBTEDLY have to rearrange his PRIORITIES. While he is a student, academic work will come high on the list. Christians should be KNOWN for their HARD WORK and HONESTY. But he must ALSO make time for NEW employments. He MUST, carve out of his busy schedule, time for DAILY PRAYER and BIBLE READING, for setting SUNDAY ASIDE, as the LORD'S DAY, that was INSTITUTED as a DAY OF WORSHIP and REST; for FELLOWSHIP with other Christians; for some kind of service, in the CHURCH and the COMMUNITY, for MAN'S sake.

ALL OF THIS IS INVOLVED, IF WE ARE TO FORSAKE SIN AND SELF, and FOLLOW CHRIST.

<u>THE CALL TO CONFESS CHRIST:</u>   We are COMMANDED, not only to follow Christ PRIVATELY, BUT ALSO TO CONFESS HIM PUBLICLY. It is NOT enough to DENY OURSELVES IN SECRET, if we DENY CHRIST IN THE OPEN. Christ said:

> 'Whoever is ashamed of Me and My words in this adulterous and sinful generation, of him will the Son of Man also be ashamed, when He comes in the Glory of His Father and with the Holy Angels'

> 'Every one who acknowledges me before men, I will acknowledge before My Father who is in heaven; but whoever denies Me before men, I will also deny before my Father who is in Heaven.   MATT 10:32-33   MARK 8:38.

The very fact that Jesus told us NOT to be ashamed of Him, shows that He KNEW we would be TEMPTED (by OURSELVES also), TO BE ashamed; and the fact that He added 'in this adulterous and sinful generation', shows He knew WHY. Christ evidently FORESAW that His Church would be a MINORITY MOVEMENT in the world; and it REQUIRES COURAGE to side with the FEW against the MANY, ESPECIALLY if the few are UNPOPULAR and you may not NATURALLY DRAWN TO THEM.

Yet, this OPEN confession of Christ CANNOT be AVOIDED. Paul declared it to be a CONDITION of SALVATION. In order to be SAVED, he wrote, we are not only to believe in our HEARTS, but also to confess with our lips, that JESUS IS LORD, 'for man believes with his heart and so is justified, and he confesses with his lips and so is saved'. CERTAINLY, if not already baptized, the convert MUST be BAPTIZED, partly to receive through the application of water, a VISIBLE sign and seal, of his inward cleansing, and NEW LIFE IN CHRIST, (rising up (out of the water) to the new life), and partly to acknowledge PUBLICALY, that he HAS trusted in Jesus Christ as his Saviour and Lord.

But the Christians open confession does NOT END with his Baptism. He must be WILLING for his family and friends to know he IS a CHRISTIAN, especially at first, by the new life he leads. This is BOUND, in due course, to lead to an OPPORTUNITY for SPOKEN WITNESS, although he should be HUMBLE and HONEST here, and NOT BLUNDER TACTLESSLY, into other people's privacy. At the same time, he will JOIN A CHURCH; ASSOCIATE HIMSELF WITH OTHER CHRISTIANS in his college or place of business; not be afraid to own up to his CHRISTIAN COMMITMENT, when CHALLENGED about it; and start SEEKING, by PRAYER, example and testimony to win his friends for Christ.

INCENTIVES: The demands Jesus makes are HEAVY; but the reasons He gives are compelling. If we are to SERIOUSLY consider the TOTAL SURRENDER Christ asks, we will need these POWERFUL incentives:

FOR OUR OWN SAKE:

Whosoever would save his life will lose it; and whoever loses his life.. will save it. For what does it profit a man. to gain the whole world and forfeit his life; For what can a man give in return for his life ?'   MARK 8:35-37

Many people have a DEEP-SEATED fear, that if they commit themselves to Jesus Christ, THEY will be the LOSERS. They FORGET that Jesus came into the world, so that WE might 'HAVE LIFE, and have it abundantly'; that Christ's purpose is to ENRICH, not to IMPOVERISH; and that Christ's service is PERFECT FREEDOM.

There ARE losses to face when we submit to Christ. We already KNOW of the SIN and SELF-CENTREDNESS that we MUST FORSAKE; we MAY lose some of our friends. BUT the RICH and SATISFYING COMPENSATIONS FAR outweigh EVERY LOSS. The ASTONISHING paradox of Christ's TEACHING, and of Christian EXPERIENCE is this: if we lose ourselves in following Christ, we ACTUALLY FIND OURSELVES. TRUE self-denial is TRUE SELF-DISCOVERY. To live for ourselves is insanity and suicide; to live for God, and for man, IS WISDOM AND LIFE. We do NOT begin to find ourselves, until we become WILLING to lose ourselves in the service of Christ and of our fellow man.

To ENFORCE this truth, Jesus placed, in contrast, the WHOLE WORLD, and the INDIVIDUAL SOUL. Jesus then asked a businessman's question of PROFIT and LOSS. Supposing you WERE to gain the whole world, and lose YOURSELF, He asked, WHAT PROFIT WOULD YOU HAVE MADE? Christ was arguing on the lowest level of PERSONAL SELF-ADVANTAGE; That to follow HIM is UNDOUBTEDLY, to have the BEST of the bargain. For to follow HIM, is to FIND OURSELVES, whereas, to hold on to ourselves, and REFUSE to follow HIM, is to lose OURSELVES, and FORFEIT our ETERNAL DESTINY, whatever MATERIAL GAINS we may have made meanwhile.

WHY IS THIS ? Well, for one thing, we CANNOT gain the WHOLE WORLD. For another, if we DID, IT WOULD NOT LAST. And thirdly, While it DID last, IT WOULD NOT SATISFY. WHAT CAN A MAN GIVE IN EXCHANGE FOR HIMSELF ?' NOTHING is valuable enough EVEN TO MAKE AN OFFER. Of COURSE it costs to be a Christian; but it cost MORE, NOT TO BE. It means losing oneself for ETERNITY.

<u>FOR THE SAKE OF OTHERS:</u>

The second incentive, We should NOT submit to Christ only for what WE get out of it, but for what we can GIVE, in association with our SOUL. 'Whoever loses his life for... the Gospel's sake' means 'for the sake of proclaiming it to others'. We already KNOW that we must NOT be ashamed of CHRIST, or HIS WORDS; NOW we are to be so proud of Jesus, that we WANT to spread His Good News TO OTHERS.

MOST of us feel OPPRESSED by the heart-rending tragedies of this CHAOTIC world. Our very SURVIVAL is questionable. The ordinary citizen often feel like HELPLESS victims of the tangled web of politics, or a faceless unit in the machine of modern society. But the CHRISTIAN need not succumb to this sense of POWERLESSNESS. Because Jesus described HIS followers as both 'the salt of the earth' and 'the light of the world'. The use of salt before refrigeration had been invented, was largely negative.. to PREVENT DECAY IN FISH OR MEAT. Christians should stop SOCIETY FROM (decaying) DETERIORATING, by helping to PRESERVE MORAL STANDARDS; INFLUENCE PUBLIC OPINION; and SECURE JUST LEGISLATION.

As the LIGHT OF THE WORLD, CHRISTIANS ARE TO LET THEIR LIGHT SHINE. They HAVE found, in Jesus, the SECRET of PEACE and LOVE; of PERSONAL RELATIONSHIPS; of CHANGING PEOPLE; they must SHARE THEIR SECRETS WITH OTHERS. The BEST contribution ANYONE can make, to the SUPPLY OF THE WORLD'S NEEDS, is to LIVE A CHRISTIAN LIFE, BUILD A CHRISTIAN HOME and RADIATE THE LIGHT OF THE GOSPEL OF JESUS CHRIST.

The GREATEST incentive of ALL, however, is FOR CHRIST'S SAKE. 'Whoever loses his life for My sake...will save it'. When we are asked to do something particularly hard, whether or not we are WILLING to do it, depends VERY MUCH on WHO ASKS US. If the request come from someone who HAS a CLAIM on us, and to whom WE are INDEBTED, we are GLAD TO AGREE. THIS is WHY Christ's appeal to us is so ELOQUENT and so PERSUASIVE. He asks us to DENY ourselves, and follow HIM, FOR HIS OWN SAKE.

This is WHY he describes the RENUNCIATION He demands, as 'TAKING UP THE CROSS'. Jesus asks no more THAN HE GAVE. He asks a CROSS for a CROSS. We should follow Him neither just for what WE can GET, nor for what WE can GIVE, but SUPREMELY, because of what HE GAVE. HE GAVE HIMSELF. Will it cost us much ? It cost HIM MORE. He left the Father's GLORY; the immunities of heaven; and the worship of countless angels; WHEN HE CAME. He humbled Himself, to assume man's nature; to be born in a stable, and laid in a manger; to work at a carpenter's bench; to make friends of rustic fisher-folk, prostitutes and sinners; to die on a common cross as a criminal; and to bear the sins of THE WORLD.

A TRUE and REALISTIC sight of the Cross, will make us WILLING to deny ourselves, and FOLLOW HIM. OUR little crosses are eclipsed by HIS CROSS. If we only catch a GLIMPS of the GREATNESS of HIS love to suffer such SHAME and PAIN for US, who deserved nothing but the wrath of God and Judgment, only ONE course of action will seem to be left. HOW CAN we DENY or REJECT such a LOVE ?

IF, then, you suffer from MORAL ANAEMIA, take my advice, and STEER CLEAR OF CHRISTIANITY. If you want to live a life of easy going self-indulgence, WHATEVER you do, <u>DO NOT BECOME A CHRISTIAN</u>. BUT, if you want a life of self-discovery; deeply satisfying to the nature GOD has given you; if you want a life of ADVENTURE, in which you have the PRIVILEGE of serving Him, and your fellow man; if you want a life in which to express something of the overwhelming gratitude you are beginning to feel for HIM, who died FOR you; THEN I would urge you to yield your life, WITHOUT RESERVE and WITHOUT DELAY, to YOUR LORD and SAVIOUR, JESUS CHRIST.

REACHING A DECISION: That a DECISION is necessary, in order to become a Christian, is an idea QUITE FOREIGN to MANY people. Some imagine that they are ALREADY Christians, because they were born in a Christian country. 'After all', they say, 'we are neither Jews, nor Muslims etc., nor Buddhists; so PRESUMABLY, we are Christians!' Others SUPPOSE that, having had a Christian upbringing, and having been taught to accept the Christian Creed, and Christian standards of behaviour, NOTHING further is required of them. But WHATEVER his parentage and upbringing, EVERY responsible adult is OBLIGED to choose; to be FOR or AGAINST Christ; gathering with Him or scattering from Him. We CANNOT remain NEUTRAL; we ARE either FOR Him or AGAINST Him. Nor can we DRIFT into Christianity. Nor can ANYBODY settle the matter FOR us. We MUST decide, FOR OURSELVES.

AGREEMENT with all that has been written here so far is NOT SUFFICIENT to be a Christian. We may concede that the evidence for the DEITY of Christ is conclusive; that Christ IS the Son of God; believe that Jesus came and died, to be Saviour of the world; and ADMIT we are sinners and need Christ as Saviour. NONE of these things makes us Christians; nor do ALL of them together, make us Christians.

To BELIEVE certain facts about the PERSON and WORK of Christ IS a necessary preliminary; true faith will translate such mental belief into a decisive act of TRUST. Intellectual conviction MUST lead to PERSONAL COMMITMENT.

At one time, I myself, thought that because Jesus had died on the Cross, by some kind of rather mechanical transaction, the whole world had been put right with God. I remember how puzzled, (even indignant), I was when it was suggested to me that I needed to appreciate Christ and His Salvation for MYSELF. The Holy Ghost (who convicts and point us to Christ), opened my eyes to see that I must do MORE than ACKNOWLEDGE I needed A Saviour; MORE even than ACKNOWLEDGE that Jesus Christ was THE Saviour I needed; it was necessary to accept Christ as MY Saviour. The personal pronoun is PROMINENT in Scriptures

'The Lord is MY Shepherd, I shall not want'.
'Lord is MY LIGHT and MY salvation'

'O God, thou art MY God'
'The surpassing worth of knowing Jesus Christ MY Lord'

One verse in the Bible that has helped many seekers, (including myself), to understand the STEP OF FAITH we must take, contains the word of Christ Himself. He says: Behold, I stand at the door and knock; if any one hears my voice and opens the door, I will come in to him and eat with him, and he with me. REV 3:20 (I was in a 'relented' stage).

This verse was ILLUSTRATED by HOLMAN HUNT in his well known picture 'THE LIGHT OF THE WORLD', painted in 1853. 'On the left-hand side of the picture is seen this door of the human soul. It is fast barred; its bars and nails are rusty; it is knitted and bound to its stanchions by creeping tendrils of ivy, showing that it has never been opened. A bat hovers about it; its threshold is overgrown with brambles, nettles and fruitless corn.. Christ approaches it in the night-time.. He is wearing a royal robe and a crown of thorns, holding a lantern in his left hand (as the light of the world) and knocking on the door with his right'. (in a letter by JOHN RUSKIN, to THE TIMES IN MAY 1854).

The context of the verse is ILLUMINATING. It comes at the end of a letter addressed by Christ through JOHN, to the Church of Laodicea, situated in what is now Turkey. Laodicea was a prosperous city, RENOWNED for its manufacture of clothing, its Medical School; (where the famous Phrygian eye powder was made), and its WEALTHY BANKS.

Material prosperity had brought in its wake, a spirit of COMPLACENCY, that had even CONTAMINATED the Christian Church, and it's Tabernacles, Pulpits, Sanctuaries, and Scriptures. Attending the church were PROFESSING Christians, who proved to be Christian's in NAME only. They were tolerably respectable, NOTHING MORE. Their religious interest was SHALLOW and CASUAL. Like the water from the hot springs of Hierapolis, that was piped to Laodicea by conduits, (that can still be seen), they WERE (Jesus said), neither COLD nor HOT; LUKEWARM only, and therefore, DISTASTEFUL to Jesus. REV 3: 15-17.

Their spiritual TEPIDITY is explained in terms of SELF-DELUSION: i.e. "I am rich, I have prospered, and I need nothing"; not knowing that they are wretched, pitiable, poor, blind, and naked'.

What a description of PROUD and PROSPEROUS Laodicea; They were BLIND and NAKED BEGGERS...naked DESPITE their CLOTHING FACTORY; blind DESPITE their PHRYGIAN EYE-SALVE; and beggars DESPITE their BANKS.

TODAY, many of us are no different. We say, as THEY did, 'I NEED NOTHING'. It would be HARD to find ANY words more SPIRITUALLY DANGEROUS. It is our SELF-CONTAINED INDEPENDENCE that, more than ANYTHING else, keeps us from committing ourselves to Christ. OF COURSE WE NEED HIM! Without Him, we are MORALLY naked (with no clothes to fit us for God's presence); blind to SPIRITUAL TRUTH; and beggars, having nothing with which to procure GOD'S FAVOUR.

But Christ can CLOTHE us, with His RIGHTEOUSNESS; touch our eyes INTO SIGHT; and enrich us with SPIRITUAL WEALTH. Apart from Him, and until we open the door to admit Him, we are BLIND and NAKED BEGGARS.

'Behold, I stand at the door and knock'. Jesus says... He is NO FIGMENT OF THE IMAGINATION: NO FICTITIOUS CHARACTER FROM A RELIGIOUS NOVEL: THIS IS THE MAN FROM NAZARETH, WHOSE CLAIMS, CHARACTER and RESURRECTION, warrant the CONCLUSION that HE IS THE SON OF GOD. He is ALSO THE CRUCIFIED SAVIOUR. REV 3: 20-22.

The hand that knocks is SCARRED. The feet that stand on the threshold, still bear the print of NAILS. And He is THE RISEN, LIVING, CHRIST. It is hard to understand how a Person of such

MAJESTY, could ever deign to visit POOR, BLIND and NAKED BEGGARS LIKE OURSELVES.

Yet, Jesus says He is standing, knocking at the door of our lives, WAITING. Notice He is standing at the door, NOT PUSHING IT, speaking to us, NOT SHOUTING. This is the more remarkable, when we reflect that the house is HIS, in any case. He is the architect; HE DESIGNED IT. He is the builder; HE MADE IT. He is the landlord; HE BOUGHT IT WITH HIS LIFE-BLOOD. So it IS His, by right of PLAN, CONSTRUCTION, and PURCHASE. We are only TENANTS. in a house that does not belong to US. He could put His shoulder to the door; HE PREFERS TO PUT HIS HAND TO THE KNOCKER. He could command us to open to Him; instead, MERELY INVITES US TO DO SO. He will not force an entry into ANYBODY'S life. He says (REV 3:18), 'I counsel you...' He could issue orders; HE IS CONTENT TO GIVE ADVICE. Such are His CONDESCENSION and HUMILITY, and the FREEDOM He has GIVEN us.

But WHY does Jesus want to come in ? He wants to be BOTH our SAVIOUR and our LORD. He DIED to become our Saviour. IF we receive Him, He will be able to apply to us, ALL THE BENEFITS OF HIS DEATH. Once inside the house, He will RENOVATE, REDECORATE, and REFURNISH it. That is, CLEANSE and FORGIVE us; our past will be BLOTTED OUT. He promises to eat with us, and allow us to eat with Him. This phrase describes the JOY of HIS COMPANIONSHIP. He not only GIVES HIMSELF to us; He asks us to GIVE OURSELVES TO HIM. We have been STRANGERS, now we are FRIENDS. There has been a closed door between us; NOW WE ARE SEATED AT THE SAME TABLE.

Jesus will also enter as our LORD AND MASTER. The house of our lives will COME UNDER HIS MANAGEMENT, and there is NO SENSE in opening the door, unless we are WILLING FOR THIS. As He steps across the threshold, we must hand Him the entire set of keys, granting Him FREE ACCESS INTO EVERY ROOM.

This involves REPENTANCE, turning, RESOLUTELY from EVERYTHING we KNOW to be DISPLEASING to Him. NOT that we make OURSELVES better before we invite Him in. On the CONTRARY, it is because we CANNOT FORGIVE or IMPROVE OURSELVES, that we NEED Him to come to US.

We MUST be WILLING for Him to do WHATEVER REARRANGING He likes, WHEN HE HAS COME IN. There must be NO RESISTANCE, and NO ATTEMPT to NEGOTIATE OUR OWN TERMS; rather an UNCONDITIONAL SURRENDER to the LORDSHIP of Jesus Christ.

WHAT WILL THIS MEAN ? In DETAIL, I can't tell you. In PRINCIPLE, it means a DETERMINATION to FORSAKE EVIL AND FOLLOW JESUS THE CHRIST.

DO YOU HESITATE ? Do you say it is UNREASONABLE TO SUBMIT TO CHRIST IN THE DARK ? NO! IT IS NOT. It is MUCH more REASONABLE than MARRIAGE. In a marriage, a man and a woman COMMIT THEMSELVES to each other, WITHOUT CONDITION. (or at least, that is the PREREQUISITE, as I understand it to be). THEY do not KNOW what the future holds for them. But they love each other (hopefully), and they trust each other. So they PROMISE to take each other, 'TO HAVE

AND TO HOLD FROM THIS DAY FORWARD, FOR BETTER FOR WORSE, FOR RICHER FOR POORER, IN SICKNESS AND IN HEALTH, TO LOVE AND TO CHERISH, TILL DEATH DO US PART'. If HUMANS can trust HUMANS, can we NOT TRUST GOD'S SON ? It is more REASONABLE to COMMIT oneself to the DIVINE CHRIST, than the FINEST and NOBLEST of HUMAN BEINGS. Christ will NEVER BETRAY or ABUSE our confidence.

So, what must we do ? To BEGIN with, we must HEAR CHRIST'S VOICE. It is TRAGICALLY possible to turn a deaf ear to Christ, and drown the insistent whisper of Christ's appeal. Sometimes we hear His voice through the prickings of the CONSCIENCE; sometimes through the gropings of the mind; it may be a MORAL DEFEAT; or the seeming EMPTINESS and MEANINGLESSNESS of our EXISTENCE; or in inexplicable SPIRITUAL HUNGER; or SICKNESS; BEREAVEMENT; PAIN; or FEAR; by which we become aware that Christ is outside the door, and speaking to us. Or His call can come to us through a FRIEND; a PREACHER; or a BOOK. WHENEVER we hear, WE MUST LISTEN. 'He who has ears to hear', Jesus says, 'let him hear'.

Next, WE MUST OPEN THE DOOR. Having heard the voice, we must open to His knock. To open the door to Jesus, is a PICTORIAL way of describing an ACT OF FAITH IN CHRIST AS OUR SAVIOUR; AN ACT OF SUBMISSION TO HIM AS OUR LORD.

It is a DEFINITE act. The door does not HAPPEN to swing open by chance. Nor is it ALREADY ajar. IT IS CLOSED, AND NEEDS TO BE OPENED. Christ will NOT open the door

Himself. There is neither HANDLE nor LATCH on the OUTSIDE of the door in HOLMAN HUNT'S picture. He OMITTED THEM DELIBERATELY, to SHOW that the handle was on the INSIDE. CHRIST KNOCKS; but WE MUST OPEN.

It is an INDIVIDUAL ACT. True, the message was sent to a Church, the nominal, lukewarm Church of Laodicea. The CHALLENGE is addressed to INDIVIDUALS within it: 'If ANYONE hears My voice and opens the door, I will come in to him'. Every man must make his own DECISION, and take the step HIMSELF. NOBODY ELSE can DO it for you. Christian parents and teachers, Pastors and friends CAN point the way; YOUR hand, and ONLY yours, can open the door, from the INSIDE.

It is a UNIQUE act. You can take this step ONLY ONCE. When Christ has entered, HE will close and bolt the door on the inside.

This is NOT to say that you emerge from this experience with fully grown wings of an angel! Nor that you will become PERFECT in the twinkling of an eye. You CAN become a Christian in a MOMENT; however, NOT a MATURE CHRISTIAN. Christ CAN ENTER, CLEANSE and FORGIVE you in a matter of SECONDS; it will take MUCH longer for your PERSONALITY/ CHARACTER to be TRANSFORMED and MOULDED to Christ's WILL. It takes only a few minutes for a bride and groom to be married; in the rough-and-tumble of their home, it may take many years for two strong wills to be dovetailed into one. So when we receive Christ, a moment of COMMITMENT will lead to a life-time of adjustment. YOUR adjustment, development and progress, WILL be determined by YOUR EFFORT and SINCERITY, LOYALTY, and FAITH. You CANNOT put in a nickel, and expect a dollar song.

It is a DELIBERATE act. Don't wait for a supernatural light to FLASH on you from heaven; or an emotional experience to overtake you. NO! Christ came into the world and died for your sins. He has now come and stands outside the door of the house of you life; your heart, and He is knocking. THE NEXT MOVE IS YOURS. His hand is already on the knocker; your hand must now feel for the latch.

It is an URGENT act. DO NOT WAIT. Time is passing. The future is uncertain. You may NEVER have a better opportunity than this. 'Do not boast about tomorrow, for you do not know what a day may bring forth'. The Holy Ghost says, 'Today, when you hear that voice, do NOT harden your heart...'   PROV 27:1 HEB 3:7-8.

DO NOT put it off until you have tried to make yourself better, or worthier of Christ's entry; or until you have solved all your problems. IF you BELIEVE that Jesus Christ IS the Son of God, AND that He died to be YOUR Saviour, THAT IS ENOUGH. The REST will follow in due time. TRUE... there IS DANGER in RASH 'bringing about' or pseudo action via your OWN hand. There is EQUAL danger in PROCRASTINATION. If in the depth of your heart you KNOW you are to act, you must not DELAY ANY LONGER.

It is an INDISPENSABLE act. However, there is MUCH MORE to the Christian life than this:

Baptism;
Getting into the fellowship of a Church;
Discovering GOD'S will;
Doing God's will;
Growing in Grace;
Growing in understanding;
Seeking to serve God;
Seeking to serve your fellow-man and Community;
To be trained-up by the Spirits of Discipline, Understanding, Wisdom, Knowledge and Intelligence;
To grow and advance through the Milk, Pablum, Strained foods, Junior foods, and the Meat/Solid food stages;
To grow and advance to the Solid, Standing, Mature, Instrument and Servant of God, filled with the Spirit of The Holy Ghost stage.

However, the step of OPENING THE DOOR, and INVITING Jesus in, is the BEGINNING; and NOTHING ELSE, INSTEAD, WILL DO. This is the FIRST step.

We can believe in Christ, intellectually AND admire Him; We can say our prayers to Him through the 'key hole' (I did for many years); We can push coins at Him under the door to keep Him quiet; We can be moral, decent, upright and good; We can be religious; we can have been Baptized and Confirmed; We can be deeply versed in the philosophy of religion; We can be scholars, theologians, educators and laypeople, even an ordained Pastor...and still not have opened the door to Christ, to come in, and indwell us. THERE IS NO SUBSTITUTE FOR THIS STEP. You must WANT and CHOOSE, to DO this step.

A titled lady responded to Billy Graham's invitation to go forward at the end of an evangelistic meeting. She was introduced to an adviser who, discovering that she had not yet committed herself to Christ, suggested that she should pray there and then. Bowing her head, she said, 'Dear Lord Jesus, I WANT You to come into my heart more than anything else in the world. Amen'.   BILLY GRAHAM

Are you a Christian; a REAL and COMMITTED Christian ? Your answer depends on ANOTHER question; not whether you go to Church or not; believe the Creed or not; or lead a decent life or not; (these are all important in their place), Rather, THIS question: WHICH SIDE OF THE DOOR IS JESUS CHRIST ON ? Is He INSIDE or OUTSIDE ? THAT is the CRUCIAL issue.

Perhaps you are ready to open the door to Christ. IF YOU ARE NOT SURE YOU HAVE EVER DONE SO, my advice to you is to MAKE SURE, even if, (as someone has put it) you will be going over, in ink, what you have already written in pencil.

My suggestion is that you get away and ALONE to pray. Confess your sins to God, (Penitential Rite), and FORSAKE them. Thank Jesus Christ that He died for YOUR sake, and in YOUR PLACE. Then OPEN THE DOOR, AND ASK Jesus to COME IN, as YOUR PERSONAL Saviour and Lord.

You will find it helpful to echo something like this prayer IN YOUR HEART:

Lord Jesus Christ, I acknowledge that I am a lost sinner,

and have gone my own way. I have sinned in thought, word and deed, in what I have done, and in what I have failed to do. I am sorry for my sins. I turn from them in repentance. With the help of Your Grace, I resolve to forsake my sins. I believe that You died for me, bearing my sins in your body, on the Cross of Calvary. I thank You for Your great Love and Gift of God.

Now I open the door. Come in, Lord Jesus. Come in as MY Saviour and Redeemer, and cleanse me. Come in as MY Lord, and take control of me and MY twelve apostles; (1. Soul; 2. Heart & Spirit; 3.brains and memory; 4.mind, emotions and will; 5.eyes; 6.ears; 7. mouth and tongue; 8.hands; 9.feet; 10.time; 11.talents;
(12). money.
Teach me how to ponder; reason; think; see; hear; speak; and pray; from the HEART, not the head.

And I will serve, as You give me strength; and obtain for me, the spirits of discipline, understanding, wisdom, knowledge and intelligence, for the rest of my life. Amen.

If you have prayed something like this prayer, and MEANT it, HUMBLY thank Christ that He HAS come in; for He SAID He would. He has given His word: 'If anyone hears My voice and opens the door, I WILL COME IN TO HIM... (REV 3:20). DISREGARD YOUR FEELINGS: TRUST HIS PROMISE: AND THANK HIM, THAT HE HAS KEPT HIS WORD.

<u>BEING A CHRISTIAN:</u> The following is written for those who HAVE opened the door of their hearts and lives to Jesus Christ.

They HAVE committed themselves to Him. They HAVE begun the Christian life.

BECOMING a Christian is one thing; BEING a Christian is another. It is with the IMPLICATIONS of BEING a Christian that we now concern ourselves.

You took a simple step; you invited Christ to come as YOUR Saviour and Lord. At that moment, what can only be described as a MIRACLE took place. GOD...without whose Grace you could not have repented and believed...GAVE YOU A NEW LIFE. You were SAVED. (see NCRC 206/1). You became a child of God, and entered HIS family.

You may not have become conscious of anything happening, as at the time of your physical birth. You were not conscious of what was taking place. SELF-CONSCIOUSNESS, the awareness of WHO and WHAT one is, is part of the process of PERSONAL DEVELOPMENT. Nevertheless, just as when you were born, you emerged as a new independent personality. When you were BORN AGAIN you became, spiritually, a NEW CREATURE IN CHRIST.

ONE of satan's darts, utilized so effectively in the Garden of Eden, involving Eve and the apple, i.e. satan utilizes a truth then perverts that truth to accomplish his own chaos and havoc for those babes in Christ, in God's Realm. This particular dart is well illustrated in the Eve and the apple scenario. It is that same dart satan utilizes with many scholars(?), theologians(?), educators(?) and laypeople, and for the same purposes. The TRUTH of God's realm is Scriptures, and God's Word is twisted, warped, stretched, battered, manhandled and taken out of context. They end up with gross theosophy and spurious speculation, produced by their OWN misguided clouded, empirical thinking, then pass THAT off as teachings of, and for, the church, and/or GOD. They take captive silly, misguided pseudo Christian's. The fodder for their thinking and modus operendi, comes from questions like:

> Is not God the Father of all men ? and
> Are not all people the children of God ?

The answer, of course, is YES and NO! (hence, their 'hook'). God IS certainly the CREATOR of ALL men, and ALL are His 'OFFSPRING' in the sense that they derive their BEING from God.   (ACTS 17:28-30).

The Bible CLEARLY distinguishes between this general relationship of God to the WHOLE HUMAN RACE, as CREATOR, and the SPECIAL relationship of FATHER to his CHILD, that God establishes with those who are NEW A CREATION, through JESUS CHRIST. JOHN explains this in the prologue to his Gospel when he writes:

> 'He (that is, Jesus) came to His own and His own received
> Him not. But to all who received Him, who believe
> in His name, He gave power to become children of God;
> who were born...of God'.   JOHN 1:11-13   GAL 3:26.

The three clauses beginning with word 'WHO' all describe the same people. The CHILDREN OF GOD are those who are born of God; and those who are born of God, are those who have received Christ into their lives, and who have believed in His name.

What does it mean to be a 'CHILD' of God in this sense? Like membership of ANY other family; it has BOTH its PRIVILEGES, and its RESPONSIBILITIES. Lets see what THESE are.

CHRISTIAN PRIVILEGES: The UNIQUE privilege of the person who has been born anew into the Family of God, is that he is RELATED to God. Lets consider this relationship.

AN INTIMATE RELATIONSHIP: We saw earlier, that our sins had ALIENATED us from God. Our sins became a BARRIER between us; we were under the JUST condemnation of the Judge of ALL the earth. But NOW, through Jesus Christ, who bore OUR condemnation, and to whom, by FAITH, we have become UNITED; we have been 'JUSTIFIED', that is, brought into ACCEPTANCE with God, and PRONOUNCED righteous. Our JUDGE has become our FATHER.

JOHN wrote 'See what love the Father HAS given us, that we should be called children of God; and so we are'. 'FATHER' and 'SON' are the DISTINCTIVE titles that Jesus gave to God and to Himself, and they are the very names that He permits us to USE! By union with Him, we are permitted to share something of His OWN intimate relationship to the Father. CYPRIAN, Bishop of Carthage in the middle of the third century AD, well expresses our PRIVILEGE when writing about the Lord's Prayer:

> 'How great is the Lord's indulgence! How great are His condescension and plenteousness of goodness toward us,

Seeing that He has wished us to pray in the sight of God in such a way as to call God Father, and to call ourselves sons of God, even as Christ is the Son of God... a name which none of us would DARE to venture on in prayer, unless He Himself had allowed us thus to pray'. CYPRIAN, BISHOP OF CARTHAGE.

Now, we CAN repeat the Lord's Prayer without HYPOCRISY. Previously, the words had a hollow sound; NOW they ring with new and NOBLE meaning. God is INDEED our FATHER IN HEAVEN, who KNOWS our needs, BEFORE we ask (and ASK we MUST; DAILY),(And He will NOT FAIL to give good things to His children... (US).

It may be NECESSARY FOR US TO RECEIVE CORRECTION AT HIS HAND, 'for the Lord disciplines him who He loves, and chastises every son whom He receives . In that discipline, He is treating us as sons, and disciplining us for OUR good. With such a Father, LOVING, WISE and STRONG, we CAN be delivered from ALL our fears. MATT 6:7-13 & :25-34 & 7:7-12 HEB 12:3-11.

<u>AN ASSURED RELATIONSHIP:</u> The Christian's relationship to God as a child to his Father, is not only INTIMATE, but also SURE. Many babes in Christ seem to do no more than HOPE for the best; It IS POSSIBLE TO KNOW FOR CERTAIN.

It is MORE than possible. It is God's REVEALED WILL FOR US. We ought to be SURE of our relationship with God, not just for the sake of OUR peace of mind and helpfulness to others; God MEANS us to be SURE. JOHN states CATEGORICALLY that THIS was the purpose in writing his first letter: 'I write this to you who believe in the name of the Son of God, that you may KNOW that you have eternal life'.

Yet, the way to BE sure, is NOT just to FEEL sure. Most people who are at the beginning of their Christian life (babes in Christ), make this MISTAKE. They rely too much on their SUPERFICIAL FEELINGS. One day they FEEL close to God; the next day they feel ESTRANGED from Him again. And since they IMAGINE that their FEELINGS ACCURATELY reflect their ACTUAL SPIRITUAL CONDITION, THEY FALL INTO A FRENZY OF UNCERTAINTY. Their Christian life becomes a PRECARIOUS SWITCH- BACK ride as they SOAR to the heights of ELATION, only to PLUNGE again into the DEPTHS OF DEPRESSION, and, unfortunately, many never develop beyond the 'babes in Christ' stage in their Christian existence; EVERYBODY loses; God, themselves, and their fellow man. This ought NOT to be so. (the COMMUNITY, CITY, PROVINCE and NATION ALSO LOSES).

This ERRATIC experience is NOT God's PURPOSE for HIS children. We have to learn to MISTRUST our FEELINGS. They are EXTREMELY VARIABLE. They change with the WEATHER, with CIRCUMSTANCES, and with our HEALTH. We are FICKLE creatures of WHIM and MOOD, and our FLUCTUATING FEELINGS often have NOTHING to do with our SPIRITUAL PROGRESS.

The basis of our KNOWLEDGE that we are in relationship with God, is NOT OUR FEELINGS, but the FACT that GOD SAYS WE ARE. The test we are to apply to ourselves is OBJECTIVE rather than SUBJECTIVE. We are NOT to grub around inside ourselves for EVIDENCE of SPIRITUAL LIFE, but to LOOK UP, and OUT, and AWAY TO GOD and HIS WORD. But. how can we KNOW and be ASSURED that we ARE God's Children ?

First, God PROMISES in His written word to give eternal life to THOSE WHO RECEIVE CHRIST. 'This is the testimony, that God gave us eternal life, and this life is in His Son. He who has the Son has the life; he who has not the Son has not the life'. HUMBLY to believe that we HAVE eternal life is NOT PRESUMPTUOUS. On the contrary, to believe God's word is HUMILITY, not PRIDE; it is WISDOM, not PRESUMPTION. The FOLLY and the SIN would be to DOUBT, for 'he who does not believe God has made Him a liar, because he has not believed in the testimony that God has borne to His Son'. 1 JOHN 5:10-12.

The Bible is FULL of the PROMISES OF GOD. The SENSIBLE Christian begins, as soon as possible, TO STORE THEM IN HIS MEMORY. Then, when he stumbles into the ditch of DEPRESSION and DOUBT, he can use GOD'S PROMISES as ropes by which to pull himself out. Here are a few verses to start memorizing. Each contains a DIVINE PROMISE:
Christ will receive us if we come to him. JOHN 6:37.
He will hold us and never let us go. JOHN 10:28.
He will never leave us. MATT 28:20; HEB 13:5-6.
God will not allow us to be tempted beyond our strength. 1 COR 10:13.
He will forgive us when we confess our sins. 1 JOHN 1:9.
He will give us wisdom when we ask for it. JAMES 1:5.

See also SOME BASIC TEXTS (Inter-Varsity Press) (a classified selection of 150 passages for memorizing).

Second, God speaks to OUR HEARTS. Listen to these STATEMENTS:

'God's love has been poured into our hearts through the Holy Spirit'...'When we cry 'Abba! Father!' it is the Spirit Himself bearing witness with our spirit that we are the children of God. ROM 5:5 & 8:15-16.
Every Christian KNOWS what this means.

The outward witness of the Holy Ghost in Scripture is confirmed by the indwelling (inward) witness of the Holy Spirit of Christ in experience. This is NOT to place any CONFIDENCE in the SHALLOW and CHANGEABLE FEELINGS; it IS, rather, to expect a deepening conviction in our HEARTS, as the Holy Spirit of Christ ASSURES us of God's love for us, and prompts us to cry 'Father!' as we seek God's face in Prayer.

Third, the same Spirit bears witness to our Sonship in Scripture, and EXPERIENCE completes His testimony in our Character. If we ARE born again into God's Family, then Christ's Holy Spirit indwells us. The indwelling of the Holy Spirit of Christ is one of the greatest PRIVILEGES of God's Children. It is the DISTINGUISHING characteristic of the babe in Christ. 'Anyone who does not have the Spirit of Christ does not belong to Him' ROM 8:9-17. And Christ's Holy Spirit will not have indwelt us long, before He begins to work a change in our manner of life. JOHN applies this test RUTHLESSLY in his first letter. If anyone PERSISTS in disobeying the Commandments of God, and is DISREGARDING his duties to his fellow men, he writes, then he is not a Christian, whatever he may say. Righteousness and love are indispensable marks of one indwelt by the Holy Spirit of Christ.

A SECURE RELATIONSHIP: Supposing we HAVE entered into this intimate relationship with God, and are ASSURED of it by God's OWN WORD, is it a secure relationship ? Or, can we be born into God's Family one moment, and repudiated from it the next ? The Bible indicates that it is a PERMANENT relationship. 'If children, then heirs', wrote Paul, 'heirs of God and fellow heirs with Christ', and went on to argue, in a MAGNIFICENT passage at the end of Romans 8:, that God's Children are ETERNALLY safe, for NOTHING WHATEVER can separate them from His love, as long as they continue to DO THEIR PART i.e. to grow in the goodness and knowledge of God. Although quite RARE, it IS possible to be 'CUT OFF' as SAUL and many others were for turning away from God, well deserving of the wrath of God, in TRUTH and JUSTICE.

Many 'babes in Christ' have asked 'what happens if or when I sin; Do I forfeit my Sonship, and cease to be God's child ? NO!...(providing)...

Think of the analogy of a human family. A boy is offensively rude to his parents. A cloud descends on the home. There is tension in the atmosphere. Father and son are not on speaking terms. What has happened ? Has the boy ceased to be a son ? No! Their relationship has not changed; it is their FELLOWSHIP that has been broken. Relationship depends on birth; fellowship depends on BEHAVIOUR. As soon as the boy apologizes, he is forgiven. And forgiveness restores fellowship.

So it is with the children of God (in most cases). When we sin, we don't forfeit our relationship to God as children, though our fellowship with Him is spoiled until we confess AND forsake our sin. As soon as we 'confess our sins, He is faithful and just, and will forgive our sins and cleanse us from all unrighteousness', for 'if anyone does sin, we have an advocate with the Father, Jesus Christ the righteous; and He is the expiation for our sins'. 1 JOHN 1:9 & 2:1-2. So DON'T wait until evening or next Sunday, to put right whatever goes wrong during the day. When you fall, (fall on your knees), REPENT and HUMBLY seek YOUR FATHER'S FORGIVENESS AT ONCE. Aim to preserve your conscience clear and undefiled.

We can be JUSTIFIED only ONCE; we need to be FORGIVEN EVERY DAY (if necessary). When Jesus washed the apostles' feet, He gave them an illustration of this. Peter asked Him to wash his hands and his head as well as his feet. But Jesus replied: 'He who has bathed does not need to wash, except for his feet, but he is clean all over'. A man invited to a dinner party in Jerusalem, would take a bath before going out. On arrival at his friend's house, he would not be offered another bath; but a slave would meet him at the front door, and wash his feet. When we first come to Christ in REPENTANCE and FAITH, we receive a 'bath' (that is JUSTIFICATION, and is outwardly symbolized in Baptism). It NEVER needs to be repeated. But as we walk through the dirty streets of the world, we CONSTANTLY need to 'have our feet washed' (which is DAILY forgiveness).

<u>CHRISTIAN RESPONSIBILITIES:</u> To be a Child of God is a wonderful PRIVILEGE. It involves OBLIGATIONS also. Peter implied this when he wrote; 'like new born babes, crave for pure spiritual milk, that by it you may grow up to Salvation'. 1 PET 2:2.

The great privilege of the child of God is RELATIONSHIP; the responsibility is GROWTH. Everybody loves children, but nobody in their right mind, wants them to stay in the NURSERY. The TRAGEDY, however, is that many Christians, born again in Christ NEVER GROW UP. Others even suffer from SPIRITUAL INFANTILE REGRESSION. Our Heavenly Father's PURPOSE, on the other hand, is that 'babes in Christ' should become 'MATURE IN CHRIST'. Our RE-BIRTH MUST BE FOLLOWED BY GROWTH. The crisis of JUSTIFICATION (our acceptance before God) MUST lead to the process of SANCTIFICATION (OUR GROWTH IN HOLINESS), What Peter terms 'growing up in Salvation'. EPH 4:15.

These are the TWO MAIN SPHERES in which the Christian MUST GROW. The first is in UNDERSTANDING, and the second in HOLINESS (WISDOM). When we BEGIN the Christian life, we probably understand very little, and we have only just come to know GOD. NOW we MUST increase in the knowledge of God, and our Lord Jesus Christ. This knowledge is partly INTELLECTUAL, and partly PERSONAL. In connection with the former, I urge you to read your Bible, morning and evening, allowing the Holy Ghost to do the teaching, as YOU are ABLE to digest. See NCRC 6/2. To neglect to GROW in your UNDERSTANDING is to COURT DISASTER.

We MUST grow in HOLINESS OF LIFE. The New Testament writers speak of the DEVELOPMENT of our FAITH IN GOD, our LOVE FOR OUR FELLOW MEN, and our LIKENESS TO CHRIST. Every son of God LONGS to become more and more CONFORMED, in his CHARACTER and BEHAVIOUR, to Jesus

Christ. The Christian life is a life of RIGHTEOUSNESS. We must OBEY GOD'S PRECEPTS, ORACLES, COMMANDMENTS, and DO GOD'S WILL. The Holy Spirit of Christ has been given to us, by God, partly for this purpose. Christ has made our bodies His temple when He dwells within us. And as we SUBMIT to His AUTHORITY, and FOLLOW HIS LEADING, He will subdue our evil desire and cause HIS fruits to appear in our lives. GAL 5:16 & :22-23.

HOW SHALL WE GROW ? There are THREE main secrets of SPIRITUAL DEVELOPMENT. They are ALSO the CHIEF RESPONSIBILITIES of the child of God. (our duty to God; our duty to the Church; our duty to our family, our duty to our community, country, and the world).

OUR DUTY TO GOD: Our relationship to our heavenly Father, though SECURE, is NOT STATIC. HE wants His children to grow up to know Him MORE and MORE, INTIMATELY. Generations of Christians have discovered that the PRINCIPAL way to DO this, is to WAIT UPON HIM EVERY DAY, in a time of BIBLE READING and PRAYER. This is an INDISPENSIBLE NECESSITY for the Christian that WANTS to make PROGRESS. We are ALL busy nowadays, BUT, we must somehow rearrange our PRIORITIES, in order to make time for our indispensable spiritual exercises/duties. It will mean RIGOROUS SELF-DISCIPLINE. Together with a legible Bible, and an alarm clock THAT WORKS, we are well on the road to VICTORY.

It is IMPORTANT to PRESERVE THE BALANCE BETWEEN BIBLE READING AND PRAYER. Through Scriptures, the Holy Ghost speaks to us, and trains us up; while through prayer, WE speak. It is also wise to SCHEDULE and make SYSTEMATIC our reading of the Bible. See NCRC 6/2. MEDITATION is also a prerequisite.

Pray before you read, asking the Holy Ghost to open your eyes and illuminate your mind to obvious necessities. Then read SLOWLY, MEDITATIVELY, and THOUGHTFULLY. Read (and re-read if necessary). Then go on to APPLY to YOUR OWN LIFE, the message of the verses you have read. Look for PROMISES to CLAIM, and COMMANDS TO OBEY; EXAMPLES TO FOLLOW: AND SINS TO AVOID. It is helpful to keep a notebook, and write down what you learn. Above all, LOOK FOR JESUS CHRIST. HE is the chief subject of the Bible. We can not only find Him revealed there, we can meet Him personally through its pages.

Prayer follows naturally. Begin by speaking back to God, on the same subject He spoke to YOU about. Don't CHANGE the CONVERSATION! If He has spoken to you of HIMSELF and HIS GLORY, WORSHIP HIM. If He has spoken to you of yourself and your sins, CONFESS THEM. Thank Him for any blessings that may have been revealed in the passage, and pray that its lessons may be learned by yourself and your friends.

When you have prayed over the Bible passage you have read, you will want to go on with OTHER prayers. If your Bible is the first great aid to prayer, your diary will be the second. Commit to Him in the MORNING, the details of the day that lies before you, and in the evening, run through the day again, CONFESSING THE SINS YOU HAVE COMMITTED, via COMMISSION or OMISSION; give THANKS for the blessings you have received, and pray for the people you have met.

God IS YOUR FATHER. Be NATURAL, CONFIDING, and BOLD. He IS interested in ALL the DETAILS of YOUR LIFE. VERY SOON, you will find it essential to start some kind of a PRAYER LIST of your relatives and friends, you feel responsible to pray for. It is wise to make your Prayer List as flexible as possible, so that people can be easily added or taken from it.

<u>OUR DUTY TO THE CHURCH:</u> The Christian life is not just a private affair of your own. If we ARE BORN AGAIN into God's Family, not only has He become our Father, but every other believer in the world, whatever his nation or denomination, has become our brother or sister in Christ. One of the commonest names for Christians in the New Testament is 'brethren'. This is a glorious truth. But it is no good supposing that membership of the universal Church of Christ is enough; we must belong to some local branch of it. Nor is it sufficient to be a member of a Christian Union or College or elsewhere (although I hope you will become active in yours). EVERY Christian's place is in a local Church, sharing in its WORSHIP, FELLOWSHIP and WITNESS.

Perhaps you ask which church you should join. If you are already linked with a church, either by upbringing or because you have been attending one recently, you would be unwise to sever this connection without GOOD REASON. If you are free to choose your church membership, however, here are two criteria to guide you. The first concern is the Pastor, the second the congregation. Ask yourself these questions: IS THE PASTOR SUBMISSIVE TO THE AUTHORITY OF SCRIPTURE, so that he seeks in his sermons, to explain its message, and relate it to contemporary life ? Does the congregation at least approximate to a fellowship of BELIEVERS, who love Christ; one another; and the world, according to the Scriptures ?

BAPTISM is the way of ENTRY into the VISIBLE Christian society. It has other meanings as well, as we have seen, but if you have NOT been Baptized, you should ask your Pastor to prepare you for Baptism. Then DO ALLOW YOURSELF to be drawn right into the Christian fellowship. MUCH may seen strange to you at first; DO NOT STAND ASIDE. Church or Chapel attendance on Sundays is a DEFINATE CHRISTIAN DUTY, and nearly EVERY branch of the Christian Church agrees that the Lord's Supper, or Holy Communion is the CENTRAL SERVICE, INSTITUTED BY CHRIST, and commemorating His death in fellowship with one another.

I hope I am not giving the IMPRESSION that fellowship is merely a SUNDAY TREAT! Love for other Christians, however unlikely it may seem in prospect, IS A NEW AND REAL EXPERIENCE. In a Christian fellowship of all TYPES, BACKGROUNDS and AGES, there are NEW depths of friendship, and MUTUAL sharing to be DISCOVERED. The Christian's closest friends will probably be CHRISTIANS, and, above all, HIS LIFE PARTNER MUST BE A CHRISTIAN TOO. 2 COR 6:14.

OUR DUTY TO THE NATION: The Christian life is a FAMILY AFFAIR, in which the children enjoy fellowship with their Father, and with each other. Let it NOT, for one moment, be thought that this exhausts the Christian's RESPONSIBILITIES. Christians are NOT a self-regarding coterie of SMUG and SELFISH PIGS, who are interested ONLY IN THEMSELVES. On the contrary, EVERY

Christian should be DEEPLY CONCERNED ABOUT ALL HIS FELLOW MEN. And it is part of his CHRISTIAN VOCATION, to SERVE them in WHATEVER way God ordains via your soul.

The Christian Church has a NOBLE RECORD of philanthropic work, for the NEEDY and NEGLECTED people of the world.. the POOR and HUNGRY; WIDOWS and ORPHANS; the SICK; VICTIMS OF OPPRESSION and DISCRIMINATION; PRISONERS; SLAVES; REFUGEES and DROP-OUTS. The world-wide followers of Christ ARE seeking, in His Name, to alleviate SUFFERING and DISTRESS. Yet, an ENORMOUS amount of work is WAITING to be done. And SOMETIMES, it must be CONFESSED WITH SHAME, others, who make no Christian profession, seem to show MORE compassion than we, WHO CLAIM TO KNOW CHRIST. These works were GIVEN TO THE CHURCH, not the government.

There is ANOTHER and PARTICULAR RESPONSIBILITY that Christians have towards 'THE WORLD' , as the Bible describes those OUTSIDE Christ and His Church: EVANGELISM! To EVANGELIZE means LITERALLY to spread the good news of JESUS CHRIST. There are MILLIONS of people that are ignorant of Christ and HIS SALVATION, in the SECULARIZED WESTERN WORLD as well. For CENTURIES, the Church seems to have been HALF ASLEEP. Is THIS the generation when Christians will WAKE UP, and win the... nation for Christ ? PERHAPS, Christ has a SPECIAL task for you to do (phenom ?) SEEK TO DISCOVER GOD'S WILL FOR YOUR LIFE, AND BE SURRENDERED TO IT, VIA THE DICTATES OF YOUR SOUL. Perhaps a REVIVAL for Canada; via POLITICS ?

God DOES intend every Christian to be a WITNESS to Jesus Christ. In his HOME, AMONG HIS FRIENDS, IN HIS SCHOOL, OR IN THE PLACE OF BUSINESS. It is also his SOLEMN RESPONSIBILITY to live a CONSISTENT, LOVING, HUMBLE, HONEST, CHRIST-LIKE LIFE, and to SEEK TO WIN OTHER PEOPLE FOR GOD. As Christians, we MUST be DISCREET, and COURTEOUS, but DETERMINED.

The way to begin IS BY PRAYER. Ask God to give you a SPECIAL CONCERN for one or two of YOUR FRIENDS. It is USUALLY wise to KEEP TO PEOPLE OF YOUR OWN GENDER.

Then pray REGULARLY and DEFINITELY for their CONVERSION; foster YOUR friendship with them, FOR ITS OWN SAKE; take TROUBLE to spend TIME with THEM; and REALLY LOVE THEM FOR THEMSELVES. Soon, an OPPORTUNITY WILL come, to take them to some service or meeting, where they will hear the Gospel EXPLAINED; or to give them some Christian literature to read; or tell them simply, what Jesus Christ has come to mean to YOU, and HOW YOU FOUND JESUS. OUR most ELEQUENT TESTIMONY, WILL BE WITHOUT EFFECT, if we are CONTRADICTING it by OUR CONDUCT; little is more influential for Christ, than a LIFE THAT CHRIST IS OBVIOUSLY transforming.

Such are the GREAT PRIVILEGES and RESPONSIBILITIES of the child of God. Born into the Family of God, and enjoying with his heavenly Father, a relationship that is INTIMATE, ASSURED and SECURE. The Christian SEEKS to be DISCIPLINED in his DAILY times of BIBLE READING and PRAYER; LOYAL IN

CHURCH MEMBERSHIP, and, at the SAME TIME, ACTIVE in CHRISTIAN SERVICE and WITNESS.

This STATEMENT OF THE CHRISTIAN LIFE, reveals the TENSION to which ALL Christian people are subject. We find ourselves CITIZENS of TWO KINGDOMS, the one EARTHLY, and the other HEAVENLY. And EACH citizenship lays upon us DUTIES that we are NOT AT LIBERTY TO EVADE.

On the one hand, the New Testament writers lay CONSIDERABLE STRESS, on our OBLIGATIONS. To THE STATE; to OUR EMPLOYER; to OUR FAMILY; and to SOCIETY AS A WHOLE. The BIBLE will not ALLOW us to RETREAT from these PRACTICAL RESPONSIBILITIES, either into MYSTICISM, or into a CHRISTIAN FELLOWSHIP, that is INSULATED FROM THE WORLD.

On the other hand, some New Testament authors remind us that we are 'ALIENS and EXILES' on earth, that 'our commonwealth is in heaven' and that we are travelling to a home. 2 COR 4:16-18; PHIL 3:20; 1 PET 2:11. Consequently, we are not to lay up treasures on earth, nor to pursue purely selfish ambitions, nor to become assimilated to the standards of the world, nor to be unduly burdened by the sorrows of this present life.

It is COMPARATIVELY SIMPLE, to ease this TENSION either by WITHDRAWING INTO CHRIST, and NEGLECTING THE WORLD; or by so INVOLVING OURSELVES in the WORLD, as to FORGET CHRIST. NEITHER of these is a GENUINE CHRISTIAN SOLUTION, because EACH involves the DENIAL of one or the other of our CHRISTIAN OBLIGATIONS.

The BALANCED Christian that takes SCRIPTURE for his guide, will SEEK TO LIVE EQUALLY AND SIMULTANEOUSLY 'IN CHRIST' and 'IN THE WORLD". The Christian CANNOT OPT OUT OF EITHER.

This is the life of DISCIPLESHIP Jesus calls us to. Jesus DIED and ROSE AGAIN, that WE may have a NEWNESS OF LIFE, GRACE and STRENGTH. GOD has given us HIS SPIRIT, so that we CAN live out THAT life, in THIS world.

FOOD FOR THOUGHT

GOD calls US to FOLLOW CHRIST, and to give OURSELVES WHOLLY and UNRESERVEDLY TO HIS SERVICE.
N.B. IN ALL INSTANCES, 'HE' IS TO BE UNDERSTOOD TO MEAN 'HE/SHE', WHEN REFERRING TO GENDER, IN ACCORDANCE WITH SCRIPTURES.

The basis for this Synthesis is a textbook utilized in a comprehensive course on Basic Christianity, provided by Professor John R. W. Stott, Sussex, England. A Holy Ghost filled solid, standing, mature instrument and servant of God; a mentor and friend in Christ. If there is any good within this Synthesis, it is from the Holy Ghost, via The Holy See, and Professor John R.W. Stott, and his teachings.

As Almighty God does ALL things WELL, within HIS Realm, satan, likewise, does all things well, within his realm, and has established a MAZE that resembles a skein of wool, i.e. a BLACK thread of deceit; lies; half-truths; counterfeiting; arrogance; vanity; pride; sensuality; empirical thinking; spiritually blinded eyes; spiritually plugged up ears; Hermeneutics; malicious cunning, etc. MILES in length, wound up into a ball, DEFYING us to untangle that skein.

This maze /ball is further compounded and complicated ...(ASSISTED)...via unthinking, stubborn and arrogant pseudo 'babes' or 'juniors' in Christ who, in ignorance (lack of wisdom), foster and promote the in-fighting between the brethren of the Universal Church of Jesus Christ, to their own peril, and to the benefit of Lucifer's realm.

In our day, these untruths, utilized by satan to create a CLOSED LOOP, ranges between: 'The King James version is the ONLY and TRUE Bible' by some of the brethren, to the blasphemy of those that deny the Deity of Christ; the Virgin Birth; and the Resurrection of Christ. The vehicles satan utilizes are misguided scholars(?), educators (?), Cardinals(?), theologians(?), bleeding-heart do-gooders and laypeople, at enmity with their souls, beguiled by satan, trapped well within their OWN empirical thinking, attempting to get God in step with the people, via gross theosophies and spurious speculations; Square pegs in round holes.

Look at our Towns and Cities; read their papers; listen to their news broadcasts.. WHAT IS WRONG ???   WHAT IS HAPPENING ???

Look at some of the PROMISES of GOD...
THE LORD IS OUR STRENGTH   PSALM 27:1
ASK, IT WILL BE GIVEN YOU   MATT 7:7
GOD GIVES FAITH   ROM 12:13

GOD ALWAYS CAUSES US TO TRIUMPH   2 COR 2:14
ALL THINGS THROUGH CHRIST   PHIL 4:13
GOD SUPPLIES ALL OUR NEEDS PHIL 4:19
GOD HELPS THE TEMPTED   HEB 2:18
CHRIST BEARS OUR CARES   1 PET 5:7
How many of us can HONESTLY say, all the above is true?

Do the Scriptures lie ? Did the sin in the world develop into such GIGANTIC proportion, that God did not foresee, or did not anticipate, and is now beyond God's capacity or capabilities ? Did God out-promise Himself, and now cannot produce ? Is God dead or asleep ? Is Christianity a con ? NO! is the answer to ALL of the above questions. TRUE Christians KNOW, ALL of the Promises of God are true, and ARE 'THERE' for us.

The 'PROBLEM' is NOT with God, His Son, or The Holy Ghost.. the 'PROBLEM' is with US...especially with those that play at their worship. A bad tree cannot bear good fruit.

WHAT IS WRONG ??? Well, lets start with the bleeding-heart do-gooders. These are those that rationalize, condone, aid-and abet (actually encouraging) sinful behaviour.
Their 'success' can be attributed to the FACT that Christ's teachings can EASILY be debased, distorted, or grossly perverted (changed), into inferior imitation (their OWN imitations). This scenario is further compounded and complicated by the FACT that the Scriptures have been TWISTED, WARPED, STRETCHED, BATTERED, MANHANDLED, and TAKEN OUT OF CONTEXT, to such a DEPLORABLE and DISGUSTING extent.

They break God's Precepts, Oracles and Commandments,

(and encourage others to do likewise), then naively ask why God is not blessing and/or helping them. And, to add insult to injury, have no concept whatsoever regarding God's Commandments, Oracles, or Precepts. COL 2:4 EPH 5:6-7. They do not know what it is to be SAVED or BORN AGAIN. See NCRC 208/1.

We must be cognizant of the implications of being created in God's likeness and image GEN 1:26. Therefore, WE have some of God's characteristics and emotions; i.e. LOVE, HURT, ANGER: how do WE feel or respond when we are lied to ? get conned ? ignored? robbed ? cheated ? gross ingratitude ? So does God! See NCRC 210/2.

We must know how to make PRAYERS, INTERCESSIONS, SUPPLICATIONS and PETITIONS, and keep these in balance with Bible reading, Meditation, and Spiritual exercises/duties, utilizing the prayer formula of MATT 6:9-13. See NCRC 207/2.

The Christian Church in the world today, falls into three categories:

1.FUNDAMEMTALISTS: Bible believing and teaching. Acknowledge the FULL and SUPREME AUTHORITY of the Bible. This term is very often used as a PUT-DOWN, thanks to satan's efforts.

2. REFORMED: Embarrassed by the Fundamentalist', broke away to form a movement to get God in step with the people, via secular humanism.

3.MODERATE/NEW AGE; Do not want to offend ANYONE, so they don't take a stand on ANYTHING. They do not seem to understand or realize, that 'NO STAND' IS a stand.
2 TIM 3:16-17 PROV 1:1-7.

We seem to have forgotten; that as GOD has ANGELS, SPIRITS, SAINTS, INSTRUMENTS and SERVANTS, and gives GRACE, BLESSINGS, URGINGS, COUNSEL, and DISCERNMENTS to those in HIS realm. satan ALSO has angels, spirits, saints, instruments and servants, and gives pseudo grace, blessings, urgings, counsel, and discernments to those in his realm.

satan can duplicate or counterfeit anything God can do, except satan cannot create life, cannot be original, cannot be honest/just or forgive sin.

Scripture is addressed to only three groups of people:
the solid, standing, mature instrument and servant of God;
the seeker or babe in Christ;
the sinner or reprobate.

We must guard against taking Scripture out of context. Scripture, like a computer, can be made to say anything we want it to say, by taking it out of context. We must not take something said to one group, and apply it to another group.. it does not apply; its out of context.

Our part God will NOT do; God's part we CANNOT do.

Some say the Old Testament is not for Christians; only the

New Testament is necessary. NOT SO! The New Testament by itself, is incomplete. Many times we read 'that Scriptures may be fulfilled'; words that point us back to the Old Testament. Characters are referred to; incidents recalled; without a knowledge of the Old Testament, the New Testament cannot make complete sense. COR 10:1-12...Paul refers to the Old Testament record of God's dealings with the Israelites on their journey from Egypt to Canaan. PSALM 78:

Behind the message of the Gospel we give to others, there must be a 'WALK' .. a life of personal Holiness and Purity, that backs up our PROFESSION. Too many 'babes in Christ' can talk the talk, but cannot walk the walk. They display hypocrisy to those around them, UNAWARES. They do a lot of harm and damage.. they make fools of themselves; a farce of their Christian experience; and a friend of Lucifer.

We can obstruct God in not only what He can do FOR us, also in what He can do THROUGH us. May I suggest the reading of JOHN E HUNTER'S book, LIMITING GOD, and my own Bible studies regarding this subject.

On the way to and off Skid Road, there are seven steps DOWN, and seven steps UP, applicable to ALL of us: LUKE 15-11-24.

DOWN	UP
1. SELF-WILL :12	7. REJOICING :23-24
2. SELFISHNESS :13	6. RE-CLOTHING :22
3. SEPARATION :13	5. RECONCILIATION :20
4. SENSUALITY :13	4. RETURN :20

5. DESTITUTION :14   3. REPENTANCE :19
6. ABASEMENT :15   2. RESOLUTION :18
7. STARVATION :16   1. REALIZATION :17

EVERY PERSON BORN INTO THIS WORLD IS A SPECIFICALLY UNIQUE PERSON. God, our family, the Church, the Community and Nation NEEDS what YOU have to give, within God's plan and realm. EACH ONE OF US is called (created) by God to become PERSONALLY and ACTIVELY INVOLVED, IN SEEKING SOLUTIONS TO THE PROBLEMS THAT CONFRONT US ALL.   2 TIM 1:9.

Each one of US has been created to do a SPECIFIC job for God...a job that has NOT been given to anyone else. If I don't do it, IT WILL NOT BE DONE, and God, our family, the Church, the community and the nation and myself will be the less for my dereliction of duty or job

WHOever, and WHAT ever we are, each one of US has a path to walk (or job to do) for God, and we CAN (and DO), shape God, our family, the Church, the community, nation, and world we live in. If not ME, who will do the job I have been created and sent to do ???

Be not overcome by evil, but overcome evil with good. ROM 12 :21.

Since it IS possible, via GOD'S help, grace, power and might, to re-shape ourselves, WE are responsible for the shape we are in.

'Who has beguiled you ? Are you so foolish as to think (or

believe) that beginning in the Spirit, you now make a finish in the flesh ?' 'Have you suffered so much in vain ? HE (GOD) who gives the Spirit to you, and works miracles among you, does He do it by the works of the Law or by the message or Faith ?' GAL 3:15 (HEARING AND BELIEVING). See   ISA 58:13-14.

Blind chance did not put us here; (in the world), a loving God did, as PART of HIS PLAN AND HIS CREATION. We HAVE what it takes...will we use it ? 'Do not let your heart be troubled, or be afraid, 'Jesus will be with you.   MATT 28:30   MARK 5:36   JOHN 14:27   2 TIM 1:9.

DON'T YOU EVEN BELIEVE IN YOU ?

NO ONE can MAKE us develop our potential, or do it for us. Others may assist us...show us the way...but the CHOICE is OURS. To follow... to strike out on our own...or to do NOTHING. We ARE what we HAVE been + what we CHOOSE to become. What's YOUR choice ?

Start from where you are right now, on the basis of what you have decided. If we don't make a START, we can't possibly get anywhere. If we don't know where we are going, THAT is where we   will end up.. NOWHERE.

EACH DAY;
Do something good you DON'T want to do.
Do something good you DO want to do.
Be quiet for Prayer 2 - 3 times a day.
Read Scriptures at least 15 minutes morning and evening.
Reach out in some way to someone else, for them.

In a short period of time, you'll be AMAZED at where you will find yourself.

Maybe you're at a low point right now, but you DON'T have to stay there. Unbelievers are not born, they are made.

The outcome of your life is not in GOD'S Hands, it's in YOUR hands. The outcome of your life is not a matter of CHANCE, it's a matter of CHOICE. (the choices YOU make along the way).

Must Jesus bear the Cross alone, STILL ? NCRC 99/2 is the message we need to get out to the iatrogenics, among others.

The characteristic of the 'babes in Christ' that are SAVED AND STUCK, is WANDERING. Often they seek or try to obtain INSTANT GODLINESS...THERE IS NO SUCH THING.

PAUL wrote about Godliness to TIMOTHY, in his first letter to that budding young Pastor PAUL was training. PAUL said 'Timothy, you must TRAIN yourself for the purpose of Godliness. 1 TIM 4:7-8.

DISCIPLINE is the secret of GODLINESS.

The word DISCIPLINE has DISAPPEARED from our MINDS, our MOUTHES, our HOMES, and our CULTURE. Yet, we MUST be willing to suffer the PAIN OF CHANGE, or we will be GIVEN, THE PAIN OF REMORSE AND REGRET.

There is no OPTION about being GODLY. PAUL'S words

constitute a COMMAND, by which The Holy Ghost tells us to DISCIPLINE OURSELVES for the purpose of GODLINESS.

GODLINESS is the GOAL that we must DISCIPLINE ourselves for; the GOAL we must move toward EVERY DAY. This means becoming more like Jesus Christ Himself... IMITATING JESUS EACH DAY; leading a life that REFLECTS Jesus, EACH DAY.

WE must come out of 'the Garden', take up our Cross, and go on to OUR Calvary, dying to self, before we can BEGIN to become a SOLID, STANDING, MATURE, Instrument and Servant of God.

If you are going to learn DISCIPLINE, you must first learn PATIENCE. We must WANT, HUNGER, and THIRST after GODLINESS.

The PROBLEM is that, although basically, our orientation is NEW, many of our day to day PRACTICES are not yet oriented toward GODLINESS.

The 'old man', (old ways of living), is STILL our unwelcome companion; we must NOT despair. We must recognize that the very word DISCIPLINE, makes it CLEAR, that GODLINESS cannot be ZAPPED...Godliness cannot be whipped up like instant pudding...GODLINESS doesn't come that way.

DISCIPLINE means WORK (success is spelled   W O R K)... it means SUSTAINED DAILY EFFORT...EXERCISE and TRAINING. The Greek word the Holy Ghost used is GYMNAZO... that the English words GYMNASIUM and GYMNASTICS were derived from. It is a term CLEARLY related to ATHLETICS.

Do you think Wayne Gretzkey became a GREAT hockey player by simply by appearing at the Oiler's rink one afternoon, after he had decided, that morning, he was going to play hockey ? Do you think that only when there is a game he practices ? You KNOW otherwise. You KNOW he spent countless hours PRACTICING...it takes SUSTAINED REGULAR PRACTICE to achieve such skills.

We must DAILY ask Jesus for the Grace and strength to DISCIPLINE ourselves, for the purpose of GODLINESS...to IMITATE Him...to be LIKE Him...CHRIST LIKE. HEB 6:12 1 COR 11:1   EPH 5:1   1 THES 1:6   2 THES 3:7 & :9.

We must MEDITATE and PONDER, (IN OUR HEART, NOT THE HEAD), in order to convert INFORMATION into KNOWLEDGE, as we progress to GODLINESS; and LOVE and APPRECIATION for God and HIS WAYS and REALM.   PROV 18:2 & 27:7   EPH 4:23   PSALM 1:2 & 64:10 & 73:13   & 119:15 & 143:5.

But remember, as a 'babe in Christ', CONCURRENT with the quest for GODLINESS, you WILL be fighting the WAR OF THE FLESH, over which you must be VICTORIOUS. ROM 7:14-25 explains this 'WAR', and the SOLUTION to that dilemma. (the Grace of God, through Jesus Christ', for which you ALSO must pray for, DAILY). If we will not ACCEPT the pain of SELF-DISCIPLINE, we will be GIVEN the pain of REMORSE and REGRET. See. NCRC 15/2.

DEUT 1:2...'There are 11 days journey from Horeb, by the way of Mount Seir unto Kadesh-Barnea'. But the NEXT verse

:3 says 'and it came to pass... IN THE FORTIETH YEAR, ON THE FIRST DAY OF THE ELEVENTH MONTH'.

HOW AMAZING...40 years and eleven months later, and the Israelites STILL had NOT reached the land of Canaan. WHY ???

What should have been a CONTINUOUS FORWARD movement...pressing on.. COUNTING of God's PROMISES.. expecting nothing but BLESSINGS, BECAME A FAILURE, due to the mean INGRATITUDE of the Israelites.

They ceased PROGRESSING, and started to WANDER. DISAPPOINTMENT; DISASTER; and DISOBEDIENCE, became the ACCEPTED NORM OF LIFE, and GOD WAS OBSTRUCTED.

There was SO much God WANTED to do for them... so much God COULD do for them...but the Israelites INSISTED on going their OWN WAY (doing things their OWN way)...Through their own stupidity, ignorance and disobedience, THEY obstructed God.   DEUT 6:24-25.. They KNEW what they were SUPPOSED to do...but they CHOSE not to...and   unless the 'babes in Christ' are VERY careful, we CAN, and WILL, be just as unexplainably STUPID as they were, in OUR relationship with the Father, the Son, or The Holy Ghost.

GOD'S plan, is a deliverance from bondage; out of the realm of satan, into the Realm of God; to a completely new life in Jesus Christ and His Church. MATT 28:19-20.

Therefore, if any man be in Christ, he is a new creature; old things are passed away; all things are become new. IF I am a true child of God, then I AM in Christ. 2 COR 5:17. IF I am a believer in Christ, then I AM in Him, and IF I am in Him, I AM a new creature...a new creation, old things pass away. THAT IS GOD'S PROMISE...IS, (not MAYBE; not COULD BE; but IS).

WE INHERIT CHRIST: Our sins have been cleansed by the atonement of Christ's shed Blood on the Cross. We have been brought near to God, as His child, through Christ. Christ IS my SAVIOUR and REDEEMER. Christ is MY ADVOCATE. Christ is the SOURCE of love, joy and peace in MY life...OUR life. All this we KNOW; and all this we TAKE. We inherit JESUS and ALL within God's Realm.   EPH 1:14.

CHRIST INHERITS US: The OTHER side of this coin can be seen in EPH 1:18-19. JESUS INHERITS US. I CANNOT function without ALL that Jesus is for me, so, in an AMAZING way, Jesus cannot fulfill HIS true purpose in MY life, without ALL that I am, at HIS disposal. WE are CHRIST'S INHERITANCE... HIS INSTRUMENTS; SERVANTS; TOOLS; WEAPONS, here on earth. The INSTRUMENTS Christ uses to IMPLEMENT HIS WILL in our FAMILIES, CHURCH, COMMUNITY, TOWN, CITY, PROVINCE, NATION and WORLD. 2 TIM 1:9.

In PSALM 78: we see the Israelites took all God offered. They asked for more; they EXPECTED more; they DEMANDED more; and God gave freely. But God got VERY little in return. The Israelites were SELFISH, BASE, MEAN and full of INGRATITUDE. They obstructed God in what God wanted to accomplish FOR them; they obstructed God in what God wanted to accomplish THROUGH them.

How about US, in THIS day and age ???   Do WE obstruct God in what He can do FOR US, and THROUGH us, via the same   SELFISHNESS ???   We TAKE so willingly; we EXPECT to be FORGIVEN; we EXPECT to be COMFORTED; we EXPECT to be BLESSED; we EXPECT to be provided with PEACE. We HOLD God to ALL of His PROMISES.

But if the Lord comes to US for HIS inheritance in US,(remember, we can't function without HIM, and He can't function without US), THAT'S a different story. We will take all the Lord GIVES, but we are BITTERLY slow to HIS NEEDS, REQUESTS, or URGINGS, if indeed, we do at all respond.

God created us; He redeemed us; we are NOT our own; He bought us with a heavy price. All of this we agree to in PRINCIPLE. But if the Lord needs us, and He calls us, we respond with 'here I am Lord; send someone else'. 2 TIM 1:9

In response to the Lord, we can be far worse than the Israelites EVER were in the desert. We withhold FELLOWSHIP, FRUITFULNESS, FINANCES, TIME, and OUR LIVES, and. God is obstructed. We talk about MY MONEY, MY TIME, MY LIFE, as if these were our prize possessions; as if we can do with them as WE please.

There are VERY searching words in PSALM 12:1. CRISP are the words 'CEASING OF THE GODLY'...'THE FAILING OF

THE FAITHFUL'. (personally, I often wonder if THIS scenario will be 'the straw that breaks the camel's back', and prompt our Heavenly Father to 'pull the pin'). Usually, the PSALMS deal with the harm done by the sinner. But HERE the cry is against the GODLY and the FAITHFUL. Today, we PLAINLY see that the Godly ARE now ceasing, and those who were once faithful, ARE now falling. Many have SUCCUMED TO SECULAR HUMANISM, and Catholic feminism, at the hands of satan, at enmity with their own souls etc. God's problem is NOT the sinner/reprobate, He can handle them with no problem whatsoever. God's problem is the failing saints, instruments and servants, and the falling seekers and babes in Christ, He dispatched into this world, to serve HIM, in ANTICIPATION.

FOR US TO KNOW THAT:
Christ was God's Son;
Christ did many miracles;
God loves us;
Christ died for us;
We can be reconciled to God through Jesus Christ;
Jesus is the light of the world;
To believe that there IS a God;
KNOWING these things does NOT reconcile us to God or SAVE us. JAS 2:19. Satan KNOWS all these things, (AND MORE), and satan goes one better than us... satan TREMBLES.

What is up in our heads, doesn't matter a bit...MANY of us who CAN talk the talk; DO NOT walk the walk. In fact, this can be very DANGEROUS and DETRIMENTAL. If we do not break out of this scenario, when we DO stand for judgement, it will do no more than 'cinch' our condemnation; our CONSCIENCE itself, will condemn us, by bearing witness AGAINST us...WE condemn OURSELVES. When God wants to SEE where we are 'at', He looks into the HEART, not the HEAD.

By deceiving OURSELVES, we help satan. Satan does not condemn us, we are ALREADY doing it; giving satan time and energy to go after someone else; he doesn't need to spend it on us. JAS 1:22 MATT 7:21-23 & :26-27   ROM 2:13.

We must be DOERS; not hearers only; deceiving OURSELVES; conning OURSELVES, via of our OWN double mind/tongue, inconsistency, and instability.
JAS 1:5-8.

FAITH is the CORNERSTONE of our relationship with God and His realm. FAITH in God is PART of our DUTY TO GOD. (see NCRC 68/1). FAITH incorporates: to BELIEVE God, to TRUST God, and to be LOYAL to God, NO MATTER WHAT...all of this mixed together,   constitutes FAITH IN GOD.

We can look around the downtown Eastside of Vancouver B.C., where Drug and Alcohol (with related syndromes) are RAMPANT. What we will be looking at, are STRONGHOLDS OF EVIL. These   'STRONGHOLDS' are certain spots or places within the district, that need to be IDENTIFIED and TORN DOWN.

Not torn down by wrecking balls or bulldozers or other heavy equipment; they will not solve THIS problem. But TORN DOWN   by instruments and servants of God, ALREADY IN PLACE, to whom THIS task has ALREADY BEEN ASSIGNED, by GOD.

Our God is NOT a God of REACTION. He is a God of ANTICIPATION. God PROVIDES ALL THAT IS NECESSARY to deal with His ANTICIPATIONS, COMPLETELY and with ALL SUFFICIENCY, utilizing the instruments and servants HE HAS IN PLACE.

Then, thanks to satan's efforts, (who ALSO anticipates), God's instruments fall, and fail God, and it all SOURS. WE obstruct God, and EVERYONE loses...God, ourselves, and mankind.

This scenario comes about, and is successful in THWARTING GOD, by the power of satan. God's instruments get 'suckered' by satan, and fall. Then satan's instruments move in, taking upon THEMSELVES, these tasks, making fools of themselves, a farce of Christianity, and a friend of satan, to their OWN PERIL. (see NCRC. 66/1).

Personally, I don't know who these Warriors are, but I DO KNOW, they are already in place.(God grant they stand).

For all intentions and purposes, these Warriors of EXORCISM are STANDING, SOLID, MATURE INSTRUMENTS AND SERVANTS OF GOD, filled with the POWER and ANOINTING of The Holy Ghost, for the exorcism path and (in the Name and POWER of JESUS), tour the district, identify the STRONGHOLDS OF EVIL, and in the NAME and POWER of JESUS, TEAR THEM DOWN. If these Warriors are to be 'suckered' by satan, that will happen long enough BEFORE the 'day of battle', so as to NOT be 'THERE' on the DAY OF BATTLE.

The 'suckered' warriors of Exorcism were of God, HAVING the POWER to do that job, but, it seems what was lacking, was the FAITH to UTILIZE that power. What is required, is the NECESSARY FAITH, coupled with the necessary SUBMISSION and OBEDIENCE to God, within the confines of God's Natural Law. HEB 11:6. Without FAITH, it is IMPOSSIBLE to please God. MATT 17:17   MARK 9:19-23   LUKE 9:38-44.

OUR part, God will NOT do; God's part, we CANNOT do. WE must possess the FAITH, in order to bring God's Natural Law into play, and FULL POWER.

God is NOT unreasonable in this...He REQUIRES faith of us, but He is willing to ACCEPT, and WORK WITH TRUE FAITH, THE SIZE OF A MUSTARD SEED, IN THE BEGINNING. (ONLY). MATT 13:31-32   & 17:19-20   LUKE 17:6.

ALL that is NOT from FAITH, is SIN. ROM 14:23   1 COR 15:14   GAL 3:9   EPH 2:8   2 THES 1:11   1 TIM 6:10   HEB 10:39   JAS 1:3.

The business of EXORCISM is a specifically UNIQUE function, to be practiced ONLY by Warriors GOD has ordained for this work. Any that FOOLISHLY, in PRESUMPTION, TAKE this work on for themselves, WILL be subject to ACTS 19:13-16. BE WARNED... if that IS your work, DO IT! if NOT, DO NOT. To reiterate, the 'WORD' (Scriptures) ITSELF, has been so TWISTED, WARPED, STRETCHED, BATTERED, MAN HANDLED, MALIGNED and TAKEN OUT OF CONTEXT, that, it hardly has any credibility at all, in the hands of the failing faithful, that are either taking Scripture out of context, to suit themselves, OR are SELF-TAUGHT via the HEAD and INTELLECT, via INTELLECTUAL SECULAR HUMANISM, rather than ALLOWING THE PARACLETE to teach them. Without The Holy Ghost being their teacher they end up with nothing but the GROSS THEOSOPHY and SPURIOUS SPECULATION, THEY HAVE TAUGHT THEMSELVES. (they had a fool for a teacher).

PSALM 12:4-5 tells us WHY the Godly and the Faithful are failing and falling. HOW MODERN…'my lips are my OWN!'… 'who is Lord over ME!'…'my time is my OWN!'…'my money is my OWN!'…'NO ONE is going to tell ME what to do!' This is the SELFISHNESS that obstructs God; when the child of God DENIES Jesus Christ the inheritance for which HE DIED.

How PATHETIC… to think OUR RESPONSE TO Calvary is the selfishness of a heart that keeps back what it does posses; and holds onto what belongs to another.. JESUS CHRIST.

MORE FOOD FOR THOUGHT

THERE ARE THREE GREAT FUNDAMENTAL MORTAL ERRORS:
1. To fail to honour and obey the dictates of our soul because of dissociation between our soul and our character/personality, heart, spirit, mind and body;
2. Wrong to others, acting against UNITY;
3. Sensuality/lust.

THERE ARE FOUR SOURCES OF DISEASE:

1. God
2. Our soul
3. satan
4. ourselves (diet...life-style etc.).

THE REAL PRIMARY CAUSE OF DISEASE OF MAN ARE SUCH DEFECTS (SIN) AS: PRIDE...VANITY...CRUELTY... SELF – LOVE...IGNORANCE (lack of Wisdom)...INSTABILITY... INCONSISTENCY...GREED...PRESUMPTION...
PRETENSION...HYPOCRISY...FROWARD   MOUTH... IMMATURITY...IMPAIRED   RATIONALE...ARROGANCE... REBELLION...DECEIT...DECEPTION...LYING...
CONTENTION...DISSENTION...ANIMOSITY... SENSUALITY/LUST...LACK OF TITHING. (INADVERTENT SIN IS ALSO SIN).
DR. EDWARD BACH, 1930.

The parallel to the SPIRITUAL growth is the PHYSICAL growth (CAN be juxtaposed): MILK... PABLUM... STRAINED FOODS.. JUNIOR FOODS...MEAT & POTATOES/SOLID FOOD, stages of development. These are the stages The Holy Ghost will teach/lead us through in our SPIRITUAL DEVELOPMENT, if we ALLOW that to be done. However, what USUALLY happens is that WE run on ahead of The Holy Ghost, on our own, teaching OURSELVES. We get a little of the MILK stage, then rush on ahead into the JUNIOR FOODS stage for a little of this 'food', then, again, rush on ahead into the MEAT & POTATOES/SOLID FOOD stage. We soon 'CHOKE', and fall flat on our backs. God loses, we lose, and mankind loses. As 'Babes' we are UNABLE to digest the 'FOOD' we have fed OURSELVES, and we choke on it. (No wonder...we had a fool for a teacher).

LUKE 2:13-14. 'Glory to God in the highest; on earth, peace'. THESE are the two things the birth of Christ, into this world, TRULY affected...GLORY TO GOD...PEACE ON EARTH.

There is NO DOUBT that the coming of Christ brought GLORY TO GOD. The angels said it did. There is no doubt about the GLORY, but to talk about PEACE ON EARTH, is ANOTHER matter.

With the world split into a MULTITUDE of ARMED CAMPS, the idea of PEACE ON EARTH seems a sheer IMPOSSIBILITY. (Iraq... Bosnia... CROATIA... AFRICA...PALESTINE...ISRAEL, to mention a few). Starting from the INTERNATIONAL level; descending through the NATIONAL level; through the PROVINCIAL level; through the MUNICIPAL level; through the DISTRICT level; through the FAMILY and DOMESTIC level; to the INDIVIDUAL level; the ABSENCE of peace is a SHOCKING reality.

Does THIS mean that Jesus failed ??? That while Jesus could produce the GLORY, He could not produce the PEACE ??? NO! The answer is STILL the same as it was in Bethlehem...NO ROOM IN THE INN.

In some instances, (or people), there is STILL no room for a Saviour and Redeemer, who is Christ the Lord. By closing the door against the PRINCE of peace, the FACT of peace is closed out also.

The BOASTFUL ones try to persuade THEMSELVES they

have peace. Like the man in DEUT 29:19, who blesses HIMSELF. What a PATHETIC attitude...he refuses the blessings of God, and blesses himself. He ASSURES himself that he WILL have peace, in SPITE of SELFISHNESS and DRUNKENNESS. THIS is the world many live in today. No wonder God is shut out and obstructed, and there is no peace.

Unfortunately, MANY Christian's have no REAL peace of heart, in SPITE of the FACT Jesus came to bring peace. They CANNOT be the blessing to others, that they OUGHT to be. The finest advertisement God has, is a life that is FULL of REAL PEACE, despite the presence of SORROW, SUFFERING and WANT.

SELFISHNESS ALWAYS produces an absence of peace. Show me someone who IS enjoying the REAL DEEP peace of God, and you will be showing me someone that is UNSELFISH in THOUGHT, WORD and DEED, and NOT simply 'playing to the audience' or playing at their WORSHIP.

To this day, within the Jewish community, a birth in Bethlehem is STILL a VERY SOLEMN, HOLY occasion. A time for REVERENCE, and a QUIET, HOLY ATTITUDE. Because (REMEMBER), they are STILL awaiting the arrival of the Messiah, who, they KNOW, is to be born in Bethlehem, according to the Prophesy regarding the Messiah. Within the Orthodox Jewish community it is not uncommon for a Jewish woman to go to Bethlehem to give birth.

At the time of Christ's birth in Bethlehem, the ONLY PLACE OFFERED to Joseph and Mary, was a STABLE. Away from the

Inn, and out of sight of the other people that were staying at the Inn.

At the time of Christ's birth in Bethlehem, a CENSUS WAS BEING TAKEN. EVERY Israelite was REQUIRED, by 'LAW' to return to the place where they were born, so that the census would be completed for tax purposes also. LUKE 2:1-3.

Bethlehem was a town on the road that the Hebrews had to travel, in order to be registered. For some of them, a 'half-way' point to the required destination. Therefore, it was also where some Hebrews would 'over-night'. There would be CELEBRATING, MERRYMAKING, DINING, DANCING, DRINKING, SINGING, with GREAT joy and happiness, as relatives and old friends exchanged greetings and friendships. No doubt, every room in the various Inns would be occupied, as well as the dining room, and the tavern/dancing floor; HEAVY PARTYING...a time of CELEBRATION.

Because of this 'census', the Inn Keepers would be busier than they had been for YEARS, and busier than they would be, for a long time to come...making nothing but. money...'laughing all the way to the bank'. And they were DETERMINED, TO DO JUST THAT, at ALL COSTS. NOTHING would be allowed to interfere with the 'windfall' the Inn Keepers were ENJOYING; 'making hay while the sun shines'.

The Inn Keepers were WELL aware of what would happen if a birth was to take place at the Inn. The EATING, DRINKING and MERRYMAKING would come to an ABRUPT HALT, as the attitude of merry making was turned into an attitude of a

VERY SOLEMN, HOLY occasion; a time for REVERENCE, and a QUIET, HOLY ATTITUDE. The guests would CEASE the DINING, DRINKING and MERRYMAKING. They would be wondering...is THIS the Messiah that they are expecting to be born in Bethlehem??? MANY WOULD BE PRAYING TO GOD, PLEADING that it WOULD be the birth of the Messiah, for whom they are, and have been waiting, for so long. There WOULD be an abrupt halt to buying/selling.

Therefore, the Inn Keeper would NOT provide accommodation to a woman that was about to give birth. However, there must have been a semblance of understanding or compassion, so the STABLE was offered, away from the Inn and partying.

Because the Inn Keeper put Joseph and Mary in a stable, NOBODY in the Inn would know or be disturbed by the birth, or put out of their room, to make room for Joseph and Mary. Everyone could carry on as usual. Because the Inn Keeper put them in the stable, nobody saw them or the baby, except those who came seeking.

The story of the STABLE/MANGER is repeated in many Christian HEARTS. They have heard the Gospel...the call of God to receive Jesus...they have opened their hearts to receive Christ, but there is no room in the Inn...they guide Jesus to the MANGER of the heart...the outside place. Jesus is NOT on the 'THRONE' (Inn) of their hearts, for all to see; they don't WANT Jesus to be SEEN. They don't want their friends or acquaintances to 'KNOW'. (ashamed ? shy ? embarrassed ? a secret? want to keep companionship with 'buddies' ?) This is a VERY

DANGEROUS game, with dangerous CONSEQUENCES. 2 TIM 2:11-12.

It is EASY to invite Jesus in, and put Him in the MANGER. THERE, just as at Bethlehem, no one in the Inn of our heart is disturbed...we can carry on as before... business as usual. Saved and stuck.

If Jesus is in the MANGER, no one in the Inn will be disturbed or annoyed...no complaints will be heard. Best of all, if Jesus is in the manger, no one will SEE Him...on the premises, but not in possession; on the site, but not in sight. Where there is no Christ presence, there can be no peace...no power.

EPH 1:18...we see that Jesus has inherited HIS people. Jesus HAS an inheritance in us...but it is NOT in the MANGER of our hearts, it is on the THRONE of our hearts (the Inn).

The angels knew Jesus for who He REALLY WAS THE LORD. The angel said this to the shepherds. LUKE 2:11.

The wise men knew where to look for a KING...they went to a PALACE to search for a THRONE. MATT 2:2. Instead, they were sent to a STABLE, to search for a MANGER. MATT 2:8.

A King doesn't rule from a MANGER, He can only reign from a 'THRONE'.

Many Christians treat their Spiritual life as a DEMOCRACY... the person in charge is an ELECTED representative, and USUALLY, they themselves are the successful candidate. But Christianity is NOT a DEMOCRACY... it is an EMPHATIC socialist

DICTATORSHIP. With God, it is HIS way, or the HIGHWAY... UNDERSTAND THIS!

There is ONE Lord only...THE LORD JESUS CHRIST. If Jesus is not Lord of ALL in my life, then He is not Lord AT ALL in my life. If Jesus is steered into the MANGER, He can't be on the THRONE.

Why do we keep turning Jesus away from the THRONE, and KEEP Him in the manger ? Because of SELFISHNESS!

If Christ is kept in the manger, its because we don't want to disturb the other 'GUESTS' in the heart, the place of everyday living...the place where people come and go, and where all of life's business is transacted. If Jesus came to take possession, WHAT A DISTURBANCE there would be, for those who place Jesus in the manger of their heart, (out of sight). They are more concerned about their 'friends' or 'behaviour' rather than allowing Christ to 'claim' HIS inheritance in them, by reigning SUPREME on the THRONE of their hearts. 2 TIM 2:12.

Jesus seeks to rule from the THRONE of our hearts, through our 12 Apostles. It is at THIS point the Christian life becomes the CHALLENGE to our INNATE SELFISHNESS.

If Jesus is to be Lord of my MIND, then my mind must be prepared to receive Him. My THINKING process must be PURE and HOLY.

Some of the books I possess may need to be DESTROYED; (not given away to someone else...DESTROYED). This is what happened in the early Christian church. ACTS 19:18-19. There is a TREMENDOUS amount of debased literature published these days; some of it finds its way into Christian homes. What is DIRTY, DOUBTFUL or DRIVEL must be burned. This will help prepare my mind for Jesus. We may need to apply 2 COR 10:5-6.

Some of our IMAGININGS and AMBITIONS may need to go. We need to SEE (in our mind's eye), Jesus' Holy Spirit standing, watching, listening, weighing, and examining, every thought that comes into our minds, every word that comes out of our mouths, and all our actions. THIS will certainly prepare our minds for the indwelling Holy Spirit of Christ.

Purity of mind is not popular these days. Yet, if we are not pure in mind, we cannot be pure in heart...if we are not pure in heart, we can't see God. PSALM 24:4 MATT 5:8. And Christ will NOT indwell an impure heart, or a heart full of ANGER, CONTENTION, DISSENTION, ANIMOSITY, DECEIT, ETC.

If Jesus leaves the manger of our heart, and moves onto the Throne of our hearts, many of the guests WILL be disturbed by His presence, and will have to go. If Jesus is to be Lord of my heart, then Jesus must be Lord over my EMOTIONS and AFFECTIONS. It is HERE the outward appearance of the indwelling Jesus will be demonstrated most.

Our EMOTIONS and REACTIONS are MANY and VARIED; like the keyboard of a piano. From the deep base of bitter anger, to the high pitch of pure tenderness. If Jesus were Lord of our EMOTIONAL life, and sat at the 'keyboard', much of our 'music' would never be played.

If JESUS were to initiate our REACTIONS to the incidents of our lives, our RESPONSE and BEHAVIOUR PATTERNS would be a bit different. There would be no SUDDEN OUTBURSTS of RAGE or CHILDISH TEMPER TANTRUMS... no PETTY JEALOUSY... no MEAN THOUGHTS.. no IMPURE THOUGHTS...no BACKBITING... no FAWNING FLATTERY, SEEKING PERSONAL ADVANTAGE OR ADVANCEMENT... no PSEUDO or FALSIDICAL BEHAVIOUR; no CONTENTION: DISSENTION; ANIMOSITY; no DECEITS; no ANGER; no MALICIOUS CUNNING.

There WOULD be a PURITY, and a HOLY QUALITY about our REACTIONS that would be OUTSTANDING. It is on this EMOTIONAL level the presence of Jesus ON THE THRONE is first noticed.

If Jesus is given HIS inheritance in our EMOTIONAL life, what a CHANGE will be SEEN. Jesus will have an opportunity to display HIMSELF. He will be incarnate in us, and able to carry on His work of bringing LOVE, HOPE, and COMFORT to the NEEDY, the HOPELESS, and the LOST. As Jesus is given control of our EMOTIONS, our whole character WILL change.. AND PEOPLE WILL NOTICE THE NEW YOU.

Jesus won't be angry with anyone who HURTS you; He will say 'Father, forgive them'...Jesus won't be bitter against INSULT... Jesus won't retaliate when ABUSED.. Jesus won't be consumed with ANXIETY... Jesus won't be fearful in DANGER... Jesus won't panic in FEAR...Jesus won't be torn with the frustration that develops because of being DOUBLE-MINDED and/or UNSTABLE.

Jesus WILL be the PEACE in our hearts as we learn to say... 'Lord Jesus, I am resting in YOU; I am leaving this to YOU; I'm counting on YOUR promises that NEVER fail'. As we SAY this, and then DO what we say, the PEACE of Christ WILL fill our hearts.   PHIL 4:7.

If you DON'T yield 'THE THRONE', its because you think Jesus CANNOT, or WILL NOT, cope with the situation. "YOUR" Jesus is too small...'this is too big...too complicated...too urgent for JESUS to handle, I have to handle this MYSELF. ..Jesus is too distant... not ABLE to handle this... NOT SO!   (IF Jesus is reigning supreme on the throne of your heart).   MATT 28:18-20.

IF you WILL yield 'the throne', there WILL be a change in your TEMPERAMENT. People WILL notice this change, and ask WHY ??? (Jesus will be magnified in you), people will WANT what YOU have... Jesus' inheritance WILL be at HIS disposal. When Jesus controls the emotions, the character/personality changes, because the personality/character is the pattern resulting from continued (learned) emotional reactions.

We must come to know THIS vital truth...CHRIST LIVETH IN ME, and reigns supreme on the 'throne' of my heart; holding absolute sway over my being.. Let Jesus put His hand on the emotional stresses and strains of your life. Jesus will ALWAYS be Himself...not moody nor involved in MOOD-SWINGS like us.

Jesus seeks to   have of our WILL as well. The mind

REASONS... the emotions REACT.. the will RESPONDS in an act of DECISION. Often, the WILL is UNREASONABLE IMPETUOUS and STUPID (at times). How many times have we blurted out a remark, then wish, with all our heart, we had never said it ??? We decide on a course of ACTION, and sometimes spend months, even years, in an AGONY of REMORSE, but it was done as an UNCONTROLLED ACT OF THE WILL.

In the WILL, more than any other area of the heart, the SELFISHNESS is displayed for all to see. (sometimes, God mocking us to our faces). It sounds so OBVIOUSLY TRUE to say 'I have a RIGHT to my OWN will'...that is what the world SAYS and EXPECTS. But consider the words of Christ (who was rich in WISDOM and KNOWLEDGE). JOHN 4:34 & 5:30 & 6:38, MATT 26:39.

Jesus possessed all things, but HE yielded HIS will to the One who had sent HIM... UNDER NO OTHER CONDITIONS could He possibly have said JOHN 8:29. We must yield OUR will, to the one that inherited US; sends US; to use US... Jesus Christ.

Only when Jesus is ALLOWED to OVER-RULE...only when Jesus is ALLOWED to REASON...only when Jesus is ALLOWED to GUIDE... IN THE AREA OF YOUR MIND...only when Jesus is ALLOWED to REACT to a given SITUITION, through your EMOTIONS.. only when Jesus is ALLOWED to RESPOND by a decision that HE made...only THEN can Jesus come into HIS inheritance in you...only THEN can you KNOW you are not obstructing God through SELFISHNESS.

Remember, we are TOLD to be IMITATORS of Jesus Christ, in THOUGHT, WORD and DEED. 1 COR 11:1 EPH 5:1 1 THES 1:6 2 THES 3:7 & :9.

Do NOT load yourself up with 'EXCESS BAGGAGE' from satan, that FORCES you to spend time and energy fighting battles God did not ordain for you to fight. If you do, you will find that when you NEED time and energy to fight battles God ordains you to fight, the time and energy required will have already been spent, and not available to you. Our God is all sufficient; but He will not provide us with time and energy to delve into what is not our business or concern, or to supply time and energy for satan to play with. If we GIVE the time and energy God provided us for HIS purposes, to Satan, that is to OUR chagrin, not God's: the consequences are OURS, not God's.

WHAT DOES IT MEAN TO BE "SAVED" ? It means that a person acknowledged being a lost sinner, on the road to hell, at enmity with God and God's ways and IS in need of the Saviour and Redeemer (Jesus Christ), and decide to deal with it. To be "SAVED" you must:

ACKNOWLEDGE your sins PSALM 32:5 ISA 1:18-19 EZEK 18:4   LUKE 18:13 ROM 3:23 & 6:23 1 JOHN 1:9.

REPENT of your sins (turn from) LUKE 13:3 ACTS 3:19 2 COR 7:10.

CONFESS your sins LEV 5:5 PSALM 32:5 PROV 28:13 1 JOHN 1:9.

FORSAKE your sins ISA 55:7.

DO PENANCE (NOT atonement) 2 CHRON 7:14 LUKE 24:47.

BELIEVE in 'the atoning work of Christ; believe in and accepting God's forgiveness PSALM 103:12 ISA 53:5 ACTS 10:43 & 16:31 ROM 10:9.

ACCEPT Christ as your personal Saviour and redeemer; receive
Him into your heart and life JOHN 1:12 & 10:9
1 JOHN 1:29 1 JOHN 2:2.

Believe that Jesus Christ IS the Son of God, the Messiah; that Jesus died on the cross, in OUR stead, bearing our sins, paying the price for each of us individually, thereby reconciling us to the Father; that on the third day, Jesus was raised from the dead, by the Father; that Jesus ascended into heaven, and sits at the right hand of the Father, alive. That Jesus is our peace with the Father, and is THERE, at our disposal, to advocate on our behalf, with the Father, The Holy Ghost and others.

<u>TO BE "BORN AGAIN".</u>

MUST BE BAPTISED;
Allow Christ to reign supreme on the 'throne' of our hearts (not tucked away in the manger);

Yield our ALL to Christ (our 12 apostles (see NCRC I01/1)) to be Christ's servant and instrument;

Being indwelt by the Holy Spirit of Christ, allowing Jesus to rule our life according to His will. We must learn to KNOW, LOVE and SERVE GOD, with all our heart, soul, mind, body and strength, walking the path God created us to walk for Him, as His instrument and servant, in association with our soul, looking forward to the second coming of Christ.

<u>TO OUR BEST, GOD ADDS THE REST...</u>

OUR BEST: COUNT THE COST, AND BE WILLING TO PAY that PRICE. Ask for mercy; Acknowledge our offenses (sin); Confess and repent of our sin; Realization of the breadth, depths and seriousness of sin;
    Sincerity of heart; Pray, asking for spiritual necessities, supplications, intercessions, petitions; Joy and gladness of heart; Witness (what God has done for you) to others; Revel in God's mercy & love; Proclaim God's praise (dueGod); Don't try to atone for your sins (already done); A contrite spirit; Humble and contrite heart; Vindicate God,(wedeserved our punishment, we had it coming).

GOD ADDS: Will have mercy on us; cleanse us of our confessed sin; God gives the necessary wisdom; will purify us; Blot out our guilt; Create a clean heart within us; Give us a steadfast spirit; Free us from blood guilt; open our lips; Will stop spurning us; Be bountiful to us; Show/give kindness to us; Re-build us (our temple); Become pleased with us. PSALM 51:1-21 (Miserere).

MERCY TRIUMPHS OVER JUDGMENT. JAS 2:13
We must learn to: THINK, REASON, SEE, HEAR, SPEAK, and PRAY, from the HEART, not the head, to be in tune with our

soul, and to master the dialectic process. See NCRC 46/1.

It is IMPERATIVE that the souls dispatched into the world get into the path; walking the path God created them to walk for Him. The calling to be a GOOD husband/father; wife/mother, is the highest, most noble call of all.

If we want to see people that would have been STARS for God, that were 'suckered' and 'snared' by satan, look on your skid roads; that is where they are. Providing they have NOT 'passed their 'time' , ' if these iatrogenics ever become reconciled to God, and into the 'path' God ordained, you will be amazed at the results and fruit they accomplish with ease. They are also prospered, and advanced, with astonishing speed, which, of course, is axiomatic.

Allow me to quote from a lecture I delivered 14 Sept 1982 re the Counselling and Rehabilitation Field: "When the children of the children with children begin to enter the mainstream, we will be faced with one of the deadliest syndromes of our century. They will have no concept whatsoever as to what family life can be, and should be.

Bad attitudes toward marriage and family values and unity will become the 'norm'. They will unwittingly LIVE and PROMOTE, bad attitudes and misunderstandings, and bad family relationships, (especially in the step- child/parent relationship) that will develop, will have been instilled in, and learned by, these children, which they will promote and foster ad infinitum.

In principle, it would fall to the Ministry of Education to

correct this dilemma. Unfortunately, the Ministry of Education will NOT be able to accomplish that intervention, due to the fact that, by that time, our whole Education Philosophy will have gone so far awry, that it will not be competent to produce Educated competent people to deal with the dilemma.

What failing/falling Christians are to Christianity, failing/falling fathers and mothers are to Society and the Nation." (end of quote).

Christianity itself has gone so far awry, that we have many 'babes' or 'juniors' in Christ, that actually thank God for what they have received from satan. This is accomplished by opting out of their obligation and responsibility to withdraw into Christ, neglecting the world; They withdraw into the world, neglecting Christ.

Find out what GOD is doing, then GO with the flow. Get in, sit down, hang on, and shut-up. NEVER obstruct or pervert that flow....you will suffer decline and destruction if you do. We must COOPERATE with God... LISTEN.

MUCH more could be said; much more needs to be said to combat the intellectualism, of secular humanism, brought about mainly, via an educational philosophy gone awry, promoting empirical thinking, disregarding dialectic thinking. Figuratively speaking, the new educational philosophy is trying to build a second floor onto a building that does not have a first floor. Wonderful folly. However, we HAVE well surpassed the attention span of most 'elite' educators (?) and theologians (?).

This Synthesis will be of no value whatsoever to illiterate, humble, obedient, God fearing and God loving peasants with a clean heart and a steadfast faith, indwelt by the Holy Spirit. There is nothing contained herein, that will be of any value to them. However, THEY have MUCH to teach many of us.

This Synthesis will be incorporated into the curriculum utilized by the Nouthetic Fraternity Club Coalition Society, to Educate and train, and to Educate Canadian's to turn our Nation back to God, restoring Canada as a Western Christian Nation, during the semester dealing with the underlining presuppositional Philosophy of the Nouthetic Counselling and Rehabilitation Technique, and in particular, the subjects of POSITIVE SIN (transgression - performance). and NEGATIVE SIN (shortcoming- presentation).

<u>FURTHER FOOD FOR THOUGHT</u>

<u>POLLUTED TABERNACLES, PULPITS, SANCTUARIES (JER 51:51)</u> It is a terrible thing that unauthorized men and women should INTRUDE into the Holy Places reserved for Priest's alone. Many ungodly men and women are now being educated to enter into the Ministry field. Such laxity of discipline; to adulterate and pollute, prompting God's wrath and vengeance.

Christ's Church is to be an assembly of believers, not an unsaved community of unconverted men and women; intruders into The Lord's sanctuaries.

The world (Lucifer's realm) would have us be more "charitable", and not to carry matters with too severe a hand . Carnal minds treat God's Precepts, Oracles and Commandments with ridicule, recommending compromise and moderation. Purity is not to be too precise; error is not to be severely denounced. They ask "what's the good of criticizing something, when it is so fashionable and everybody does it ??? (to their own eternal ruin).

What do the Scriptures (from which The Church derives ALL it's POWER and AUTHORITY) have to say regarding women praying with their heads uncovered ???   regarding women preaching or teaching ???

If we would follow The Lord wholly, we must go into the 'wilderness' of His Realm, and leave the carnal world (Lucifer's realm), behind us, leaving its maxims, pleasures, and religion, and go to the place where the Lord calls the members of HIS Church (HIS Realm). Let the call be sounded. 2 COR 6:17 PROV 1:22-33. Take heed, those at enmity with God.

Humanistic secular wisdom delights to trim and rearrange the doctrines of the Cross into a system more artificial and more congenial with the depraved tastes of fallen human nature. Instead of improving, carnal wisdom pollutes.

All alterations and amendments of The Lord's own words are defilements, and pollute   the Lord's own Words.

The proud heart of unregenerate man is VERY anxious to have a hand in the justification of the soul before God.

There is an inherent blasphemy in seeking to add to what Christ Jesus, in His dying moments, declared to be finished.

The fire of Christ's Church must not be smothered beneath the ashes of a worldly conformity. We must never underestimate God's severity towards those who will lead astray Christ's Church.

We must beware of those that weave the spider's web. (ISA 59:5). To quote C. H. Spurgeon: "See the spider's web and behold in it a most suggestive picture of the hypocrite's religion. It is meant to catch his prey. foolish persons are easily entrapped by the loud professions of pretenders, and even the more judicious cannot always escape. Custom, reputation, praise, advancement, and other flies are the small game which hypocrites take in their nest. A spider's web is a marvel of skill. Look at it and admire the cunning hunter's wiles. Is not a deceiver's religion equally amazing ? How does he make so barefaced a lie appear to be truth ? A spider's web comes from the creature's own bowels. The bee gathers her wax from flowers. The spider sucks no flowers, yet she spins out her material to any length. Even so hypocrites find their trust and hope within themselves. They lay their own foundation and hew out the pillars of their own house, refusing to be debtors to the sovereign Grace of God. But a spider's web is very frail. It is not enduringly manufactured. It is no match for the servant's broom or the traveler's staff. Hypocritical cobwebs will soon come down when the broom of destruction begins its purifying work. This reminds us of one more thought, that such cobwebs are not to be endured in the Lord's house. He will see to it that they and those who spin them will be destroyed forever. Oh, my soul, be resting on something better than a spider's web. Let the Lord Jesus be your eternal hiding place".

Again, to quote C. H. Spurgeon: "Some Christians look back on the past with pleasure but regard the present with dissatisfaction. Once they lived near to Jesus, but now they feel they have wandered from Him. They say, "O that I were as in months past!" They complain that they do not have peace of mind or that they have no enjoyment in the means of Grace or that conscience is not so tender or that they have not so much zeal for God's Glory. The cause of this mournful state of things are manifold. It may arise through NEGLECT OF PRAYER, for a neglected prayer closet is the beginning of all Spiritual decline. Or it may be the result of IDOLATRY. The heart has been occupied with something else more than with God. The affections have been set on things of earth instead of the things of Heaven. A jealous God will not be content with a divided heart. He must be loved first and best. He will withdraw the sunshine of His presence from a cold, wandering heart. Or the cause may be found in SELF-CONFIDENCE and SELF-RIGHTEOUSNESS. Pride is busy in the heart, and self is exalted instead of lying low at the foot of the Cross. Christian, if you are not now as you "were in months past", do not rest satisfied with wishing for a return of former happiness, but go at once to seek your Maker and tell Him your sad state. Ask His Grace and strength to help you walk more closely with Him. Humble yourself before Him, and He will lift you up. Do not sit down to sigh and lament. While the Beloved Physician lives, there is hope and certain recovery for the worst cases. "O that I WERE AS IN MONTHS PAST" (Job 29:2).

If you are not as close to God as you once were, make no mistake; determine WHO moved away from WHO; Did God move away from you ??? or did you move away from God ???

We must never unwisely make preferences in the Persons of the Blessed Trinity. Some think of Jesus as if He were the embodiment of everything lovely and gracious, while our Heavenly Father they regard as severely just and destitute of kindness...WRONG! None of the Persons of the Trinity act apart from the rest; they are one.

We must keep alive the truth, light, and teaching of the Holy See (Joel 1:3); and expose the works of darkness. We must keep rank with true believers, walking well the very thin line between being loyal to God our Father, and doing all in our power to bring the Gospel of Salvation to even those who have forsaken God, endeavoring to help them to save their souls via turning back to God through Jesus Christ, their Saviour and Redeemer, with empathy, compassion and service to our follow man, imitating Jesus Christ, as is our duty and responsibility.

Oh the anguish, pain, chaos and disunity caused by 'scholars' who worship their work, work at their play; play at their worship, at enmity with their soul, lacking Godliness. Deign O God to rescue them; for your name's sake, let mercy triumph over judgment.

In contending with certain sins, there remains no mode of victory but by flight. Who would enter the leper's prison and sleep amid its horrible corruption unnecessarily ? Only he who DESIRES to be leprous would court contagion. The wings of a dove may be of more use than the jaws of a lion. I am to resist satan, but the lusts of secular humanism I must flee, or they will surely overcome me. (GEN 39:12).

Anger is not always sinful, but it has a tendency to run wild. Sometimes it is Elijah's fire from heaven. We do well when we are angry with sin, because of the wrong that it commits against our Good and Gracious God.   JONAH 4:9   PSALM 97:10.

It is to be feared, if our anger is <u>NOT</u> commendable or justified.

Those of God's Realm are NOT to be collaborators with those in Lucifer's realm, rendering themselves contemptible and reprehensible.

Lucifer's plan is to stop us from running our race in God's realm, thereby stopping us from accomplishing God's plan for our life. Sin is intended, by satan, to entangle us; to stop us from running our course...easing us off to the side lines as spectators or cheerleaders; out of the race of God's realm, into the sidelines of satan's realm. Repentance alone is not enough to get us back into the race. We must also throw off the 'excess weight' and sin. We must not make God angry; He may hand us over to satan. We collaborate with satan by allowing self-will to reign instead of Scriptural authority, and fickle emotions to reign, instead of sound judgment.

The instrument of our Sanctification is the Word of God... Scriptures.

What God has divided, we should not try to unite. We must come out from among the ungodly, and BE a peculiar people. Do NOT shrink from tempestuous winds of trial. (1 PET 5:10).

Be sober, be watchful ! For your adversary the devil, as a

roaring lion, goes about seeking someone to devour. Resist him, steadfast in the faith, knowing that the same suffering befalls your brethren all over the world. 1 PET 5:8-9). GRASP the promises of God; thresh them out via MEDITATION; feed on them with joy.

A life of 30 years of Prayer and Holiness was not enough for Jesus...there was still Calvary to be accomplished, before He finished His course for God. Each one of us must come out of the Garden, and go on to OUR Calvary.

The Holy Spirit provides men and women with wisdom for our pilgrimage through this world... (RUTH 2:17).

As Ruth went out to gather the ears of corn, so we must go forth into the fields of Prayer, Meditation, hearing and reading Scriptures, to gather Spiritual food.

The gleaner gathers her portion ear by ear...gains are little by little. Every ear helps to make a bundle, and every Gospel lesson assists in making us wise concerning Salvation.
The gleaner keeps her eyes open. If she stumbles along in a 'dream', she would not have a load to carry home rejoicing. We must be watchful in religious exercises; that they may not become unprofitable to us. We must rightly value our OPPORTUNITIES, and glean with DILIGENCE ! 3X 2X

THE GLEANER STOOPS FOR ALL SHE FINDS, and so must we. Proud spirits criticize and object, but humble minds glean and receive benefit. A humble heart is a great help towards profitably hearing the Gospel. The word of Salvation is only received with meekness. Pride is a vile robber, not to be endured for a moment.

What the gleaner gathers, she HOLDS. If she dropped one ear to pick up another, her day's work would be of little value. She is as careful to RETAIN as to OBTAIN; therefore, her gains are great. We often forget all that we hear! The second truth pushes the first out of our head, so that our reading and hearing (the Scriptures) become much learning with little application . Do we realize the importance of storing up the truth ? A hungry belly makes the gleaner wise... if there is no corn in her hand, there will be no bread on her table. We have an even greater need... Lord, help us to feel it, that it may urge us onward to glean in fields which yield so great a reward to DILIGENCE.

Days of sloth ruinously destroy that which was gleaned in times of zealousness. We need to beware of lean prayers, lean praises, lean duties, and lean Spiritual experiences; these will eat up the fat of our comfort and peace. GEN 41:4.

If we draw no fresh supplies from heaven, the old corn in our 'granary' is soon consumed by the famine in our soul. We must feed in the right meadows, and spend time with The Lord in His service; in His company; in His fear (reverential awe); and in His way.

Lions cannot be tamed if they are too well fed. (secular humanism). They must be brought down from their great strengths, and THEN they will submit to the tamer's hand.

We must not permit Mr. Carnal Security to feast at our tables. If we do, rest well assured, a rod is being prepared for each of us; God becomes distressed about our backsliding.

SLACK ABIDING produces

BACKSLIDING

Yet, faint not, heir of rebuke, when you are rebuked. Rather, recognize the loving hand which chastens, and say like the prodigal son, "I will arise and go to my father". (LUKE 15:18). Think about David... finish our course by the Grace of God. We must not be rudderless when in rough waters.
Get a grip on yourself; stop it; get back on the track.

Do you serve in God's Realm or Lucifer's realm ??? On God's side or satan's side ??? Are you half way into each realm; walking the middle of the road (a betweenity) ??? Just lukewarm ??? REV 3:15-17.

For example; Wives... do not claim or take dominion over your husbands. Husbands... do not ALLOW your wife to take dominion over you. But remember... YOU are RESPONSIBLE AND ANSWERABLE to God, for the Spiritual and material welfare of your wife and children, AND HOW YOU TREATED THEM. Your wife is your helpmate; your 'other self '; the two are ONE FLESH. Love your wife and care for her, as Christ loves and cares for HIS Church.

This Synthesis is dedicated to His Blessed Holiness, Pope John Paul II, with all due respect and support in Jesus Christ, our Saviour and Redeemer.

It's purpose is to, if at all possible, prevent the fall of the Roman Catholic Church, which will be inevitable, if the unfaithfulness; secular humanism; rebellion; disobedience; apostasy, and heresy, along with the gross theosophy and spurious speculation, that has entangled, and is binding tighter and tighter, the Roman Catholic Church , does not cease.

It is <u>CLEARLY</u> understood, the gates of hell shall <u>NOT</u> prevail against the Church of Jesus Christ, (but perhaps rattle the Church violently), and if necessary, <u>WILL</u> be re-established at the Second Coming of our Lord Jesus Christ.

However, if the present trend of certain Cardinals, Bishops, theologians, Priests and lay people continues, and because this movement is growing larger every day, rest well assured, our Heavenly Father will <u>NOT</u> tolerate such an insult to Christ, and the resulting Church <u>WILL</u> fall from favour, as did Israel of old, and for the same reasons. BARREN GAIN; BITTER LOSS.

And the blood of that fall <u>WILL</u> be required, at the hands of <u>EACH AND EVERY ONE </u>that contributed to the fall of the Church of Christ, and rebelled against His Holiness , Pope John Paul II.

It is also understood, that there will remain, a remnant of the faithful few, that will receive their reward from that same Heavenly Father, with His Holiness Pope John Paul II leading the procession.

My prayer is that the dissident will take heed, and repent, allowing God's Mercy to Triumph over His Judgment.

R. A. PRATT, Ph.D.,F.B.F.S.

ISBN 1412089746-3

9 781412 089746